# Texts and Monographs in Computer Science

# Texts and Monographs in Computer Science

# A Guide to Modula-2

## Kaare Christian

With 46 Illustrations

Springer-Verlag
New York Berlin Heidelberg Tokyo

Kaare Christian
Department of Neurobiology
The Rockefeller University
New York, NY   10021-6399
U.S.A.

*Series Editor*

David Gries
Department of Computer Science
Cornell University
Ithaca, NY   14853
U.S.A.

CR Classification: D.3

**Library of Congress Cataloging-in-Publication Data**
Christian, Kaare
  A guide to Modula-2.
  (Texts and monographs in computer science)
  Includes index.
  1. Modula-2 (Computer program language) I. Title.
II. Title: Guide to Modula-two. III. Series.
QA76.73.M63C494   1986          005.13′3          85-25201

Printed and bound by R. R. Donnelley & Sons, Harrisonburg, Virginia.
Printed in the United States of America.

9 8 7 6 5 4 3 2 1

ISBN 0-387-96242-5   Springer-Verlag   New York Berlin Heidelberg Tokyo
ISBN 3-540-96242-5   Springer-Verlag   Berlin Heidelberg New York Tokyo

For Robin, Kari, Arli

# Preface

Modula–2 is a simple yet powerful programming language that is suitable for a wide variety of applications. It is based on Pascal, a successful programming language that was introduced in 1970 by Niklaus Wirth. During the 1970's Pascal became the most widely taught programming language and it gained acceptance in science and industry. In 1980 Dr. Wirth released the Modula–2 programming language. Modula–2 is an evolution of Pascal. It improves on the successes of Pascal while adding the MODULE — a tool for expressing the relations between the major parts of programs. In addition Modula–2 contains low–level features for systems programming and coroutines for concurrent programming.

Programming languages are important because they are used to express ideas. Some programming languages are so limited that certain ideas can't be easily expressed. For example languages that lack floating point arithmetic are inappropriate for scientific computations. Languages such as Basic and Fortran that lack recursion are unsuitable for text processing or systems programming.

Sometimes a programming language is useable for a certain application but it is far from ideal. A good example is the difficulty of writing large programs in pure Pascal. Pascal is a poor language for large jobs because it lacks facilities for partitioning a program

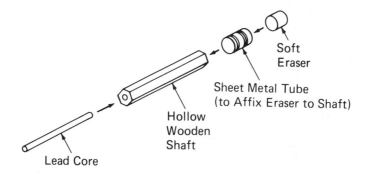

Figure 1. An exploded diagram.

into separate pieces that can be developed independently.

The major problem confronting serious computer programmers is the management of complexity. Writing a program to count the number of blanks in a text file is easy in any language — writing a database, a spreadsheet, a compiler or an operating system is fundamentally harder. Complexity is usually managed by division. The military dictum is "divide and conquer." A complex task is divided into several subtasks, the subtasks are further divided, and so on until each unit of the program is easy to understand.

However subdivision is a trap unless the relationships between the separate pieces are clearly specified. Lets suppose that you want to understand the mechanism of a cuckoo clock. A cuckoo clock lying in pieces on your workbench is no easier to understand than a working clock on the wall. The heap of pieces presents a mass of detail with no meaning while the working clock refuses to divulge its secrets. A better way to understand a cuckoo clock is to look at an exploded diagram. An exploded diagram shows all the parts in detail, with lines and arrows showing how the parts fit together. Modula-2 is like an exploded diagram. It expresses the details of the simplest subtasks while simultaneously expressing the relationship of each subtask to the rest of the program.

Perhaps the most impressive aspect of Modula-2 is its suitability for a diverse range of applications. Modula-2's low-level features make it ideal for systems programming — it has better control and data structures than Forth — it is clearer and simpler than C. Modula-2's coroutines make it valuable for embedded systems that require concurrency without the overhead of large operating systems or large languages such as ADA. The simplicity and style of Modula–2 make it an ideal teaching language. Many languages allow programs to become large and complicated by allowing separate compilation — Modula–2 manages large programs because MODULES clearly define the interface between themselves and the rest of the program.

Modula–2 is a procedural programming languages. This means that Modula–2 programs specify exactly how a problem is to be solved. An alternative approach is logic programming, which expresses logical relationships and leaves it up to the language to find a solution. There are four fundamental topics that must be understood before you can use a procedural language. These are *algorithms, data, control flow,* and *procedures.* Each of these ideas can be defined in a sentence, but mastery is often elusive. In an introductory book on programming the author presents these four topics at great length. Although short definitions help to orient the students, these basic ideas don't begin to take hold until examples are studied and programmed.

I have focused this book on the Modula–2 language. I don't cover algorithms, data, control flow, or PROCEDURES in as much detail as most books for beginners. I expect that most readers will have encountered these ideas previously, or that this book is being used in conjunction with other materials that cover these elementary aspects of programming. The focus here is on one particular language, not on the ideas that are common to many languages.

I have tried to very clearly explain those areas of Modula–2 that may surprise programmers who have experience in other programming languages. Although people who have programmed in Basic may understand the general idea of a procedure (function), they may need help to understand Modula–2's facilities for ordinary and function procedures, and for value and variable parameters. People with experience in Fortran or Forth may be surprised by the large assortment of data types in Modula–2. Pascal programmers may need coaching to understand Modula–2's facilities for separate compilation. I have tried to take all of these backgrounds into account in designing the level of presentation throughout the book.

This book is a complete guide for Modula–2, organized by language features so that it easily serves as a reference. I have tried to localize each discussion so that material on a given topic isn't scattered throughout the book. I have carefully chosen the order of presentation so that each part builds on what has come before. The Modula–2 novice should start at the beginning and read forward — the lay of the language will quickly become apparent.

Part I introduces an informal, robust subset of Modula-2. This subset is sufficient for writing many useful programs. Chapter 1 starts with a discussion of the evolution of Modula-2. MODULES, IMPORT and EXPORT and widely used InOut library MODULE are also covered in Chapter 1. Chapter 2 presents Modula-2's view of data while Chapter 3 talks about control flow in Modula-2. The final two chapters in Part I cover PROCEDURES and ARRAYS.

Part II examines MODULES, the major new feature of Modula-2. The first chapter in Part II describes local MODULES. Then there is a pair of chapters describing the two halves of Modula-2's global MODULES. Global MODULES enable separate compilation, which is discussed and demonstrated in these chapters. The fourth chapter in Part II describes the facilities of the global MODULES that form a part of most Modula-2 implementations. The final chapter of Part II contains several MODULES that form the longest example program in the book, an algebraic desk calculator with variables.

Part III presents Modula-2's advanced data TYPES. Pascal was admired for its rich assortment of data TYPES; Modula-2 continues this tradition. Modula-2 includes all Pascal's data TYPES plus several new ones. Each chapter in Part III close with an extended example.

Part IV details Modula-2's systems programming features. More than elsewhere, the emphasis of Part IV is on techniques because many readers aren't familiar with the ideas that underly concurrent and low-level programming. Part IV also includes significant example programs. There are two versions of a virtual terminal program plus several interrupt handlers.

The Appendices provide several useful summaries of key language features. Naturally there is a syntax description of Modula-2 that references the fuller descriptions in the body of the text. In addition there are summaries of Modula-2's reserved words, and standard identifiers, descriptions of the standard functions, a useful table detailing the compatibilities and operations for Modula-2's data types, and a discussion of the differences between the variants of Modula-2.

There are examples throughout the book, in fact this book is about 25% (by weight) examples. I try to avoid using program *fragments* as examples because fragments often raise as many questions as they answer. The alternative is to include examples that are complete programs or PROCEDURES. Most of my examples are short illustrations of one aspect of the language in *isolation*. In addition there are more than fifteen longer examples showing more realistic use of the language.

A secondary goal of this book is to present several generally useful programming techniques. One example presents an algebraic desk calculator that uses recursive descent to analyze numeric expressions. Other examples introduce the quicksort, ordered binary trees, binary searches, co–routines, circular buffers, stacks, linked list buffers, and device drivers. Two of the more interesting examples are a virtual terminal program and a program to solve maze puzzles.

Let me comment briefly on programming style. This is a book on Modula–2, not an applications program. Most of the program examples in the book are short and clean. I realize that real world problems and solutions are murkier than those presented here. This book is for learning — ten thousand line applications programs are a poor introduction. Most of my short examples have few comments. This is because they are "commented" in the text. The fifteen longer examples display more realistic programming style and a more realistic use of comments.

Everyone seems to agree that gotos are harmful. I haven't used any in the examples in this book because Modula–2 doesn't have a goto statement. However fewer people agree that deep nesting of PROCEDURES and MODULES is also an obscure programming practice. I find it hard enough to worry about a MODULE'S or PROCEDURE'S surrounding scope, its virtually impossible to understand constructions involving six or eight layers of surrounding context. Some people claim that nesting PROCEDURES twenty deep can promote clarity. I disagree. None of my programs are nested deeper than two.

My first exposure to Modula–2 was using the RT–11 compiler written by Professor Wirth and colleagues. Most of the examples were first tried using that system. Later a derivative of that compiler for PDP$^{TM}$–11 based Unix$^{TM}$ systems was released by the University of New South Wales. Much work for this book was done using that system. Still later I was able to make that compiler function on a VAX$^{TM}$ with Berkeley Unix$^{TM}$ 4.2 using the University of Pittsburgh compatibility software. A much better version of Modula–2 for the VAX$^{TM}$ has recently been released to educational institutions by the Digital Equipment Corporation Western Research Laboratory. Many of the examples in this book were refined using DECWRL Modula–2.

In the past several years commercial software developers have produced versions of Modula-2 for the MS-DOS™ IBM PC environment. I have tried most of my longer examples using the Modula Research Institute compiler, and my PC interrupt handlers were built using the Logitech compiler. The Volition Systems version of Modula-2 for the PC is well liked by its users.

The syntax diagrams in this book were originally created by Philip Femano on an Apple™ Macintosh™ computer using the MacPaint™ software. Phil's excellent drawings were updated by Robin Raskin, and then printed on a QMS® Lasergrafix™ printer at four times the original Macintosh™ resolution. As a result of Philip's success with the syntax diagrams, I decided to draw the figures myself (except for Figure 1 and Figure 1.1.) using my Macintosh™. The resolution of these drawings isn't as high as a professional artist would produce using pen and ink, but for me the added element of control is more important.

I typeset this book using the Unix™ Operating System's troff typesetting software on a QMS® Lasergrafix™ 1200 laser printer. The major font is ten point Computer Modern Roman, and the font used for program examples is Union. References in the body of the text to Modula-2 keywords, such as PROCEDURE, are in small caps.

Many of the book's longer examples are available in machine readable form. Contact the author (Box 138, The Rockefeller University, 1230 York Ave., New York, New York 10021) for price and media availability.

Many friends and colleagues contributed to this book. I was first introduced to Modula-2 by Dr. Robert Schoenfeld, the head of the Electronics Laboratory at the Rockefeller University. Bob also contributed by carefully reviewing the book. Other reviewers include Hugh McLarty of Logitech Inc., Ralph Guggenheim of Lucasfilms Ltd., Malcolm Harrison of the Courant Institute, Paul Haahr of Princeton University, Mark Cohen and Dan Ts'o of the Rockefeller University, Philip Femano, Vice President of Zamano Labs, Richard Bielak, and Eric Rosenthal. Dr. Wirth patiently answered my qestions and provided guidance. Thanks must also go to Torsten Wiesel for his generous support. Jim Gaughan provided early guidance for this project.

January 1985                                      Kaare Christian
                                                  New York, New York

# Contents

Chapter 3

## Control Flow in Modula-2                                           71

Chapter 4

## PROCEDURES                                                          94

Chapter 5

## ARRAYS                                                             128

Chapter 18

## Coroutines                                                     357

Chapter 19

## Device Drivers                                                 367

# Appendices

# Part I

# Moving to Modula-2

Perhaps the biggest problem in learning a new programming language is getting over the initial hurdle. In order to do anything useful with a programming language you have to know "most" of the language. I have tried to lower the hurdle by collecting a usable subset of Modula–2 in Part I of this book.

Part I covers simple data TYPES, flow of control statements, PROCEDURES and ARRAYS. These topics are sufficient for many useful programs. Most of the topics in Part I will be familiar to anyone with some programming experience. However the level of coverage in Part I is such that inexperienced readers should be able to follow the material. Part I avoids difficult features such as SETS, RECORDS, POINTERS, and systems programming.

Experienced Pascal programmers may wish to skim Chapters 2, 3, and 4 (Data, Control Flow, and PROCEDURES) because this material is almost the same as Pascal. Chapter 5 discusses ARRAYS. Although some of Modula–2's ARRAY handling resembles Pascal, ARRAY parameters and strings are different and should be examined carefully. Appendices III, VII, and VIII summarize much of the material in Chapter 2.

# Chapter 1

# Modula-2 and Pascal

Modula-2 was introduced in 1980 by its author Niklaus Wirth. Wirth is a well known computer scientist as a result of the widespread acceptance of his earlier programming language, Pascal. Modula-2, like Pascal, is a small, simple, consistent language. Modula-2 is an improvement of Pascal. It is an excellent learning language and it is also an excellent language for large, commercial and scientific applications.

Pascal is renowned as a learning language. It is taught widely in the United States, Canada, and Europe, it is the subject of innumerable scholarly papers, and it has become the standard language in which to express computer algorithms (an *algorithm* outlines the procedure for performing a certain operation) in scientific papers. In addition Pascal has become an extremely important *production language*.

Most programming languages bear the scars of the battle between simplicity and features. Simplicity is often admired but it is usually sacrificed to add more features to a language. PL/1, Cobol, and Ada teach us that features usually win. Modula-2 contains only a handful of features not found in Pascal, thus Modula-2 is, like Pascal, a small language.

The most important new feature of Modula–2 is the MODULE. MODULES allow programs to be divided into small pieces that are developed independently (separate compilation, see Section 8.1) and they offer an alternative to PROCEDURES for organizing data.

The other major area of enhancement might be called *systems programming*. Modula–2 includes several features that allow machine dependent programming (See Part IV), concurrent programming (See Chapter 18), and relaxation of Modula–2's strict TYPE checking (See Section 2.3 and Section 16.4).

## 1.1. Modula-2 and Pascal

Let's start our discussion of Modula–2 by looking back to Pascal. Pascal was introduced by Niklaus Wirth in the early Seventies. His goal was to provide a clean and elegant language for learning to program. Naturally many features that would be mandatory for a commercial language were omitted. Pascal proved to be an academic success, and eventually a commercial success. Students who learned to program in Pascal were often reluctant to use clumsier tools professionally. As Pascal became successful, it also became controversial. Many language implementors added features to pure Pascal to make their implementation attractive commercially. The success of Pascal is partly due to the abundance of good implementations, but there are few truly standard implementations.

Now in the Eighties Niklaus Wirth has introduced a successor to Pascal. Modula–2 retains Pascal's essential feature — simplicity — yet it manages to possess considerable power and flexibility. Modula–2 is about as large a language as pure Pascal, and it is smaller than many of the bloated Pascal dialects. Modula–2 is *much* simpler than large do–it–all languages such as ADA (footnote: ADA is a trademark of the United States Department of Defense). Several Modula–2 implementers have suggested that a Pascal programmer can learn to use Modula–2 effectively in about a week.

Pascal and Modula–2 embody *structured programming*. The key idea of structured programming is that virtually all programming algorithms can be expressed by a few constructs: subtasks are handled by PROCEDURES, repetitive operations are expressed as loops, and decision making is expressed using the IF statement. These few constructs form a common bond between programmers and they make it easier for one programmer to understand the work of another. These constructs have proven to be easier to work with and more reliable than the notorious goto statement. Today structured programming is so accepted that Wirth boldly omitted the goto statement from Modula-2.

Structured programming addresses the *algorithmic* aspects of programming. It is a toolkit for expressing step–by–step processes. Recently many people have increasingly focused on the organizational aspects of programming. It's easy to organize a twenty line textbook example, it's much harder to organize a 100,000 line statistics package. Try to imagine working on a 100,000 line program. (As a reference, consider the size of this book, about 15,000 lines.) The difference between a textbook example and a major software system is similar to the difference between Frank's corner grocery and General Foods.

In Frank's grocery there's just Frank and his friend Alice who works the evening shift. Naturally they communicate informally. Frank gives Alice a few pointers when her shift starts. Sometimes Alice leaves a note for Frank to read in the morning. The organization is different at General Foods. There they have presidents, V.P.s, managers, workers, departments, committees, and an endless paper chase. These encumbrances are necessary because General Foods is a massive corporation. A huge program requires more effective management tools than typical textbook program examples.

Modula-2's most important new feature is the MODULE. MODULES enable a program to be organized as a group of semi–autonomous units. They also make it possible for a group of people to work together on large programs, and they are responsible for many of Modula-2's other features such as systems programming.

Modula-2 is a major improvement on Pascal without being a much larger language. The history of programming languages shows us that once a language is popular, it never falls out of use. Pascal is likely to continue to be an important language even as Modula-2 gains in popularity because of its superiority. Fortunately if you know one, it is possible to move to the other without too much trouble.

## 1.2. MODULES

MODULES are important because they allow you to organize your programs. Modula–2 contains the following types of MODULES:

> *Program* MODULES
> *Local* MODULES
> *Global* MODULES:
> > The DEFINITION part
> > The IMPLEMENTATION part

MODULES are simply collections of data and PROCEDURES. The difference between the different types of MODULES is their context. A Program MODULE contains the main routine for a program. A local MODULE is nested inside another MODULE. A global MODULE is an independent entity — it usually implements a service for a program MODULE or another global MODULE.

It is possible to write programs in Modula–2 that are housed in a single program MODULE. This is analogous to the approach that is taken in Pascal. However for complicated tasks it is much better to partition the task into semi–autonomous units. The overall organizational idea of the program is then expressed in a program MODULE and each of the semi–autonomous subtasks is expressed in a global MODULE.

A global MODULE is like a specialty shop in a city. The locksmith knows about locks, the baker understands flour and sugar, the tailor works with cloth. Each global MODULE does one job well. (A Pascal program is somewhat like a department store because numerous unrelated services are stuffed into a single package.)

The specialty shop analogy nicely explains the two parts of a global MODULE. The DEFINITION part of a global MODULE is the bakery's menu — it lists the wares of the bakery. The menu might entice you to buy pumpernickel bread, but it won't detail the bakery's secret recipe for pumpernickel. The IMPLEMENTATION part of a global MODULE is the back room where the baking takes place. Obviously the recipes for the bakery's products are well known in the back room.

Global MODULES are used to implement semi–autonomous subtasks. The main issue in a global MODULE is the interface between the MODULE and the rest of the program. If the global MODULE is completely autonomous no interface is necessary. This situation doesn't arise in practice. (Just as there aren't any completely isolated bakeries — you can't have a bakery without customers.) On

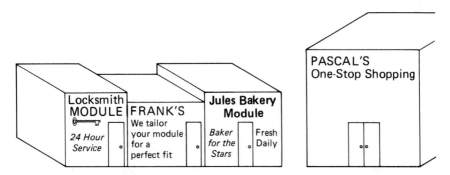

Figure 1.1. A Modula–2 MODULE is like a specialty shop, whereas a Pascal program is more like a department store.

the other extreme one can imagine a overly dependent global MODULE. Such a MODULE would be too intertwined with the rest of the program. (Imagine the bakery jammed into your living room!) Naturally it would have a horrendous, overly complicated interface.

The ideal global MODULE has a simple relationship to the rest of the program. Because the interface of a global MODULE is so important, they are designed in two parts: the DEFINITION part to manage the interface and the IMPLEMENTATION part to perform the chores. In more formal terms we say that the DEFINITION part of a global MODULE shows the visible features and the IMPLEMEN-TATION part hides the rest.

It is possible to write global MODULES that implement *general* services and then use these MODULES in many different programs. Many important Modula–2 facilities, such as I/O, math support, operating systems interfaces, and systems programming support are global MODULES, which are delivered with all Modula–2 systems. The most common global MODULES are discussed in Chapter 9.

For example, many programs need to use random numbers. (When random numbers are generated by computer they are

properly called pseudo–random numbers because the sequence of
numbers looks random even though it is generated by a predictable method.) Here is the DEFINITION MODULE for a random
number generator.

(* Example 1.1 *)

```
DEFINITION MODULE random;

PROCEDURE Random( ) : INTEGER;

END random.
```

Notice that this DEFINITION MODULE doesn't actually make the
random numbers, it simply defines the interface to the random
number generating routine. This particular DEFINITION MODULE
states there is a software routine called Random that delivers a
random number to the client. (In this case a client is a routine that
needs a random number source.) Note that a DEFINITION MODULE
doesn't guarantee that the advertised service works correctly —
the guarantee is that the interface to the service is as stated. Thus
the above DEFINITION MODULE guarantees that the routine named
Random will produce a number each time it is activated. Random
may be broken, for example it might always produce the number
zero, but it is guaranteed to produce a number.

For every DEFINITION MODULE there is a corresponding IMPLE-
MENTATION MODULE. It's easy to tell the difference between a DE-
FINITION MODULE and an IMPLEMENTATION MODULE — the former
always start with the keyword DEFINITION whereas the latter always start with the keyword IMPLEMENTATION. Here is one possible implementation of the Random IMPLEMENTATION MODULE.

(* Example 1.2 *)

```
IMPLEMENTATION MODULE random;

VAR
    a,b,c : REAL;

CONST
    Max = 32767.0;
    FirstA = 30000.0;
    FirstB = 17000.0;

(*
 * Random number algorithm of
 *         Andrew, Talley and Metropolis
```

```
    *)
PROCEDURE Random() : INTEGER;
BEGIN
    c := a + b;
    IF c > Max THEN c := c - (Max+1.) END;
    c := c * 2.;
    IF c > Max THEN c := c - Max END;
    a := b;
    b := c;
    RETURN TRUNC(c)
END Random;

BEGIN (* The initialization of a and b *)
    a := FirstA;
    b := FirstB;
END random.
```

This is one of the simplest methods for generating random numbers. Notice that the clients of this MODULE don't know about the variables named a, b, and c. In addition the clients aren't aware of the actual method used to create the sequence of random numbers. This minimizes the likelihood that a client MODULE will erroneously depend on the internal structure of the service. (If the baker baked in your living room, you might tend to order plain pastries to minimize the muss and fuss. Moving the baker to a bakery frees you, the client, to order without concern for the details of production.)

One advantage of separating the IMPLEMENTATION part from its interface DEFINITION is that it is possible to repair, improve, or replace the IMPLEMENTATION part without "disturbing" the client programs.

One important characteristic of a random number generator is its period. The period is the length of the random number sequence that is produced before the generator stumbles back to its starting conditions. We can detect the beginning of a period by monitoring the variables named a and b. When a and b resume their initial values, the generator has returned to its initial conditions and it is about to start a new period. Obviously it is desirable for a random number generator to have a long period, thus it is useful to measure the period. The following is an alternate version of random that has been modified to measure its period length.

```
                                          (* Example 1.3 *)
IMPLEMENTATION MODULE random;
FROM InOut IMPORT WriteString, WriteLn;
FROM RealInOut IMPORT WriteReal;

VAR
    a,b,c,N : REAL;

CONST
    Max = 32767.;
    FirstA = 30000.;
    FirstB = 17000.;

PROCEDURE Random( ) : INTEGER;
BEGIN
  IF (N > 0.) AND (a = FirstA) AND (b = FirstB) THEN
      WriteString("Sequence Length: ");
      WriteReal(N,10);
      WriteLn;
      HALT;
  END;
  N := N + 1.;
  c := a + b;
  IF c > Max THEN c := c - (Max+1.) END;
  c := c * 2.;
  IF c > Max THEN c := c - Max END;
  a := b;
  b := c;
  RETURN TRUNC(c)
END Random;

BEGIN (* The initialization of a, b, and N *)
    a := FirstA;
    b := FirstB;
    N := 0.;
END random.
```

This version of random interfaces to client MODULES exactly as
does the first because its DEFINITION has not been changed. Thus
this version can be used anywhere the first version is used. In fact
there is no way for a client to tell the difference. Global MODULES
are discussed in Chapter 7 and Chapter 8.

A *local* MODULE is a MODULE that exists inside some other MODULE. The purpose of a local MODULE is to improve the internal organization of MODULES. Local MODULES allow you to partition the enclosing MODULE into several pieces, without the inconvenience of starting a new global MODULE. Local MODULES are usually nested inside large global MODULES, thus there is no realistic way to show a small example here. Local MODULES are discussed in Chapter 6.

A Modula-2 program consists of a program MODULE and several global MODULES. The program MODULE usually expresses the basic outline of a program. Programming styles vary; some people place a large amount of detail in their program MODULES, others move the details to the global MODULES.

A program MODULE starts with the keyword MODULE followed by the name of the program and a semicolon. Next come the IMPORT lists, followed by the body of the program, and then the closing. Note that the closing phrase of a MODULE (or PROCEDURE) always contains its name. This is designed to improve readability.

The sequence of phrases in a Modula-2 program can be described using syntax diagrams. Here is the syntax diagram that describes the structure of program MODULES.

**ProgramModule**

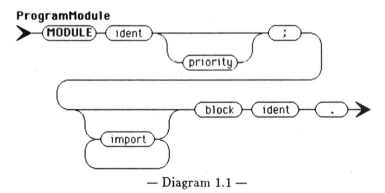

— Diagram 1.1 —

Paths through syntax diagrams usually describe valid Modula-2 constructs. Syntax diagrams are discussed in Section 1.6.) (The priority that is mentioned in Diagram 1.1 is only used for certain systems programming situations. It is usually omitted. See Section 17.2.)

Here is an example program. This program MODULE prints the series of random numbers generated by the PROCEDURE named Random from the previous example.

(* Example 1.4 *)

```
MODULE dorandom;
FROM random IMPORT Random;
FROM InOut IMPORT WriteInt, WriteLn;

BEGIN
  LOOP
    WriteInt(Random(),8);
    WriteLn
  END
END dorandom.
```

It's easy to tell that this is a program MODULE because it starts
with the keyword MODULE. (Local MODULEs also start with the
keyword MODULE but they are always nested inside of a MODULE
or PROCEDURE.)

This particular program MODULE picks up the Random PROCEDURE
from the random global MODULE and (as usual) it uses I/O facilities from the InOut global MODULE. (The InOut MODULE is a
standard Modula-2 facility for performing input and output. It
will be available for almost any version of Modula-2.)

Here is another example. This program reads in and averages a
series of numbers. It uses the ReadInt routine and the WriteInt
routine from the standard global MODULE named InOut.

(* Example 1.5 *)

```
MODULE doave;
FROM InOut IMPORT ReadInt, WriteInt, WriteLn, Done;

VAR
    n, sum, x : INTEGER;

BEGIN
    n := 0;
    sum := 0;
    ReadInt(x);
    WHILE Done DO
        n := n + 1;
        sum := sum + x;
        ReadInt(x)
    END;
IF n > 0 THEN WriteInt(sum DIV n,8); WriteLn END
END doave.
```

**Exercise 1.1.** List the items that doave MODULE imports from
InOut.
□

## 1.3. IMPORT and EXPORT

If the building blocks of a Modula–2 program are MODULES, then
the mortar that binds the blocks is import and export. Without
import and export, a MODULE would be isolated. EXPORT allows a
MODULE to list internal items that are accessible from outside the
MODULE. Similarly import allows a MODULE to list external items
that the MODULE needs to use.

All MODULE types (local, global, and program) can import things
from other MODULES. The rules for export are more involved. All
items listed in the DEFINITION part of a global MODULE are automatically exported. Explicit export is limited to local MODULES.
Export is *not* allowed in program MODULES or in the IMPLEMENTA-
TION part of a global MODULE.

Each MODULE creates a conceptual wall that divides the world into
two parts, inside and outside. The outside world is known as the
*surrounding scope.* For a local MODULE, the surrounding scope is
usually another MODULE. For a global MODULE or a program
MODULE the surrounding scope is the environment in which the
program executes.

In Modula–2 you can import or export MODULES, PROCEDURES,
TYPES, variables, or constants. Although all of these are useful,
PROCEDURES often are the major interface between one MODULE
and another. Programs typically import and export variables,
constants, and TYPES less frequently. For example the InOut global MODULE (See Section 9.1) exports one constant, two variables,
and fifteen PROCEDURES.

Most of your first Modula–2 programs will need to import various
things from Modula–2's global MODULES. The mechanism for im-
portation in Modula–2 is an IMPORT list immediately following the
program heading. The syntax diagram for an IMPORT list is

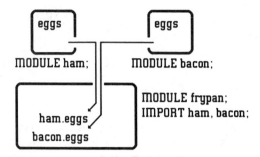

Figure 1.2. Importing whole MODULES leads to the use of qualified identifiers.

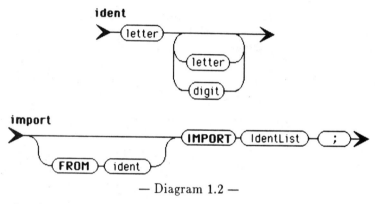

— Diagram 1.2 —

The simplest IMPORT list is the word IMPORT followed by a list of imported MODULES. For example the following IMPORT list might be used in the frypan program MODULE to import all the exports from the ham MODULE and the bacon MODULE.

( * Example 1.6 * )

```
IMPORT ham, bacon;
```

Using the simple IMPORT list means that ham's exports must be referred to (within frypan) using *qualified* identifiers. A qualified identifier (sometimes called a qualident) is formed by taking the name of the source MODULE followed by a period followed by the name of the identifier. Here is the syntax diagram that describes identifiers and qualified identifiers.

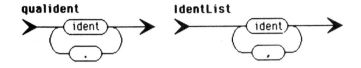

— Diagram 1.3 —

If the MODULE named ham contains an exported item named eggs then eggs must be referred to in the frypan MODULE using the qualified identifier

(* Example 1.7 *)

ham.eggs

The advantage of a qualified identifier is that it always forms a *unique* name. For example if ham and bacon both have variables named eggs, ham's eggs is referred as above while bacon's eggs is referred to as

(* Example 1.8 *)

bacon.eggs

Qualified identifiers are good because they are always unique, but they are verbose. When there aren't name clashes it's often easier to use *un*qualified identifiers. Using an unqualified identifier requires an IMPORT list containing the FROM phrase.

For example if the MODULE named skillet contains the *un*qualifying IMPORT list

(* Example 1.9 *)

FROM ham IMPORT eggs;

then within skillet you can refer to eggs simply as eggs. When the FROM phrase is used, each IMPORT statement is limited to importing items from a single global MODULE and every imported item must be listed. Notice that ham can only import unqualified one of the two eggs. If both must be imported, at least one of them must be referred to using a qualified identifier. Using the FROM phrase obligates you to make sure there aren't any name collisions.

Here is a more realistic example to demonstrate both forms of import. The example is a program named Hello that outputs a short message. It imports the WriteString and WriteLn PRO-CEDURES from the InOut global MODULE. WriteString outputs a

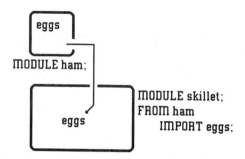

Figure 1.3. Selective import from a MODULE leads to the use of unqualified identifiers.

text message and WriteLn advances to the next line. (The complete list of objects in InOut can be found in Section 9.1, a more descriptive discussion of InOut is in Section 1.4 of this chapter.)

Let's first use the simple form of the IMPORT list to import all of InOut's exports.

(* Example 1.10 *)

```
MODULE hello;
IMPORT InOut; (* IMPORT all of InOut's EXPORTs *)

BEGIN
   InOut.WriteString('Hi, I am a Modula-2 Program!');
   InOut.WriteLn
END hello.
```

Notice that the two references to the PROCEDURES from InOut use *qualified* identifiers: InOut.WriteString and InOut.WriteLn.

If these routines are used extensively it becomes unpleasant to type the qualified identifier each time. Here is another version of the hello program that uses unqualified names.

(* Example 1.11 *)

```
MODULE hello1;
(* unqualifying IMPORT *)
FROM InOut IMPORT WriteString, WriteLn;

BEGIN
   WriteString('Hi, I am a Modula-2 Program!');
   WriteLn
END hello1.
```

Notice the FROM phrase in the IMPORT list. This allows *unqualified* references to WriteString and WriteLn.

## 1.4. An Overview of the InOut global MODULE

In Modula–2 I/O operations aren't built into the language. Instead I/O operations are contained in a set of global MODULES that are provided with each Modula–2 system. If you don't like the supplied I/O facilities you can write your own! The standard I/O MODULES are customized so that they work on a particular system, but they perform essentially the same functions on all systems. A Modula–2 program that relies on the standard I/O MODULES should be easily portable from one system to another.

The simplest level of I/O in Modula–2 is provided by the global MODULE named InOut. InOut provides PROCEDURES to read and write characters, character sequences, and whole numbers. These facilities are adequate for many programs and they are used extensively in the examples in the remainder of this book. InOut and several other standard I/O MODULES are discussed in Chapter 9.

There are two main limitations to the I/O routines in InOut:
- Only one input file may be open and only one output file may be open. You can switch from one input to another (or one output to another) within a program, but InOut only allows one at a time.
- All I/O is sequential. It is not possible to back up to the beginning of a file, move to an arbitrary point, etc.

Programs that work with several files simultaneously, or that need more flexible operations, should use the alternative I/O MODULES detailed in Chapter 9.

The services provided by the InOut MODULE are described in the InOut DEFINITION MODULE. You can read and comprehend a DEFINITION MODULE even if you don't have a detailed understanding of everything in the MODULE. Feel free to peruse the version of the InOut DEFINITION MODULE in Section 9.1.

Here is a list of the most common facilities in the InOut global MODULE.
- The variable named Done is set to TRUE when input operations succeed. Done is set to FALSE when the end of the input data is encountered, or when other input errors occur.
- The Read PROCEDURE inputs a single character from the input source.
- The ReadInt and ReadCard PROCEDURES input whole numbers from the input source. The input numbers are in text (not binary) form.

- The `ReadString` PROCEDURE inputs a sequence of non-blank (non–control) characters.
- The `Write` PROCEDURE outputs a single character.
- The `WriteInt` and `WriteCard` PROCEDURES output text representing whole numbers. The field width must be specified as a second parameter.
- The `WriteLn` PROCEDURE advances the output to the next line.
- The `WriteString` PROCEDURE outputs a string (a sequence of characters).

`InOut` contains four or five other features that are less important at this point in your Modula–2 learning.

`InOut`'s facilities are easy to use, as demonstrated in the following section.

## 1.5. Example — The Underline Filter

Here is a program that shows how items from `InOut` are used in a small, but useful application. A friend of ours does most of her writing on a small computer connected to a slow, cheap printer. This particular printer has few "features," but it is capable of underlining. If you send this particular printer a special control code (Control–S) it will subsequently underline the text that it receives. When the printer receives another Control–S it reverts to normal print mode.

At one stage in our friends work she transported her text to a larger computer to print it on a high quality printer. Unfortunately the high quality printer on the large computer uses a different scheme for underlining. On this second printer you can underline a given letter if you precede it with an underscore and a backspace.

Thus our problem is to convert files from the control character underlining format to the backspace–underscore underlining system. Let's start by developing a specific plan for our program.

- Ordinarily, the program will read a letter from the input file. If the letter is not the underline control code (Control–S) it is immediately copied to the output file.
- In underline mode, the program will read a letter from the input file. If the letter isn't the underline control character the program will write the following to the output file: an underscore, a backspace, and the letter itself.

- When the special underline control character is encountered, it will not be copied to the output. If the program is in ordinary mode it will enter underline mode, otherwise the program will return to ordinary mode.

A program that reads an input, makes some changes, and then writes the changed information to the output is often called a filter. This filter changes text from one underline format to another.

(* Example 1.12 *)

```
(*
 * Convert text bracketed by CtrlS to
 *     Underscore-Backspace underline format
 *)

MODULE Underline;
FROM InOut IMPORT Read, Write, Done;

(*
 *    Please <CtrlS>HELP<CtrlS> me.   -->
 *        Please _<BS>H_<BS>E_<BS>L_<BS>P me.
 *)

CONST
   BackSpace = 10C;
   CtrlS = 23C;

VAR
   ch : CHAR;
   UnderLining : BOOLEAN;

BEGIN
  UnderLining := FALSE;
  Read(ch);
  WHILE Done DO
    IF ch = CtrlS THEN
      UnderLining := NOT UnderLining
    ELSE
      IF UnderLining THEN
        Write('_');
        Write(BackSpace)
      END;
      Write(ch)
    END; (* IF *)
```

```
   Read(ch)
  END (* WHILE *)
 END Underline.
```

Notice that the Done variable from InOut is checked following each Read. Thus the filter stops processing as soon as the end of the data is encountered.

## 1.6. Syntax Diagrams

The last few sections in this chapter cover some of the basic details of the Modula-2 language. If you already know Pascal, you can probably skim this material because it is similar to Pascal.

The *syntax* of a language defines the rules for constructing sentences. I use *syntax diagrams* throughout this book to show you the syntax of Modula-2. These diagrams are sometimes called *railroad diagrams* because they look like possible layouts for a railroad yard.

Part of the difficulty of programming is *understanding* the ideas of the language, but part of the difficulty is *expressing* your ideas in the language. Computer languages require more precision than conversational languages. A missing comma in an English sentence doesn't usually alter the meaning much but incorrect syntax in Modula-2 is unacceptable.

Syntax diagrams don't have much to say about the *meaning* of Modula-2, they are merely a convenient way to express the syntax of the language. It is allowable (and common) to write programs that contain serious logical flaws even though they adhere to Modula-2 syntax.

Syntax diagrams show the *order* of symbols in a program. Within a syntax diagram, something in *italics* refers to another syntax diagram, anything else must appear exactly as in the diagram. If you stay on the tracks you will *usually* (but not always) stay within the bounds of the language. In some cases legal phrases are disallowed because of their meaning or context. (For example ConstExpressions have the same syntax as expressions even though ConstExpressions must represent fixed values.)

Just as there are only a few basic shapes for train tracks in a switch yard, there are only a few basic railroad diagrams. The next few sections present the four types of railroad diagrams that are used in this book.

## 1.6.1. Sequence

The simplest syntax diagram dictates that elements must appear in a fixed *sequence*. For example a LoopStatement consists of the word LOOP followed by a StatementSequence followed by the word END. (Many of the names for syntax items are actually several words run together, such as LoopStatement.) The syntax diagram for a LoopStatement is

**LoopStatement**

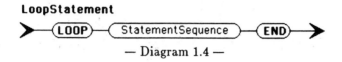

— Diagram 1.4 —

## 1.6.2. Optional Paths

Sometimes elements are *optional*. For example in an EXPORT list the word QUALIFIED is optional. Optional elements are indicated in a syntax diagram by placing a switch on the railroad tracks. The syntax diagram for the Modula–2 EXPORT list is

**export**

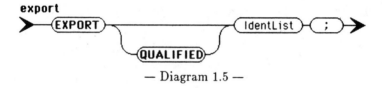

— Diagram 1.5 —

## 1.6.3. Alternative Paths

Syntax Diagrams can also express the idea of *alternatives*. For example a digit is either an octalDigit (base eight digit 0 – 7), or the digit 8 or the digit 9. The syntax diagram for a digit is

**digit**

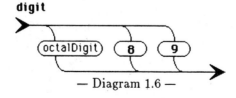

— Diagram 1.6 —

### 1.6.4. Repetitive Paths

The final form for syntax diagrams expresses the idea of *repetition*. Any item that may be repeated (zero, once, or several times) is drawn in a circle. For example a base ten integer is written as a single digit possibly followed by more digits. The syntax diagram for a decimalinteger is

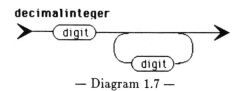

— Diagram 1.7 —

All the syntax diagrams are collected together in Appendix IX, which also contains an index to the diagrams. The syntax diagrams also appear throughout this book near the discussions of the relevant topics.

**Exercise 1.2.** Make syntax diagrams to describe the following situations:

a. Every morning I wake up and brush my hair. Then I sometimes take several bites of my cereal. Some mornings I remember to brush my teeth and wash my face, and then I go to work.

b. Drive to Grandmothers by taking the highway to Shelter Rock Road, to Orange Drive, and then Turnip Place. Remember to take the service road of the highway if the highway itself is crowded.

c. When you are on a hike and you get tired, use the rest step. After moving your weight to one leg, completely straighten the leg so that you are supported without using muscle power. Rest for an instant, then move the other leg forward, relax the first leg, transfer weight, and then completely straighten the leg to give it a rest.

d. Pressure breathing is used at high altitudes to scoop in extra oxygen. Take a quick large breath and hold it, wait several heartbeats, then forcefully expell the air and then start over.

e. When working hard at high altitude, take a rest step followed by two pressure breaths. For really hard work, or at the end of a long day, take a rest step followed by four pressure breaths.

☐

## 1.7. The Elements of a Modula-2 Program

The purpose of a programming language is to establish a middle ground — a programming language is more rigorous and detailed than natural language but much more comprehensible (to humans) than the computer's native tongue. Most of this book focuses on the ideas that underlie Modula-2, and on practical use of the language. However this section discusses the basic elements of a Modula-2 program; the programming language equivalents of participles and punctuation.

A Modula-2 program is simply a sequence of words (symbols). There are four basic symbol types in a Modula-2 program:

identifiers
reserved words and operators
numbers
strings

*Reserved words* and punctuation symbols are part of the Modula-2 language. They are the landmarks that you use to express your program ideas. Modula-2's reserved words are fully capitalized such as the word MODULE. *Identifiers* are symbols that provide names for things in your programs. Most identifiers are created by programmers although a handful are standard features in versions of Modula-2. *Numbers* are simply numeric constants and *strings* are simply text constants. Numbers and strings are discussed in Section 2.5 and Section 5.6.

In addition to the four basic symbol types listed above there are *comments* and *white space*. Comments are used by program authors to document their work. They are ignored when the program is translated to an executable form. Thus comments don't count as a basic symbol — they are just a soapbox for programmers.

White space consists of spaces, tabs, or line breaks. It doesn't count as a basic symbol type; it only serves to separate one symbol from another. When two adjacent symbols are *both* composed of alphanumeric (letters and numerals) characters then they must be separated by white space: spaces, tabs, or line breaks. For example the heading of the donothing program (see below) must be expressed as

(* Example 1.13 *)

```
MODULE donothing;
```

and *not* as

```
                                              (* Example 1.14 *)
    MODULEdonothing;
```

When a punctuation symbol is next to an alphanumeric symbol then white space separating them is optional. For example you can either write

```
                                              (* Example 1.15 *)
    MODULE donothing   ;
```

or

```
                                              (* Example 1.16 *)
    MODULE donothing;
```

Most programmers use *indentation* and *white space* to enchance the *readability* of a program. However you are free to use whatever style you prefer — Modula-2 ignores the appearance (page layout) of a program. In general, line breaks are ignored unless they are necessary to separate one symbol from another. You can't continue a *symbol* across a line although *comments* (see below) can range across several lines.

The following is the entire donothing program that was alluded to above.

```
                                              (* Example 1.17 *)
    MODULE donothing;
    BEGIN
    END donothing.
```

In the donothing program the first line break doesn't serve any purpose other than to make the program appear attractively. However the second line break does serve to separate the symbols BEGIN and END. The donothing program could also be written on a single line:

```
                                              (* Example 1.18 *)
    MODULE donothing;BEGIN END donothing.
```

Placing the program on three lines makes it easier for you or I to understand it because the layout on the page helps us understand the structure of the program.

The program could also be written as

(* Example 1.19 *)

```
MODULE
donothing
;BEGIN END
donothing
.
```

Although this form of the donothing program is equivalent *logically* to the first two, it is poor style.

*Comments* are an essential part of all non–trivial programs because they are used to document the programmer's intent. Although comments may help a human reader to understand a program, they don't have any effect on the operation of a program. You can place anything inside a comment including another comment. Comments begin with the constructed brace " (* " and end with the brace " *) ". Comments may extend over one line or many and they can be placed between two symbols in a program.

Here are three comments:

```
(* A one line comment *)

(* A two line
comment. *)

(*
* Comments often are used as headings
* ******** ***** *** **** ** ********
*)
```

*Nested* comments exist when one comment encloses another. Thus a large section of code can be logically removed from a program by placing it inside comment braces. This works in Modula–2 even if the code already contains comments.

```
                                        (* Example 1.20 *)
(*************************************************
        Skip the following loop -- kc 9/13/84

   (* Print a brief table of squares *)
   FOR I := 0 TO 9 DO
        WriteCard(I*I,4) (* Note that I is squared *)
   END;
**************************************************)
```

**Exercise 1.3.** If you were using a language in which comments did *not* nest, how would you "comment out" the following FOR loop?

```
                                        (* Example 1.21 *)
   (* Print a brief table of squares *)
   FOR I := 0 TO 9 DO
        WriteCard(I*I,4) (* Note that I is squared *)
   END;
```

(Remember that in Modula–2 comments *do* nest. This example shows the importance of nested comments.)
☐

**Exercise 1.4.** Explain why some people think that nested comments are an error prone feature of a programming language. What do you think?
☐

## 1.7.1. Identifiers

*Identifiers* are simply names. Most identifiers are invented by the programmer although there are a few *standard* identifiers that are part of Modula–2. A valid identifier is a sequence of letters and digits with the first character a letter. The syntax diagram that describes this simple rule was presented in Section 1.3. A digit is one of the numerals 0 through 9 and a letter is either lower case or upper case a through z. Letters do not include any punctuation symbols or other special symbols.

All this simply serves to tell us that the following words are identifiers

Wilson     peach     x30     NewValue     temp     i     zyx

whereas *none* of the following are identifiers

       ;    []    n_peach_trees    get$int    4stars

The first four of these words are *illegal* because they contain characters other than letters or digits and the last is *illegal* because it doesn't start with a letter.

Modula–2 distinguishes between upper case and lower case letters. Thus the following

        GetInteger GETinteger getinteger GETINTEGER

are four different identifiers. In Pascal all the above would be equivalent (because Pascal does not distinguish between upper case and lower case); in Modula–2 these are four separate identifiers referring to four separate items.

Some programmers have a difficult time adjusting to Modula–2's case distinction rules. The compiler will usually object if you mistakenly enter an identifier using two different capitalizations. Some people capitalize the key variables and reserve lower case for the lesser variables.

## 1.7.2. Modula-2 Reserved Words and Standard Identifiers

Modula–2's *reserved words* are used to mark the major features of the language. All these words have special meanings that will be explained throughout the remainder of this book. Notice that Modula–2's reserved words are either *fully* capitalized words or special symbols. Capitalization is important in Modula–2 — the word "and" is not a reserved word but it might be a bad choice for one of your own identifiers because of its confusion with the reserved word AND.

# Modula–2's Reserved Words

| | | | | |
|---|---|---|---|---|
| + | = | AND | FOR | QUALIFIED |
| − | # | ARRAY | FROM | RECORD |
| * | < | BEGIN | IF | REPEAT |
| / | > | BY | IMPLEMENTATION | RETURN |
| := | < > | CASE | IMPORT | SET |
| & | < = | CONST | IN | THEN |
| , | . | DIV | MOD | TYPE |
| ; | : | DO | MODULE | UNTIL |
| ( | ) | ELSE | NOT | VAR |
| [ | ] | ELSIF | OF | WHILE |
| { | } | END | OR | WITH |
| ^ | \| | EXIT | POINTER | |
| (* | *) | EXPORT | PROCEDURE | |
| , | " | ~ | | |

All implementations of Modula–2 include standard identifiers. These identifiers name features that are found in all versions of Modula–2.

# Modula–2's Standard Identifiers

| | | | | |
|---|---|---|---|---|
| ABS | CHR | HIGH | LONGREAL | PROC |
| BITSET | DEC | INC | MAX | REAL |
| BOOLEAN | EXCL | INCL | MIN | SIZE |
| CAP | FALSE | INTEGER | NIL | TRUE |
| CARDINAL | FLOAT | LONGCARD | ODD | TRUNC |
| CHAR | HALT | LONGINT | ORD | VAL |

Some of the standard identifiers refer to the data TYPES that are built into Modula–2. The other standard identifiers refer to operations that are common enough to be part of all Modula–2 installations.

**Exercise 1.5.** The following Modula–2 program clears the screen of a Zenith model Z19 computer terminal.

```
                                           (* Example 1.22 *)
MODULE clrscrn;
(* Clear the screen of a Z19 Terminal *)
FROM InOut IMPORT Write;

CONST
    ESC = 33C;

BEGIN
  Write(ESC);
  Write('E')
END clrscrn.
```

Make a list of the symbols in the program. Indicate whether each symbol is an identifier, reserved word, etc., and list the number of times each symbol is used.

□

# Chapter 2

# Data in Modula-2

Let's define *data* as information that is stored and manipulated by a computer. Manipulation of data is performed by programs — that's where Modula–2 comes in. Within a Modula–2 program there are two different forms of data: *constants* and *variables*.

- A *constant* datum consists simply of a value and possibly a name that refers to that value. Obviously the value of a constant does not change as a program executes.
- A *Variable* is a datum whose value can change while a program executes. Variables (except dynamic variables — see Chapter 14.) in Modula–2 programs have names. The value of a variable is established by an *assignment* statement (See Section 2.4).

Outside a computer there are many different types of information. We are all familiar with numbers, letters, words, sentences, books, pictures, music, paintings, bills, etc. Each of these items is a form of information that we have become accustomed to managing. However inside a computer information is handled much more formally. At the lowest level of abstraction, a computer can only store ones and zeroes. Although some programs work extensively with these fundamental logic values, most programs want to handle numbers, text, and other higher level entities.

To provide a level of abstraction above the machine's own, Modula–2 (and virtually all other languages) have an assortment of data TYPES. A data TYPE defines a certain set of values and the operations that can be applied to those values. For example the common whole number TYPE named INTEGER has as its values the positive and negative counting numbers that can be represented on a particular machine. On sixteen bit computers the Modula–2 INTEGER TYPE encompasses the values between −32768 and +32767. Modula–2 provides the usual *operations* for INTEGERS including addition, subtraction, comparison, multiplication, division, conversion to floating point form, etc. Appendix VI lists the operations that Modula–2 provides for its data TYPES.

Modula–2's primary data TYPES include whole numbers, floating point numbers, and characters. More complicated data TYPES include RECORDS, ARRAYS, SETS, POINTERS, enumerations and subranges.

## 2.1. Declarations and Variables

Modula–2 MODULES and PROCEDURES have two distinct parts:
- The *declaration* part
- The *statement* part

Statements in Modula–2 (and most other languages) are used to specify a series of actions. Although the details of this process may be hard to master, the basic idea is familiar to everybody. We've all given directions to a lost motorist or outlined a solution to a tricky international issue on a social studies test.

Declarations are trickier. In most languages declarations are used to define the various data elements that are used in the program. Declarations dictate how many of which data TYPE are going to be used in the program and they provide names for the data elements. This is somewhat like *creating* a landscape containing a lost motorist.

Defining the data elements that will be used in a program is one role of Modula–2 declarations. The other roles are more unusual — Modula–2 declarations are also used to introduce new data TYPES, PROCEDURES and local MODULES. The only universal aspect of a Modula–2 declaration is that it associates a name with something. The other functions of Modula–2 declarations are listed in Figure 2.1.

### Modula–2 Declarations

- A *constant* declaration associates a name with a constant value. (Constant values have, by implication, a certain TYPE.)
- A *variable* declaration sets aside storage for a variable of a given TYPE.
- A TYPE declaration defines the characteristics of a data TYPE.
- A PROCEDURE declaration defines:
    1. A group of local declarations. Local variables are created each time the surrounding PROCEDURE is invoked. Local PROCEDURES can only be invoked from within the surrounding PROCEDURE.
    2. A set of operations that are performed each time the PROCEDURE is invoked.
    3. The parameters (if any) that are passed to the PROCEDURE and the value (if any) that is returned from the PROCEDURE.
- A MODULE declaration defines:
    1. A group of local declarations. The variables in a MODULE are created whenever the surrounding scope of the MODULE is activated.
    2. A set of operations that are performed whenever the surrounding scope of the MODULE is activated.
    3. The IMPORTS and EXPORTS of the MODULE.

Figure 2.1.

The names that are invented in a declaration are used in different ways, depending on what the name refers to:
- A *constant's* name refers to the value of the constant.
- A *variable's* name refers to the variable.
- A TYPE name is used to declare variables with that TYPE.
- A PROCEDURE name is used to invoke the PROCEDURE.
- A MODULE name is used to refer to its exports.

All of these uses will be discussed in much more detail in later sections of this book.

MODULES and PROCEDURES contain a heading (followed by IMPORT and EXPORT lists in a MODULE) followed by a *block*. Blocks contain two parts: the beginning contains declarations and the end contains statements. Here is the syntax diagram for the declaration part of a block.

**declaration**

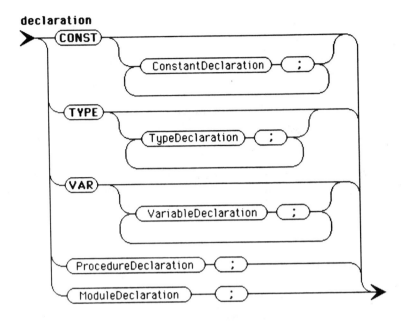

— Diagram 2.1 —

Except for dynamically allocated variables (Chapter 14), all variables in Modula-2 must be declared. It is usually an error to use a name in a program that doesn't appear in a declaration. There are three exceptions

- Keywords
- Standard Identifiers
- Imported Identifiers

Many older languages such as Fortran and Basic are much more cavalier about declarations. In these more relaxed languages you don't have to declare all of your variables, or you only need declarations for certain variables.

Modula-2's requirement for "full disclosure" makes it easier to write, read, and maintain good software. Explicit declarations allow safer programming because they enable the compiler to perform basic verifications. For example, programmers often mistype the names of variables. Declarations provide the compiler with a list of valid names, enabling the compiler to detect many errors.

Modula-2 allows you to place declarations in any order you choose, provided that something that is referenced in one declaration is declared earlier in the program. (There is one small relaxation of this rule — see Chapter 14, which discusses the order of

POINTER declarations.) Thus Modula–2 allows you to group declarations logically.

*Variable* declarations are a list of names followed by the name of the data TYPE.

**VariableDeclaration**

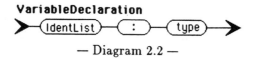

— Diagram 2.2 —

I have already mentioned that the Modula–2 data TYPE called IN-TEGER is used for positive and negative whole numbers. The following program declares four INTEGER variables: i, j, Xcount, and NLIST;

(* Example 2.1 *)

```
MODULE VarDemo;
VAR
    i,j : INTEGER;
    Xcount : INTEGER;
VAR
    NLIST : INTEGER;
BEGIN
END VarDemo.
```

Modula–2 declarations are flexible. The word VAR indicates that the following phrases declare variables. There may be numerous variable declaration sections within the declaration part of a block. (Notice that the statement part of VarDemo's block is empty.)

## 2.2. Eight Useful Data TYPES

This section presents the rules, capabilities, and quirks of Modula–2's built–in data TYPES for numbers, text, and truth values. The built–in data CARDINAL and INTEGER TYPES are used to store whole numbers. The REAL TYPE can store numbers with a fractional part, or large numbers. CHARS store single characters of text, and BOOLEANS record TRUE/FALSE values. There are also three long data TYPES that extend the range of the three standard precision numeric types.

These data TYPES are important because they are used in virtually every program. They are also important because they are the foundation upon which Modula–2's more involved TYPES, such as

ARRAYS (Chapter 5) and RECORDS (Chapter 13), are built.

Modula–2 has different data TYPES for several reasons. One reason is efficiency. It is easier for the compiler to translate programs into machine language if it knows how much storage to allocate for each TYPE and what operations might be performed on each TYPE. Another reason is clarity. It is easier for other people to read your Modula–2 programs because each datum has a clearly defined TYPE.

The final reason that I will mention is TYPE checking. A programmer's attitude towards TYPE checking is often a clue to their programming origins. People who are introduced to programming using Fortran, Basic, or C often have a casual attitude towards TYPE checking. People who first encounter ADA, Pascal or Modula–2 learn early the value of strict checking.

TYPE checking means the language checks your *usage* of variables and constants to make sure that your operations and expressions are reasonable. For example Modula–2 prohibits arithmetic operations on characters and it prohibits expressions mixing REALS with INTEGERS. The rules will be developed more thoroughly in Section 2.3. Modula–2 has various facilities for circumventing TYPE checking when necessary. See Section 2.3 and Section 16.4.

Modula–2 is sensitive to mixed operations because they have been identified as the cause of subtle programming errors in other languages. Because of Modula–2's strict TYPE checking, programs that pass muster with the compiler are more likely to work than in looser languages. This is one of the most important qualities of Modula–2.

Some languages have the philosophy that "anything goes." Many of the most ingenious, and least robust programming tricks involve *implicit* TYPE conversions. For example one particular programming language codes the value FALSE as zero. In that language a "trick" for checking to see if several logical variables are all FALSE is to add them together. If the sum is zero they are all presumed to be FALSE. This is a programming style that Modula–2 hopes to discourage with strict TYPE checking. Whenever such tricks are necessary, as they occasionally are, they are brought to everyone's attention because they must be performed *explicitly* using Modula–2's TYPE conversion facilities. This is a major improvement over Pascal, which completely lacks explicit TYPE conversions. In Pascal necessary TYPE conversions are performed by using subterfuges that fool the compiler and make the program unintelligible.

Each of the numeric data TYPES has a limited range. None of them can store an arbitrarily large value. The maximum and minimum value for the numeric data TYPES is implementation and machine dependent. In most situations these variations are unimportant, but for those occasions when it matters Modula–2 has two built in standard functions that allow a program to adapt to different Modula–2 implementations.

The standard Modula–2 function MAX takes as its parameter the name of any scalar data TYPE, and it returns the largest possible value of that data TYPE. (A scalar data TYPE represents an ordered series of values. The scalar TYPES include all the numeric TYPES, CHARS, enumerations, subranges.) For example the expression

(* Example 2.2 *)

```
  i  >  (MAX(INTEGER) DIV 2)
```

tests the (INTEGER) variable named i to see if it is larger than half the maximum value that an INTEGER can attain.

Similarly the standard PROCEDURE named MIN takes as its parameter the name of any scalar TYPE, and it returns the smallest value of that TYPE. MIN and MAX are lightly used, but indispensable.

Many people will find more information in this section than they need to write simple Modula–2 programs. This section and the next may be skimmed the first time through the book. You should also know that much of the information presented in this chapter is summarized in the Appendices.
- Appendix III lists the standard functions.
- Appendix VI lists the operations that apply to Modula–2's data TYPES.
- Appendix VII and Appendix VIII summarize the rules of TYPE compatibility.

For each of the data TYPES I will present the operators that can be used with the TYPE and I will also mention the Modula–2 standard functions that apply to that TYPE.

## 2.2.1. BOOLEAN

The BOOLEAN TYPE contains but two values: TRUE and FALSE. There are two roles for BOOLEANS in Modula–2:

- To store truth values
- To formalize Modula–2's decision making rules

I believe that the second role is more important than the first. Anything (CHARS, INTEGERS, strings) could be used to store truth values, the important thing is to have a clear set of rules and operations for making decisions.

BOOLEAN values can come from two types of Modula–2 expressions:

- *Comparisons* of INTEGERS, CARDINALS, CHARS, REALS, BOOLEANS (and other TYPES) yield BOOLEAN values.
- *Logical* operations on BOOLEAN values yield BOOLEAN values.

Modula–2 includes the following *comparison* operators.

$$= \quad \# \quad <> \quad < \quad <= \quad > \quad >= \quad IN$$

The sharp (#) is a synonym for < >, which means "not equal." The operator IN is the membership operator for SETS and it is only used with SETS. The other operators have the customary meanings. These operators (except IN) can compare INTEGERS, CARDINALS, REALS, CHARS, and BOOLEANS. Comparisons follow two simple rules

1. The *operands* of a comparison must be compatible.
2. The *result* of a comparison is always a BOOLEAN value.

*Logical* operations test BOOLEAN values. A BOOLEAN value can be a BOOLEAN constant, a BOOLEAN variable, or an expression that yields a BOOLEAN result. Modula–2 includes the following logical operators

$$NOT \quad \tilde{} \quad AND \quad \& \quad OR$$

NOT is the BOOLEAN negation operator. The ~ (tilde) symbol is a synonym for NOT. NOT TRUE is FALSE and NOT FALSE is TRUE. AND (whose synonym is &) is the logical AND operator and OR is the logical OR operator. The BOOLEAN expression

```
p AND q
```

is TRUE if *both* operands are TRUE and FALSE otherwise. The BOOLEAN expression

```
p OR q
```

is TRUE if *either* operand is TRUE; it is FALSE otherwise. The

BOOLEAN operators AND and OR have the following definitions:

| p AND q | means | IF p THEN q ELSE FALSE END |
| p OR q | means | IF p THEN TRUE ELSE q END |

As a consequence of these definitions, it is possible to have BOOLE-AN expressions that are perfectly behaved even if the second operand is undefined. Modula-2's BOOLEAN expressions are executed from left to right and the expression is only evaluated far enough to determine its value. This is called *short circuit* evaluation. Short circuit evaluation differs from the usual rules of logic because it terminates execution of a proposition as soon as its value is determined.

There are several situations where operands may be undefined. For example an ARRAY index must be within a certain range; ARRAY values are undefined outside the range. Another example is variant RECORDS; only one alternative is valid at any given time. A final example concerns POINTERS that might point at nothing at all. Examples showing the importance of short circuit evaluation are shown in Chapter 5, Chapter 13, Chapter 14.

Another tricky area that trips many programmers is side effects. A side effect is a secondary result of some operation. For example many Modula-2 programs use the input routines from InOut to collect their input data. Each time one of these input routines is called, some amount of data is collected from the input source and handed to the program. The program's position in the input stream is advanced as a side effect of calling any of the input routines in InOut. Contrast this with the behavior of a math routine such as sin. Computing the sine of an angle doesn't have any side effects. Calling ReadInt (from InOut) ten times may produce ten different numbers, calling sin(0.) ten times will always yield the answer zero.

The side effects of I/O operations are well understood, expected, and they make I/O more convenient. However some PROCEDURES have more subtle side effects. For example PROCEDURES often communicate results by modifying global (universally accessible) variables. You must be aware of a PROCEDURE'S side effects to use it safely. Side effects are not necessarily bad, but they must be carefully understood.

The previous discussion of equivalent BOOLEAN expressions assumes that there aren't any side effects. The expression Q AND Q is logically equivalent to the expression Q if Q is a variable. However calling a PROCEDURE named Q() once may not be equivalent to

calling it twice. Therefore you must be extremely careful when
you form expressions involving PROCEDURE calls.

**Exercise 2.1.** Use the definitions of AND, OR, and NOT to simplify
the following BOOLEAN logical expressions involving the BOOLEAN
variables P, Q, and R:

```
P OR FALSE
NOT TRUE AND P
NOT((NOT Q) OR Q)
(P OR Q) AND (P OR R)
(P OR Q) OR (P OR R) AND Q
```

□

**Exercise 2.2.** P() and Q() are PROCEDURES that return a
BOOLEAN value, and they have unpredictable side effects. What
simplifications can you make to the following expressions that are
guaranteed not to change the meanings?

```
P() OR FALSE
NOT TRUE AND P()
NOT((NOT Q()) OR Q())
```

□

**Exercise 2.3.** Here is an expression involving a PROCEDURE
named Q() that returns a BOOLEAN value.

```
(NOT Q()) OR Q() OR Q()
```

How many times will Q() be called:
    a. If Q() always returns TRUE.
    b. If Q() always returns FALSE.

□

**Exercise 2.4.** Here is a BOOLEAN expression from the random
program in Example 1.3.

```
(N > 0.) AND (a = FirstA) AND (b = FirstB)
```

The variable named N is zero but once, the first time this expression is evaluated. However a is rarely equal to FirstA. How
could you rewrite this expression so that it will run faster? Why
will it run faster?

□

## 2.2.2. INTEGER

An INTEGER is a whole number that can attain positive and negative values. INTEGERS can range from MIN(INTEGER) to MAX(INTEGER) The range is usually defined by the word size of the underlying machine. On sixteen bit computers the range is usually from −32768 to 32767.

The comparison operators discussed in the previous subsection apply to INTEGERS. The result of comparing two INTEGERS is a BOOLEAN value. It is illegal to compare an INTEGER with a CARDINAL.

Five *arithmetic* operations apply to INTEGERS:

$$+ \quad - \quad * \quad DIV \quad MOD$$

All five arithmetic operators require that *both* operands are INTEGERS. The *result* of an INTEGER arithmetic operation is always another INTEGER. Addition, subtraction and multiplication act as you would expect but we need to scrutinize division and remainder.

INTEGER division in Modula–2 is *truncating*. Thus

```
5 DIV 2
```

yields the answer 2. This makes sense considering that INTEGERS never have a fractional part. Since the fraction is thrown away, it also makes sense that

```
-5 DIV 2
```

yields the answer −2. The symbol DIV is used for INTEGER division to emphasize that INTEGER division truncates.

The MOD operator yields the *remainder* from INTEGER division. (MOD stands for modulus.) Thus

```
5 MOD 2
```

yields the answer 1. The second operand of MOD must always be *positive*.

The following program uses DIV and MOD to compute change. For example if I buy a cream soda for $0.66 and I pay with a dollar, the soda jerk must return $.34 in change, one quarter, one nickel, and four pennies. Here is a program to perform that calculation.

(* Example 2.3 *)

```
MODULE MakeChange;
FROM InOut IMPORT WriteInt, WriteLn, WriteString,
    ReadInt, Done;

VAR
    Cents : INTEGER;
    Quarters, Dimes, Nickels, Pennies : INTEGER;

BEGIN
    WriteString("Make Change."); WriteLn;
    WriteString("Enter the amount in cents");
    WriteString(" (0 - 99): ");
    ReadInt(Cents);
    IF NOT Done THEN RETURN END;
    IF (Cents >= 0) AND (Cents < 100) THEN
        Quarters := Cents DIV 25;
        Cents := Cents MOD 25;
        Dimes := Cents DIV 10;
        Cents := Cents MOD 10;
        Nickels := Cents DIV 5;
        Cents := Cents MOD 5;
        Pennies := Cents;
        WriteString("Quarters: ");
        WriteInt(Quarters,2); WriteLn;
        WriteString("Dimes:    ");
        WriteInt(Dimes,2); WriteLn;
        WriteString("Nickels: ");
        WriteInt(Nickels,2); WriteLn;
        WriteString("Pennies: ");
        WriteInt(Pennies,2); WriteLn
    ELSE
        WriteString("Sorry, not enough change.");
        WriteLn
    END
END MakeChange.
```

Since mixed operations aren't allowed in Modula–2, you have to be careful when you write expressions that involve the comparison operators and the arithmetic operators. It is *legal* to compare arithmetic expressions but it is *illegal* to perform arithmetic on the results of a comparison. The rules for expressions are discussed more fully in a later section of this chapter. For now you should note that the expression

```
(5 * 10) <= (2 * 2 * 2 * 2)
```

is *legal* because it compares the results of two INTEGER arithmetic operations but the expression

```
(5 < 10) * (2 > 1)
```

is *illegal* because it performs arithmetic on the result of comparison operations.

Several standard functions can be applied to INTEGERS. (Note that many of these standard functions also apply to other data TYPES.)

• The ABS function returns the absolute value of an INTEGER. Thus

```
ABS(10)
```

has the value ten while

```
ABS(-200)
```

has the value 200.

• The ODD function returns the BOOLEAN value TRUE if its INTEGER parameter is odd. Thus

```
ODD(30)
```

has the value FALSE while

```
ODD(31)
```

has the value TRUE. The parameter for the functions ABS and ODD can either be a variable, a constant, or an expression.

• The standard INC and DEC PROCEDURES are provided to increment or decrement INTEGER (or CARDINAL, CHAR or enumeration) variables. Their parameter *must* be a variable, they cannot be passed constants or expressions. (The parameter may involve an expression that picks out a particular element in an ARRAY.) If nsamples is an INTEGER variable with the value ten, then the PROCEDURE

```
INC(nsamples)
```

will increase the value of nsamples to eleven. Similarly the PROCEDURE DEC can be used to decrease the value of a variable by one.

INC and DEC can also be used with a second parameter that indicates how much the variable should be incremented or decremented. The first parameter or INC or DEC must be a variable; the second, if it is present, may be a variable, constant, or an expression. (Note that ordinary PROCEDURES have a fixed number of parameters — a few standard PROCEDURES such as INC and DEC allow various numbers of parameters.)

For example the PROCEDURE call

```
DEC(nsamples, 3)
```

will decrease the value of nsamples by 3.

**Exercise 2.5.** What do INC and DEC do if their parameter is already as large as possible? Write a program that declares an INTEGER variable and then assigns it the highest possible INTEGER value on your machine. (Use the MAX standard PROCEDURE.) Pass your variable to INC and then output the results. What do you expect to happen? Note that this exercise is an exploration of the behavior, at the limit, of your particular Modula–2 system. Don't ever rely on this result (trick) in a real program.
□

**Exercise 2.6.** Modify the MakeChange MODULE to handle half dollars.
□

**Exercise 2.7.** How would you modify the MakeChange MODULE to avoid the MOD operator?
□

### 2.2.3. CARDINAL

The CARDINAL TYPE represents whole number values that are *non-negative*. CARDINALS are like INTEGERS with one small exception, INTEGERS may be negative whereas CARDINALS cannot. Using CARDINALS instead of INTEGERS has two advantages. The first advantage is style — declaring variables to be CARDINALS expresses your intention that they should never have negative values. The second advantage of CARDINALS is more substantive — on most computers CARDINAL numbers can be twice as large as the largest possible INTEGER. On typical 16 bit computers MAX(INTEGER) is 32767 while MAX(CARDINAL) is 65535.

The biggest disadvantage of CARDINALS is that many people are careless when they conclude that "a certain value will never be negative." A good example of this is Example 15.8, which wouldn't work if the variables bot and top in the qsort PROCEDURE were declared as CARDINALS. (The problem is the next to last IF statement in the PROCEDURE.)

CARDINALS use the same arithmetic and comparison operators as INTEGERS. The BOOLEAN function ODD can be used with CARDINALS to determine if a given value is odd or even. However, the function ABS is obviously not allowed (or needed) with CARDINALS. The standard functions INC and DEC apply to CARDINALS and work as you would expect.

Whole number constants are assumed to be INTEGERS when they are used in situations that require INTEGER values and they are assumed to be CARDINALS in situations that require CARDINAL values. Thus whole number constants are compatible with both CARDINALS and INTEGERS. However, keep in mind that CARDINALS and INTEGERS have different ranges. Whole number constants that are negative are assumed to be INTEGERS and whole number constants larger than MAX(INTEGER) (32767 on 16 bit computers) are assumed to be CARDINALS.

Many people are surprised to learn that CARDINALS and INTEGERS are incompatible TYPES. To mix CARDINALS and INTEGERS together in an expression you must use TYPE transfer functions (see below).

**Exercise 2.8.** Here are two lines from a PROCEDURE (Example 15.8.) that implements a sorting routine.

```
IF first<(bot-1) THEN qsort(first,bot-1,comp,swap) END;
IF (bot+1)<last THEN qsort(bot+1,last,comp,swap) END;
```

The variables first, bot, and last are declared as INTEGERS. The range of all three variables is from zero to some small positive value. What values of first and bot would make the first IF statement fail if bot were declared as a CARDINAL? Does first (in this same qsort PROCEDURE) need to be an INTEGER? What about last? Why?
□

**Exercise 2.9.** What is the BOOLEAN value of the following expression if c is a CARDINAL variable?

```
c >= 0
```

□

**Exercise 2.10.** a. What is the value of the following expression?

```
5 > (3-4)
```

b. If the CARDINAL variables a, b, and c have the values 5, 3, and 4, what is the value of the following expression?

```
a > (b-c)
```

□

**Exercise 2.11.** Write a program that calls DEC to decrement a CARDINAL variable whose value is zero. What result do you expect, and what result do you actually get?
□

## 2.2.4. CHAR

The CHAR TYPE represents single characters. Every computer system uses a character set for sending information to and from printers, terminals, etc. The two most common character sets are ASCII (American Standard Code for Information Interchange) and EBCDIC (Extended Binary Coded Decimal Interchange Code). EBCDIC is used primarily on IBM mainframe computers and computers that are compatible with IBM mainframes. The examples in this book assume the ASCII character set, the prevailing character set outside of IBM. The ASCII code table is shown in Appendix IX.

A *single* character surrounded by quotes is a constant string whose TYPE is compatible with CHARS. The following are valid single character constant strings:

$$'a'  \quad "X" \quad "." \quad ''''$$

The surrounding quotes can either be single quotes (') or double quotes ("), and they must be the same on each end.

It's possible to enter the ASCII octal code number for CHAR constants. The octal code for the character (See Appendix IX) is followed by that the suffix "C".

Here are two CHAR constants specified by their ASCII code.

$$15C \quad 12C$$

The ASCII code 15C signals a carriage return operation and the code 12C represents the line feed function. Either notation can be used for *printable* characters; the octal code must be used for control characters and other *unprintable* characters.

Modula-2 allows two operations on CHARS:
- CHAR variables may be assigned a value.
- CHARS may be compared.

It is not possible to perform *arithmetic* on CHARS without using the TYPE transfer facilities. Therefore *neither* of the following is legal.

```
'a' - 'A';
60C + 8C;
```

Performing arithmetic on CHARS requires the TYPE transfer functions discussed in Section 2.3.3.

Several standard PROCEDURES apply to CHARS. The CAP PROCEDURE returns a capital letter if it is passed a lower case letter, and it returns the same letter if it is passed an upper case letter. The parameter for CAP may either be a variable, a constant, or an expression.

Here is a program that capitalizes its text input.

(* Example 2.4 *)

```
(*
 Capitalize text
 *)

MODULE Caps;
FROM InOut IMPORT Read, Write, Done;

VAR
    ch : CHAR;

BEGIN
  Read(ch);
  WHILE Done DO
    IF (ch >= 'a') AND (ch <= 'z') THEN
      Write(CAP(ch))
    ELSE
      Write(ch)
    END; (* IF *)
    Read(ch)
  END (* WHILE *)
END Caps.
```

**Exercise 2.12.** Modify Caps to avoid using the CAP PROCEDURE.
□

**Exercise 2.13.** Write a program to discover what CAP returns when it is passed something other than a letter. Try a digit, a punctuation symbol, and a control character. Note that this is an exploratory exercise, it is not wise to write a program that relies on this behavior.
□

The standard INC and DEC PROCEDURES apply to CHARS as well as INTEGERS and CARDINALS. If ch is a CHAR variable whose value is 'e', then

    INC(ch)

sets the value of ch to 'f'.

A sequence of characters surrounded by quotes is called a *string*.

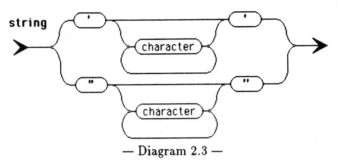

— Diagram 2.3 —

The following are valid strings:

    '"R.U.R." by Karel Capek'
    "Rossum's Universal Robots"
    "robot"
    'a'
    "X"
    " "

The number of characters in the string is said to be the length of the string. Strings of length one are compatible with the CHAR TYPE, all other strings are fundamentally different from CHARS. Note that the fourth and fifth strings shown above are one long, thus they are compatible with CHARS. The sixth string shown above is the empty string.

Note there is no mechanism in Modula–2 for defining constant strings that contain ASCII control codes although (as we saw immediately above) it is possible to define CHAR constants to represent ASCII control codes. Strings are treated much as if they were an ARRAY OF CHAR variables and they are discussed more in Section 5.6.

## 2.2.5. REAL

The REAL data TYPE is used to represent numbers that may have a fractional part, or numbers that may exceed the allowed range for INTEGERS (or CARDINALS). REAL numbers are at once more and less satisfying than INTEGERS. The frustrating aspect of REALS is their lack of precision. Because of their internal representation, many common fractions cannot be represented exactly as REALS. An even worse problem is the unavoidable error that creeps into calculations involving REALS.

On the other hand, REALS are satisfying because of their lack of restrictions. REALS can be large or small and they can have a fractional part. Modula–2, like most languages, allows you to decide which representation (REAL, INTEGER, or CARDINAL) is appropriate for your numeric variables.

The following *arithmetic* operators apply to REAL operands.

$$+ \quad - \quad * \quad /$$

Modula–2 uses the DIV operator for INTEGER or CARDINAL division and the / operator for REAL division. This forces you to acknowledge in your program that whole number division *truncates* while REAL division is as exact as the underlying computer hardware. Obviously there isn't a MOD function for REAL numbers.

Note that arithmetic operations involving REALS must only involve REALS; in particular it is *not* permissible to add an INTEGER to a REAL. (Note that addition or subtraction of INTEGERS from REALS is allowed in Pascal.) This rule applies to constants as well as variables. The standard FLOAT PROCEDURE is used to promote a whole number to a REAL when necessary. (See Section 2.3.2.)

Comparing two computed REALS for equality (or inequality) is risky. Computations involving REALS (especially division operations) tend to accumulate small errors. Computations are repeatable, but the results of two different computations that should lead to the same result might actually result in different answers. Also you should be aware that two REAL expressions that compare as equal on one computer may not be *exactly* equal on a different type of computer.

Here is a program that demonstrates how error can creep into a calculation.

(* Example 2.5 *)

```
MODULE RealDemo;
FROM InOut IMPORT WriteInt, WriteLn;
FROM RealInOut IMPORT WriteReal;

(*
 * show the loss of accuracy in
 *      floating point arithmetic
 *)
CONST
    Max = 9;

VAR
    f : REAL;
    i : INTEGER;

BEGIN
    f := 100.;
    FOR i := 0 TO Max DO
        WriteInt(i,5); WriteReal(f,20); WriteLn;
        f := f / 3.;
    END;
    WriteInt(Max+1,5); WriteReal(f,20); WriteLn;
    FOR i := Max TO 0 BY -1 DO
        f := f * 3.;
        WriteInt(i,5); WriteReal(f,20); WriteLn;
    END;
END RealDemo.
```

In algebra the following equation is true for all x.

```
x = (x / 3) * 3
```

However when errors creep into a calculation, expressions that are algebraicly equal may not be exactly equal. The program produced the following output.

```
 0    100.0000000000000
 1     33.3333320617676
 2     11.1111106872559
 3      3.7037036418915
 4      1.2345678806305
 5      0.4115226268768
 6      0.1371742039919
 7      0.0457247346640
 8      0.0152415782213
 9      0.0050805262290
10      0.0016935087042
 9      0.0050805262290
 8      0.0152415791526
 7      0.0457247383893
 6      0.1371742188931
 5      0.4115226566792
 4      1.2345679998398
 3      3.7037041187286
 2     11.1111125946045
 1     33.3333396911621
 0    100.0000228881836
```

The last ten lines in this table should mirror the first ten. Unfortunately the error creeps relentlessly to the left, and by the final line in the table there are only seven accurate digits. Note that no error was visible on the same computer when the defined constant Max was set to seven instead of nine!

The standard function ABS can be used with REALS to return an absolute value. When ABS is supplied with an INTEGER parameter, the result is an INTEGER but when ABS is supplied with a REAL parameter the result is a REAL. ABS has this flexibility because it is built into Modula-2. PROCEDURES that you write can't accept various parameter TYPES or return various result TYPES.

The standard functions ODD, INC, and DEC *cannot* be used with REALS.

### 2.2.6. Long Data TYPES

The three numeric data TYPES mentioned above are adequate for
most programming chores, but there are situations that require a
greater range. On a typical sixteen bit computer, the INTEGER
TYPE has a maximum value of 32,768. For situations requiring
larger whole numbers, Modula-2 has the LONGINT data TYPE. On
a typical sixteen bit computer, a LONGINT has a maximum value
of 2,147,483,648.

Modula-2's other long data TYPES are LONGCARD and LONGREAL.
Both of these are similar to their standard precision counterparts,
except for the obvious difference in scale. The long data TYPES
may not be available in some versions of Modula-2.

## 2.3. TYPE Compatibility and TYPE Transfer Functions

A feature of Modula-2 that may be new to some programmers is
strict TYPE checking. There are several situations where TYPES
are checked for compatibility. The most obvious example is an *expression* involving several variables or constants. TYPES are also
checked

- When a value is *assigned* to a variable.
- When *parameters* are passed to PROCEDURES.
- When values are *returned* from function PROCEDURES.
- When ARRAY *indices* are used.

There are two types of compatibility in Modula-2, *true* compatibility, which is very strict, and *assignment* compatibility, which is
less strict. You will have an easier time learning Modula-2 if you
master the two following rules:

- True compatibility is required in expressions.
- Assignment compatibility applies when a value is assigned to
  a variable.

As a general rule, two variables are compatible only if they are declared to be the same TYPE. Different data TYPES in Modula-2 are
*incompatible*. Assignment compatibility is less strict than true
compatibility because CARDINALS and INTEGERS are assignment
compatible.

If i and j are INTEGER variables and c and d are CARDINAL variables it is acceptable to write

(* Example 2.6 *)

```
i := c + d;
c := i + j;
```

because INTEGERS and CARDINALS are assignment compatible. The first expression above leads to a CARDINAL result that is *assignment* compatible with the INTEGER variable i. The second expression above leads to an INTEGER result that is *assignment* compatible with the CARDINAL variable c. It is *illegal* to write

(* Example 2.7 *)

```
i := i + c;
c := i + c;
```

because INTEGERS and CARDINALS aren't compatible. Both *expressions* immediately above mix the INTEGER variable i with the CARDINAL variable c.

Modula–2 allows you to create your own data TYPES. (See Section 5.1.) Programmer defined TYPES are good for several reasons — they increase program readability, they can be used to increase program portability, and they create a new TYPE that may be incompatible with other TYPES. Making TYPES incompatible with each other might sound like a disadvantage. Actually it is an advantage because many subtle programming errors are caused by mixed operations that occur without the knowledge, understanding, or consent of the programmer. These forms of error are less likely in Modula–2 because mixed expressions must be managed explicitly by the programmer.

Modula–2 contains TYPE *transfer functions* so that data of one TYPE can be converted to another. TYPE transfer functions allow programmers to perform mixed operations as necessary by explicitly specifying TYPE conversions. These functions are necessary because Modula–2 is picky about *mixed expressions*.

Modula–2's TYPE transfer facilities *behave* as if they were *function* PROCEDURES. The TYPE transfer functions take a parameter (which is not altered) of one TYPE and then return another type with the same (or equivalent) value. Parameters for these PRO-

CEDURES may be either constants, variables, or expressions.

| Common Modula-2 TYPE Transfer Functions | | |
| Function | Parameter TYPE | Result TYPE |
| --- | --- | --- |
| INTEGER(p) | CARDINAL | INTEGER |
| CARDINAL(p) | INTEGER | CARDINAL |
| FLOAT(p) | CARDINAL | REAL |
| TRUNC(p) | REAL | CARDINAL |
| CHR(p) | CARDINAL | CHAR |
| ORD(p) | CHAR, INTEGER, or any enumeration | CARDINAL |

In addition to the TYPE transfer facilities in this table, Modula-2 allows you to use TYPE names as transfer functions. This capacity is discussed in Section 16.4. VAL is another useful TYPE transfer function that is primarily used with enumeration TYPES. VAL is discussed in Section 11.1. The six TYPE transfer functions from the table are discussed in the following sections.

## 2.3.1. INTEGERS and CARDINALS

The INTEGER and CARDINAL TYPE transfer functions are used to convert between INTEGERS and CARDINALS. The following expressions are legal in Modula-2, assuming that Ival is declared as an INTEGER variable and Cval is a CARDINAL. The first two are CARDINAL expressions while the third is an INTEGER expression.

                                                    ( * Example 2.8 * )
```
CARDINAL( Ival )
CARDINAL( Ival ) DIV Cval
INTEGER( Cval ) + Ival
```

The last of these could also be written

                                                    ( * Example 2.9 * )
```
INTEGER( Cval + CARDINAL( Ival ) )
```

Converting a negative INTEGER to a CARDINAL, or converting a CARDINAL greater than MAX(INTEGER) to an INTEGER is likely to produce mystifying results.

Since INTEGERS and CARDINALS are assignment compatible, it is permissible to write a mixed assignment

                                              (* Example 2.10 *)
```
Ival := Cval
```

You can also use the TYPE transfer functions to label the mixed assignment

                                              (* Example 2.11 *)
```
Ival := INTEGER(Cval)
```

In Section 2.4 it is explained that the left hand side of an assignment statement must be a variable. Therefore is *not* legal to write

                                              (* Example 2.12 *)
```
CARDINAL(Ival) := Cval
```

## 2.3.2. REALS and CARDINALS

TRUNC and FLOAT are used to convert between CARDINALS and REALS. Assume that Cval is a CARDINAL and that Rval is a REAL. The first two expressions represent CARDINALS while the third and fourth are REAL.

```
TRUNC(Rval)
TRUNC(Rval) - 5
2.2 + FLOAT(Cval)
Rval + FLOAT(3)
```

The last expression could also be written

```
Rval + 3.
```

TRUNC and FLOAT are unique among the TYPE transfer functions listed in the table because they actually perform calculations to convert between CARDINALS and REALS. Calculations are necessary because the two TYPES use different internal representations. The other TYPE transfer functions in the table merely relax the Modula-2's strict TYPE compatibility rules — calculations aren't necessary (on most systems).

### 2.3.3. CHARS and CARDINALS

Converting CHARS to CARDINALS (and vice versus) is a common programming task. Modula–2 contains the TYPE transfer function CHR to convert a CARDINAL to a CHAR TYPE and the function ORD to convert a CHAR to its corresponding CARDINAL value.

The following are legal in Modula–2, assuming that Ch is a CHAR variable and Cval is a CARDINAL. The first two are CHAR values, the last three are CARDINAL values.

```
CHR(Cval)
CHR(Cval + 60B)
ORD(Ch)
ORD(Ch) - 60B
ORD(Ch) - ORD('0')
```

The CHR and ORD TYPE transfer functions are particularly important because arithmetic is not allowed using CHAR variables or constants. Thus in Modula–2 it is *legal* to write the expression

```
60B + 8B
```

whereas it is *illegal* to write

```
60C + 8C
```

Similarly it is *illegal* to write

```
'0' + CHR(8)
```

Arithmetic on CHARS is performed by converting the CHARS to CARDINALS, performing the arithmetic, and then converting the result back to CHAR.

```
CHR(ORD('0') + 8)
```

The standard functions INC and DEC can also be used with CHARS to perform addition and subtraction of numeric constants to CHAR variables, but the method outlined above is more flexible.

ORD can be used with INTEGERS and enumeration TYPES (as well as with CHARS) to produce corresponding CARDINAL numbers. ORD used in combination with the VAL TYPE transfer function produces several different TYPE transfers. ORD and VAL are especially useful with enumeration TYPES. Since enumeration TYPES are user defined, a flexible TYPE transfer system ORD and VAL) is required. Examples will be shown in Chapter 11.

**Exercise 2.14.** Which statements in the TypeDemo MODULE are illegal because of TYPE incompatibility? Which statements only work sensibly for certain values of the expressions on the right hand side?

(* Example 2.13 *)

```
MODULE TypeDemo;

VAR
   intvar : INTEGER;
   cardvar : CARDINAL;
   realvar : REAL;
   charvar : CHAR;
   boolvar : BOOLEAN;

BEGIN
   (*1*) intvar := 3;
   (*2*) cardvar := 3;
   (*3*) cardvar := -3;
   (*4*) intvar := 50000;
   (*5*) intvar := 40B;
   (*6*) intvar := 40C;
   (*7*) cardvar := cardvar - intvar;
   (*8*) cardvar := cardvar - CARDINAL(intvar);
   (*9*) realvar := 0;
   (*10*) realvar := realvar + 2;
   (*11*) realvar := realvar + 2.;
   (*12*) charvar := CHR(ORD('0') + cardvar);
   (*13*) charvar := charvar + CHR(1);
   (*14*) boolvar := charvar < '9';
   (*15*) boolvar := boolvar < (ORD(charvar) < 177B);
   (*16*) boolvar := realvar < FLOAT(2.0);
   (*17*) boolvar := boolvar = boolvar;
END TypeDemo.
```

□

**Exercise 2.15.** How would you use TYPE transfer facilities to convert
   a. A CHAR to an INTEGER.
   b. A REAL to an INTEGER.

□

## 2.4. Assignments, Expressions, and Precedence

The previous sections of this chapter have discussed some of Modula–2's data TYPES and declarations. Declarations serve to establish an environment for a program and they serve as a form of communication between a programmer and the compiler, but they don't actually do very much. In this section the emphasis shifts to using the data in a Modula–2 program.

There are two ways for a variable to attain some value. The direct method is to use an assignment statement. In an assignment statement a *value* is established by an *expression* and then that value is assigned to a variable. The less direct method is to pass a variable to a PROCEDURE. If the PROCEDURE uses a VAR parameter, any assignments to the PROCEDURE parameter will change the value outside the PROCEDURE. VAR parameters to PROCEDURES are discussed in Section 4.3.

Here is the syntax diagram for assignment statements.

**assignment**

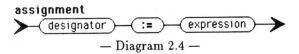

— Diagram 2.4 —

The left hand side of an assignment statement is something that can be assigned a value. (The term designator is discussed more in Section 13.1.) In Modula–2 the following can be assigned values:

> A simple variable
> A RECORD or an element of a RECORD
> An ARRAY or an element of an ARRAY
> A SET
> Something pointed at by a POINTER

The left hand side of an assignment must *never* be a constant, an expression, a TYPE name, a PROCEDURE name, a MODULE name or an individual member of a SET variable.

Obviously the key part of an assignment statement is the expression. Expressions are often extremely simple. The following assignment statement sets the variable named HoursPerWeek to the expression forty.

(* Example 2.14 *)

    HoursPerWeek := 40

Assignment statements resemble ordinary *algebraic equalities*;

you should actively resist this notion. Assignment statements indicate that a value from the right hand side *becomes* the value of the variable on the left hand side. It is illegal to place any thing but a variable on the left hand side. For example, the following two statements look plausible but are actually *illegal*.

(* Example 2.15 *)

```
5 := x;
x + y := 30;
```

The first is illegal because 5 is a constant and the second is illegal because x + y is an expression. Constants and expressions are allowed on the right hand side of an assignment, but never on the left.

The distinction between algebraic equalities and assignment statements is emphasized by using the := (pronounced "becomes") notation in the assignment statement. The = operator (pronounced "has the same value as" or "equals") is reserved in Modula–2 to *test* the equality of two operands — it is not used for assignment.

The right hand side of an assignment statement can be a complicated expression such as the following.

(* Example 2.16 *)

```
HoursPerWeek := HoursPerMonth + 2 - Seniority MOD 7
```

The easiest way to make the compiler understand your intent when you form expressions is to follow these rules:
- Parenthesize to make your meaning clear.
- Don't perform operations with mixed data TYPES.
- Remember that *arithmetic* operations on a given TYPE yield that TYPE.
- Remember that *comparison* operations on any TYPE yield the BOOLEAN TYPE.

The remainder of this section is a more detailed discussion of expressions. You might want to skip the following material during your first reading. The easy rules outlined above are adequate for most Modula–2 programs.

**expression**

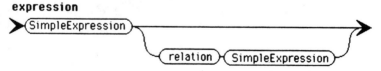

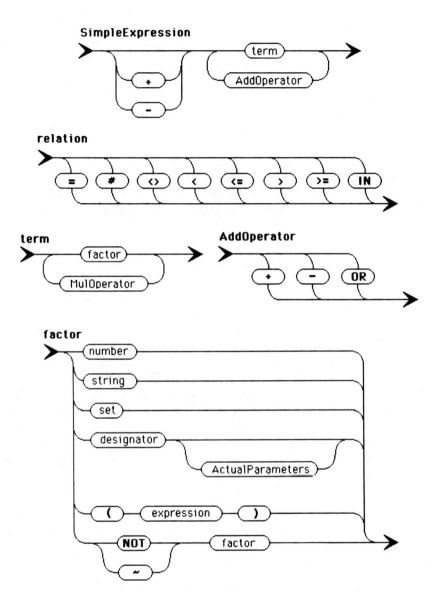

MulOperator

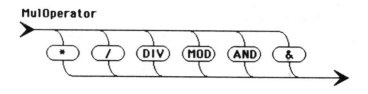

— Diagram 2.5 —

In Diagram 2.5 expressions are defined as SimpleExpressions, SimpleExpressions are defined as terms, and terms are defined as factors. One approach to understanding the inner mechanics of expressions is understanding Diagram 2.5. An alternative way to understand the inner mechanics of expressions is *operator precedence*.

Precedence describes the order in which operations are performed in an expression. For example if the expression

    5 + 6 * 7

is evaluated strictly from left to right then the result is seventy-seven (five plus six equals eleven, eleven times seven is seventy-seven). Another approach is to decide that multiplication takes precedence over addition, and then perform the multiplication first. If the preceding expression is evaluated with multiplication having precedence over addition, then the result is forty-seven (six times seven is forty-two, forty-two plus five is forty-seven). Programming languages must choose one approach or another. Most programming languages, including Modula–2, choose the more natural operator precedence over the simpler left to right method.

In Modula–2 there are four levels of precedence: the NOT operator has the highest precedence, followed by the MulOperators, the AddOperators, and then the relational operators.

In expressions with operators of varying precedence the high precedence operations are performed first. When an expression involves operators with equal precedence the operations are performed from left to right. Parentheses can (and should) be used to clarify expressions.

| Modula–2 Operator Precedence | |
|---|---|
| Precedence | Operator |
| Highest | NOT ~ |
| | * / DIV MOD AND & |
| | + − OR |
| Lowest | = # <> < <= > >= IN |

Modula–2 differs from many languages in its treatment of the unary minus. Unary minus is used to indicate negation (e.g. −5) as opposed to subtraction (e.g. x−5). The minus shown in the table above is the subtraction operator, not the unary minus. The unary minus doesn't follow a simple operator precedence rule that could be expressed in the table.

In many languages the unary minus operation has the highest precedence, equivalent to the precedence of NOT in Modula–2. Diagram 2.5 reveals the inner mechanics of the Modula–2 unary minus — it can only be applied to the *first* term of a SimpleExpression. (Take this as a given if Diagram 2.5 is not for you.) Therefore in Modula–2 it is *not* legal to write

```
x * -5
```

because 5 isn't the *first* term of a SimpleExpression. Instead one must use the bulkier expression

```
x * (-5)
```

or the equivalent expression

```
- x * 5
```

I recommend the following three simple rules for unary minus. Following these rules is the easiest way to use unary minus correctly.

1. Unary minus is allowed at the *beginning* of an expression. (e.g. −7 + x)
2. Unary minus is allowed *following* a comparison operator. (e.g. x <> −3)
3. In *all* other cases the unary minus and the following term must be enclosed in parentheses. (e.g. 3 MOD (−y))

The following examples will clarify some of the expression rules. In these examples, the variables x, y, z, and w are presumed to be INTEGERS and the variables p, q, and r are presumed to be

BOOLEAN.

| Expression | Means | Result |
|---|---|---|
| x+y+z | (x+y)+z | INTEGER |
| x+y*z | x+(y*z) | INTEGER |
| x-y+z-w | ((x-y)+z)-w | INTEGER |
| x*y*z | (x*y)*z | INTEGER |
| x*y+z*y | (x*y)+(z*y) | INTEGER |
| x+y*z+w | (x+(y*z))+w | INTEGER |
| x<y+z | x<(y+z) | BOOLEAN |
| p OR q AND r | p OR (q AND r) | BOOLEAN |
| NOT p AND q | (NOT p) AND q | BOOLEAN |
| x+y<z+w | (x+y)<(z+w) | BOOLEAN |
| x<y#p | (x<y)#p | BOOLEAN |
| p AND NOT q | p AND (NOT q) | BOOLEAN |
| x<-y+3 | x<((-y)+3) | BOOLEAN |

Now let's show some expressions that appear to be legal but are actually *illegal*. As before x, y, and z are INTEGERS and p, q, and r are BOOLEANS.

Because of the Modula–2 precedence rules, the expression

    x<y AND z<5

actually means

    ( x < (y AND z)) < 5

This is illegal because the AND operator works with BOOLEAN operands whereas y and z are INTEGERS. The proper way to indicate that x must be less than y and that z must be less than five is

    (x<y) AND (z<5)

Another form of expression that is *illegal* in Modula–2 is

    x < y < z

Because expressions are evaluated left to right, this actually means

    (x < y) < z

The result of comparing x and y is a BOOLEAN, and it is then illegal to compare this BOOLEAN result with z, an INTEGER. If you want to perform a *range test* you must use the more laborious expression

```
(x < y) AND (y < z)
```

Since BOOLEANS can be compared, it *is* legal to write

```
p < q < r
```

if p, q, and r are BOOLEANS. In Modula-2 this means

```
(p < q) < r
```

Because the NOT operator has the highest precedence, it is illegal to write

```
NOT x = y
```

This is illegal because it means

```
(NOT x) = y
```

and the NOT operator can only be applied to BOOLEANS, not IN-TEGERS. Parentheses are often used to reduce the binding force of the NOT operator.

```
NOT (x = y)
```

A better way to convey the idea of inequality is

```
x <> y
```

**Exercise 2.16.** What value is represented by the following expressions?

| | | | |
|---|---|---|---|
| a. | 5 + 6 * 10 | k. | 30 * 5 DIV 2 |
| b. | 5 < 6 | l. | 3. / 2. |
| c. | 5 + 3 - 4 + 7 - 2 | m. | ORD('a') + 25 |
| d. | 5 + 3 - 2 * 2 + 5 | n. | 10 DIV 15 >= 4 |
| f. | 3 DIV 5 | o. | NOT ( 3 > 5 ) |
| g. | 3 MOD 2 | p. | 20 MOD 20 |
| h. | 10 DIV 2 DIV 2 | q. | 3 > 5 - 3 |
| i. | 3 < 10 DIV 3 | r. | (3 < 1) <= (5 > 2) |
| j. | (x<y)AND(5<2) | s. | (y=y)OR(x=y) |

□

**Exercise 2.17.** Rewrite the expressions in the previous example using parentheses as necessary to *clarify* their meanings. Be careful not to alter their meanings.
□

**Exercise 2.18.** Which of the following expressions are *illegal* in Modula-2? Why?

a.    5 / 10

b.    20000 + 30.
c.    'a' - 'A'
d.    NOT('A' > 'a')
e.    5 < 10 < 20
f.    5 < 10 AND 10 < 20
g.    FLOAT(30 DIV 4) > 3.2
h.    -20 < -10
i.    ORD('0') + 1C
j.    CHR(ORD('a')-ORD('c'))
k.    NOT 3 < 2
l.    30.1 MOD 2.
m.    TRUNC(8) < 2.
n.    (1 + (2 + (3 + (4) + 5))))
o.    5 < 10 = TRUE

□

## 2.5. Constants

Constants are an important part of most programs. They are used to initialize variables to a known value, to declare specified numbers of items, to indicate how many times certain operations should be performed, to provide fixed criteria for comparisons, etc. Constants are as flexible as variables with just one exception — their value cannot be changed.

Modula–2 has numeric, single character, multiple character (string), BOOLEAN, enumeration, and SET constants. Unlike some languages, Modula–2 does *not* have constant ARRAYS or constant RECORDS. This limitation of Modula–2 has often been criticized. Modula–2's lack of ARRAY and RECORD constants is a reflection of the limited number of operations that are available for these TYPES. Modula–2 also lacks POINTER constants — an omission that has not drawn much criticism.

*Explicit constants* are simply constants that appear directly in the program at the appropriate places. For example a program to compute the area of a circle might include the equation

```
area := 3.14159 * radius * radius;
```

In this equation the number 3.14159 is an explicit constant. Modula–2 also allows you to provide a symbolic *name* for a constant so that the name can be used wherever you would normally write the constant. Named constants are discussed in the following section. Let's first talk about the rules for writing an explicit constant.

Modula–2 has two forms of numeric constants: whole numbers and floating point numbers. In syntax diagrams whole numbers are called INTEGERS and floating point numbers are called REAL numbers. The syntax for numeric constants is shown in the following diagram.

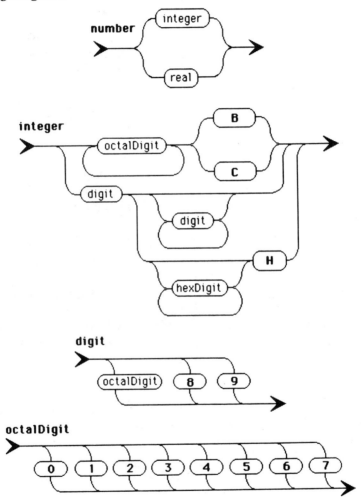

**hexDigit**

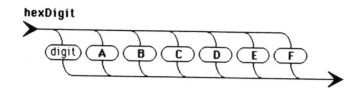

— Diagram 2.6 —

*Whole numbers* can be represented in decimal (base 10), in octal (base 8) or in hexadecimal (base 16). Octal numbers use the suffix "B" (or "C" for CHARS), hexadecimal numbers use the suffix "H", and decimal numbers don't use a suffix.

A *decimal* whole number is simply a sequence of the digits "0" through "9". The following are valid decimal whole numbers:

$$0 \quad 33 \quad 502 \quad 33000 \quad 12$$

Note that decimal whole numbers consist *only* of numerals. The word "33,000" is not a valid decimal INTEGER because of the comma. The word "33." is not a valid decimal INTEGER because of the period, but it is a valid REAL number (see below).

A *hexadecimal* (base sixteen) number is a sequence of hexadecimal digits ("0" through "9", and "A" through "F") followed by the suffix "H". If the first digit of a hexadecimal number happens to be any of the digits "A" through "F" then the number must be preceded by a zero. This makes it easy to distinguish numbers from identifiers — numbers always start with one of the numerals 0 through 9 whereas identifiers always start with an alphabetic character. The following are examples of hexadecimal INTEGERS:

$$\text{0H} \quad \text{33H} \quad \text{0FH} \quad \text{3300H} \quad \text{0DECH}$$

The symbol DECH is *not* a hexadecimal INTEGER because it doesn't start with one of the numerals "0" through "9"; the compiler assumes that DECH is an identifier.

An *octal* INTEGER is a sequence of octal digits ("0" through "7") followed by either a "B". The following are valid octal INTEGERS:

$$\text{0B} \quad \text{33B} \quad \text{177560B}$$

A REAL constant is used to represent numbers that have a fractional part, or numbers whose magnitude exceeds the limited range allowed for whole numbers.

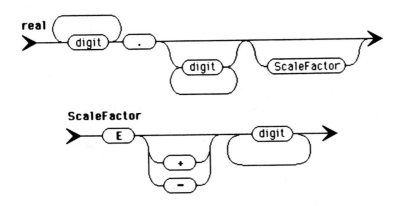

— Diagram 2.7 —

As you can see from the syntax diagram, the hallmark of a REAL number is the decimal point. A REAL number always consists of one or more decimal digits followed by a decimal point. The decimal point may be followed by more decimal digits representing the fractional part of the number and there also may be a trailing exponent representing the scale factor of the number. Let's first look at some REAL numbers without scale factors:

            1.0    0.    456.879    12000.    128.

Scale factors make it easy to represent large or small numbers. A scale factor consists of the letter "E", optionally followed by a plus or minus followed a power of ten in decimal. For example, the REAL number 1.E6 is read as "one time ten to the sixth power" and it represents one million. It could equivalently be entered as 1000000. but it is somewhat safer to tell the computer about the six zeroes rather than enter them by hand.

Here is the REAL number 133000. entered in several formats using scale factors:

    133000.E0    1.33E5    1.33E+5    0.133E6    1330000.E-1

**Exercise 2.19.** There are innumerable ways to write REAL numeric constants incorrectly. Explain what is wrong with each of these constants?

    1.33e5  .333E6  133000E0  133E.3  0FFH.E0  017.77BE0

☐

## 2.5.1. Named Constants

A named constant is created using a declaration. The declaration defines the name of the constant and its value. Like explicit constants, named constants only have an implied TYPE.

There are two major advantages to named constants:

- A well chosen name makes a program more readable.
- The value of a named constant can be updated by changing a single declaration.

The name of a constant should be chosen to express the *usage* of the constant, not its *value*. In my opinion it is worthless to declare the following constant.

```
CONST
    TEN = 10;
```

The symbolic name TEN conveys no more meaning (and possibly less) than the number 10. A more useful name for a constant illustrates its usage in a program. For example the declaration

```
CONST
    Nrows = 10;
    Ncols = 6;
```

names two constants that might be used in a matrix multiplication program. The symbolic name Nrows helps unravel the mystery of the program wherever it is used.

In a program the value of a named constant appears in just one place, the declaration. However the name may be used throughout the program. For example the Constants MODULE shown below contains a constant named xres. In a real program xres might be used in dozens of calculations. If the program had to be updated for a new graphics system with a different x resolution, only one declaration would have to be changed. However if explicit constants were used throughout a program the programmer would have to browse through the program to change them manually. Obviously it's better to change one declaration, than to change dozens of numbers scattered throughout a program.

**ConstantDeclaration**

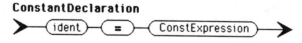

**ConstExpression**

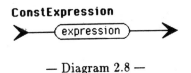

— Diagram 2.8 —

Diagram 2.8 shows the syntax for constant expressions and constant declarations. Notice that the rule for forming a ConstantExpression is the same as that for forming any expression. The caveat (not expressed in the syntax) should be obvious — a ConstantExpression must be formed from constants.

Constant declarations are indicated by writing the word CONST followed by a list of phrases. Each phrase is the name of the constant, followed by an "=", followed by the value, followed by a semicolon.

Here is a program MODULE that declares several numeric constants.

(* Example 2.17 *)

```
MODULE Constants;

CONST Pi = 3.14159;
      xres = 256;
      yres = 196;
      Npixels = xres * yres;


BEGIN
END Constants.
```

Evidently Pi is a floating point constant, and the others are whole number constants. The constant Npixels has the value 50176. Notice that Npixels is defined after xres and yres because it depends on them.

You could use the named constant Pi in a program to compute the area of a circle.

```
area := Pi * radius * radius;
```

**Exercise 2.20.** Expand the Constants MODULE to print the value of xres, yres, and Npixels using the facilities of the InOut MODULE.
□

**Exercise 2.21.** Write a program MODULE that defines constants for the following ASCII characters:

CarriageReturn
LineFeed
Backspace
Tab
FormFeed
Escape
Delete

(See Appendix IX.)
□

# Chapter 3

# Control Flow in Modula-2

Unless instructed otherwise, a computer will process the operations in a program in order, one after another. However most programming tasks have repetitive elements, and most involve alternatives. Repetitive elements are managed by instructing the computer to return to a earlier point in the program. Alternatives are managed by directing the computer to go to one of several places in a program. In either case the programmer is controlling the flow of execution of the program.

A computer executes a program somewhat like people read technical material. Phrases are read word by word, from start to finish. However the work as a whole is read more eclectically. Some parts may be skipped, some must be repeated, some must be worried over again and again until they are understood. Often the reader skips from one place to another to pursue interesting topics. Whereas we can adjust our own "flow of control" while reading, computers must be told exactly how to proceed through a program.

*Structured programming* is a technique for writing programs. It has become universally accepted because it helps programmers to write clearly and to produce more reliable software. Structured programs are constructed from universally recognized flow-of-control building blocks. These building blocks better express the sequence of the operations better than their predecessor, the goto statement. A goto statement directs the computer to move its point of execution from one location in a program to another. The goto is simple and powerful, but it is often used so cleverly that confusion is the universal result.

Theoretical studies have shown that any program that uses gotos can be rewritten using structured control flow statements. Experience has shown that programs constructed from standardized repetitive and decision making building blocks are easier to write, easier to understand, and easier to rewrite than their convoluted goto laden predecessors. Another benefit is that structured programs are easier to translate into efficient machine language form.

Many people have defined structured programming to be programming that avoids using the goto statement. In that sense of the term *all* programming in Modula–2 is *structured* because Modula–2 doesn't even have a goto statement. However structured programming is much more than a lack of goto's. One goal of structured programming is to improve the clarity and correctness of programs. Another goal is to manage complexity so that ever more challenging subjects can be tackled. Obscure programs can be written using beautiful control structures just as clear programs can be written with gotos.

Modula–2's structured programming building blocks address the following issues:

1. Conditional execution of statements.
2. Iterative (repeated) execution of statements.
3. Grouping of statements and data into PROCEDURES.

Modula–2 contains the following statements.

**statement**

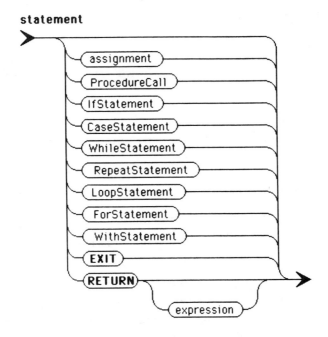

— Diagram 3.1 —

Most of these statements serve to define the flow of control within a program. IF, WHILE, CASE, WHILE, REPEAT, FOR, LOOP and EXIT are discussed in this chapter. Procedure calls and the RETURN statement are discussed in the following chapter. The WITH statement is discussed in Section 13.1.

Five of Modula–2's control flow statements (IF, CASE, WHILE, REPEAT, and FOR) should be familiar to anyone who has programmed in Pascal. I am going to discuss them first. Modula's new iterative structure is the LOOP/EXIT statement that is discussed in the final section of this chapter.

Throughout this chapter I try to show you when you should use each of these structures. Each is appropriate in different situations so I try to provide guidance that will help you write better programs.

## 3.1. The IF Statement

The IF statement allows a programmer to specify *alternative* execution paths based on the value (TRUE/FALSE) of a control expression.

**IfStatement**

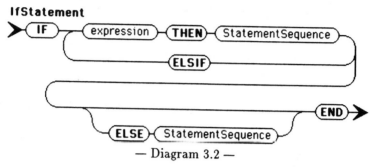

— Diagram 3.2 —

The expression in an IF statement must have BOOLEAN results. Control flows to one or another of the *StatementSequences* based upon the BOOLEAN value of the given expression. Naturally a StatementSequence is just one or more statements, separated by semicolons.

**StatementSequence**

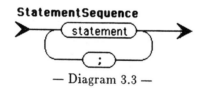

— Diagram 3.3 —

There may be zero, one, or several ELSIF clauses, but only zero or one ELSE clauses. Only the StatementSequence associated with the first TRUE expression is executed. If none of the expressions are TRUE then the ELSE clause's StatementSequence (if it exists) is executed.

The syntax diagram for the IF statement shows you how to express IF statements correctly. Syntax diagrams are useful for showing you how you can express your thoughts in Modula-2, but they aren't useful for describing what happens when your program is executed. Another useful diagram is the *flowchart*. It shows the possible control paths in a program (or program segment). In days of yore flowcharts were used to explain whole programs. This usage has declined in popularity because clear, structured languages like Modula-2 help make the program obvious to a reader. However I do believe that flowcharts are useful visual aids

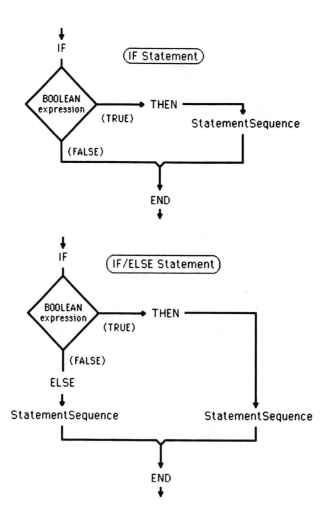

Figure 3.1.

to explain the Modula–2 control flow statements.
Here are two Modula–2 IF statements.

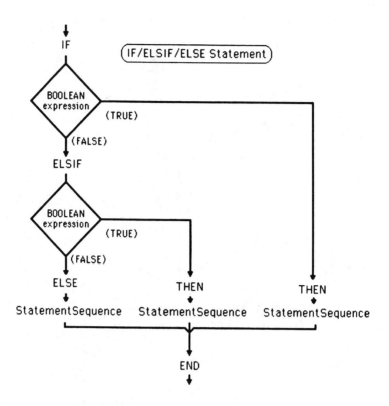

Figure 3.1. (continued)

(* Example 3.1 *)

```
IF x = 10 THEN x := 0 END;

IF x = z THEN
    x := 0
ELSIF x = y THEN
    x := 1
ELSE
    y := y - 1
END;
```

Modula–2 is not very picky about semicolons. The semicolon is used as a statement *separator*, not as a statement *terminator*. Since Modula–2 allows *null* statements (See Diagram 3.1), it is acceptable to write

                                              (* Example 3.2 *)
```
IF x > y THEN
    max := x; min := y;
ELSE
    max := y; min := x;
END
```

Strictly speaking, the last semicolons on the second and fourth lines are unnecessary and they are simply ignored. (Note that the declaration part of a Modula-2 program is much pickier about semi-colons than the statement part.)

**Exercise 3.1.** Given that x, y, z, and m are all INTEGER variables, explain the purpose of the following *nested* IF statements.

                                              (* Example 3.3 *)
```
IF x<y THEN
    IF x<z THEN m := x ELSE m := z END
ELSE
    IF y<z THEN m := y ELSE m := z END
END
```

□

**Exercise 3.2.** Rewrite the previous example using more complicated expressions (rather than nested IF statements) to accomplish the same result.

□

## 3.2. The CASE Statement

The CASE statement causes control to flow to one of several StatementSequences based on the value of an expression. The CASE statement is not as general as the IF statement, but for certain situations it is preferable because it is clearer (more expressive). (A secondary reason to use the CASE statement is efficiency — it may encourage the compiler to produce better code.)

**CaseStatement**

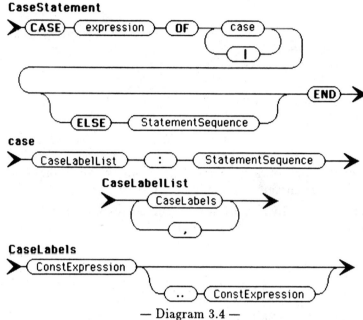

— Diagram 3.4 —

The vertical bar is used to separate the individual alternatives. It is not acceptable to place a vertical bar after the last alternative. In a CASE statement there is only one expression. In effect the result of the expression is compared with the constants in the CaseLabels and an associated StatementSequence is executed if there is a match. It is illegal for the same constant to appear in two separate CaseLabels, and the expression and the CaseLabels must be compatible TYPES. The expression (and the CaseLabels) may not be REAL.

```
MODULE DoCmds;                           (* Example 3.4 *)
FROM SupportMod IMPORT appendcmd, printcmd,
     deletecmd, movecmd, linenumber, errmsg, CmdCh;
BEGIN
  CASE CmdCh() OF
     'a' : appendcmd |
     'p' : printcmd |
     'd' : deletecmd |
     'm' : movecmd |
     '=' : linenumber |
     (* following commands not implemented *)
     'c','x','v','h' :
     ELSE errmsg    (* unknown command *)
  END
END DoCmds.
```

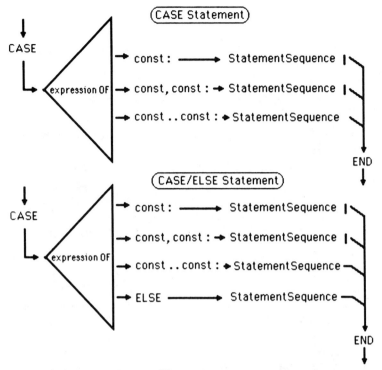

Figure 3.2.

This CASE statement could also be coded using an IF statement.

```
                                        (* Example 3.5 *)
MODULE DoCmds1;
FROM SupportMod IMPORT appendcmd, printcmd,
      deletecmd, movecmd, linenumber, errmsg, CmdCh;

VAR
     ch : CHAR;

BEGIN
     ch := CmdCh();
     IF ch = 'a' THEN appendcmd
     ELSIF ch = 'p' THEN printcmd
     ELSIF ch = 'd' THEN deletecmd
     ELSIF ch = 'm' THEN movecmd
     ELSIF ch = '=' THEN linenumber
     (* do nothing: c, x, v, and h not implemented *)
     ELSIF (ch = 'c') OR (ch = 'x') OR
```

```
          (ch = 'v') OR (ch = 'h') THEN
     ELSE errmsg
     END
  END DoCmds1.
```

Programmers are often forced to choose between using a CASE statement and using an IF statement. The CASE statement is preferred when there are several distinct alternatives identified by constants. The CaseLabels are often character constants or enumeration values (See Chapter 11). The CASE statement should only be used when the CaseLabel values are closely spaced. An IF statement should be used for comparing a variable with a list of scattered values. The CASE statement emphasizes that a single option among many will be selected — the IF statement is more general.

**Exercise 3.3.** Example 3.5 showed a complicated IF statement that is functionally the same as the CASE statement in Example 3.4. One difference is the use of the variable named ch to hold the results of the CmdCh PROCEDURE during the series of tests in the IF statement. Why is this temporary variable necessary? Why wasn't a similar variable necessary in the CASE statement version of the program? Does this difference argue for or against the use of the IF statement equivalent in this example?
□

**Exercise 3.4.** Rewrite the following IF statement as a CASE statement.

```
   IF (ch >= 'a') AND (ch <= 'z') THEN ch := CAP(ch) END;
```
□

## 3.3. The WHILE Statement

The WHILE statement causes a StatementSequence to be repeatedly executed while a certain condition exists.

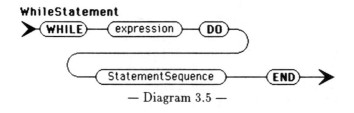

**WhileStatement**

— Diagram 3.5 —

The control expression must produce a BOOLEAN result. If the expression is TRUE then the StatementSequence is executed and the process is repeated. If the expression is found to be FALSE then control passes to the statement following the symbol END. A group of statements that is executed repeatedly is called a *loop*, a WHILE loop in this case. The term *iterate* means to do something repeatedly. One pass through a loop is often called an *iteration*.

In a WHILE loop the StatementSequence will be executed as long as the given expression is TRUE. Note that the StatementSequence will never be executed if the expression is FALSE when the WHILE statement is first encountered. In virtually all cases the execution of the StatementSequence causes the expression to eventually become FALSE so that the WHILE loop terminates.

(* Example 3.6 *)

```
MODULE Filter;
FROM Subs IMPORT ReadLine, eof, ProcessLine;
BEGIN
     ReadLine;
     WHILE NOT eof DO
          ProcessLine;
          ReadLine
     END
END Filter.
```

In this WHILE loop the ReadLine PROCEDURE eventually exhausts the input, causing the BOOLEAN variable named eof (end of file) to become TRUE, thereby terminating the loop. Notice that if the file is empty the first ReadLine statement will cause eof to be TRUE and the loop will never be executed.

WHILE statements are used primarily when the number of iterations of the loop is *not* known in advance. The FOR statement is better if the number of iterations is known. Consider the problem of determining experimentally how many coin tosses are necessary before a run of five heads emerges. In the following example the routine flip returns TRUE for heads and FALSE for tails. We take it as given that flip models a *fair* coin toss. When the loop completes, the variable Attempts indicates how many coin tosses were necessary. Because we are modeling a random process, we expect to get different answers each time we run this program.

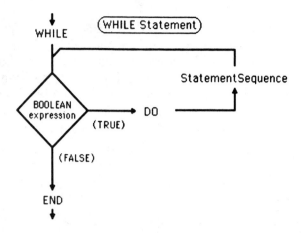

Figure 3.3.

(* Example 3.7 *)

```
MODULE Toss;
FROM Flip IMPORT flip;
FROM InOut IMPORT WriteCard, WriteLn;

VAR
   HeadCnt, Attempts : CARDINAL;

BEGIN
   HeadCnt := 0;
   Attempts := 0;
   WHILE HeadCnt < 5 DO
     INC(Attempts);
     IF flip() THEN
       INC(HeadCnt)
     ELSE
       HeadCnt := 0
     END
   END; (* WHILE *)
   WriteCard(Attempts,5); WriteLn;
END Toss.
```

**Exercise 3.5.** Put some output statements (imported from InOut) inside the Toss program's WHILE loop so that you can watch the search for a sequence of five heads.
□

**Exercise 3.6.** The following program is a generalization of the toss program. In the following we determine experimentally how many tosses are necessary to reproduce a given sequence. The method is to think of each step in the sequence as a given state. The states are numbered, state zero means nothing has been accomplished, state one means the first element of the sequence has been seen, state two means the first two elements (in order) have been encountered, etc.

(* Example 3.8 *)

```
MODULE States;
FROM Flip IMPORT flip;
FROM InOut IMPORT WriteCard, WriteLn;

VAR
    State, Attempts : CARDINAL;
    Heads, Tails : BOOLEAN;

BEGIN
    State := 0;
    Attempts := 0;
    WHILE State # 5 DO
      INC(Attempts);
      Heads := flip();
      Tails := NOT Heads;
      CASE State OF
          0: IF Heads THEN INC(State) END |
          1: IF Tails THEN
                INC(State)
             ELSE
                State := 1
             END |
          2: IF Tails THEN
                INC(State)
             ELSE
                State := 1
             END |
          3: IF Heads THEN
                INC(State)
             ELSE
                State := 0
             END |
          4: IF Tails THEN
                INC(State)
```

```
              ELSE
                  State := 1
              END
         END (* CASE *)
      END; (* WHILE *)
      WriteCard(Attempts,5); WriteLn;
   END States.
```

What is the sequence of heads and tails that leads out of the
WHILE statement? Why do some of the cases in the CASE statement revert to state zero whereas others revert to state one?

Could this program have been written without the variables
named Heads and Tails? If so then how do they contribute to the
solution?

Describe several other situations where the notion of states might
be useful for organizing a program.

Note, another method for solving this problem appears in Exercise
5.3.

□

**Exercise 3.7.** Modify the program in the previous example to
detect the sequence

□

**Exercise 3.8.** Rewrite the original Toss MODULE to use a CASE
statement to detect the pattern 'HHHHH'.

□


## 3.4. The REPEAT Statement

The REPEAT statement is similar to the WHILE statement. In both
cases the StatementSequence is executed repeatedly. One
difference is that the condition for a WHILE loop is at the start of
the loop whereas the condition governing a REPEAT loop is at the
end. Thus the StatementSequence of a WHILE loop will not be executed if the condition is initially FALSE whereas the StatementSequence of a REPEAT loop will *always* be executed at least once.
The other important difference is the sense of the conditional test
— in a WHILE loop the iteration continues so long as the condition
is TRUE whereas in a REPEAT loop the iteration continues so long
as the condition is FALSE.

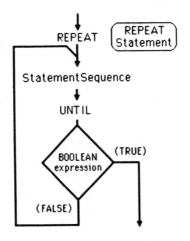

Figure 3.4.

**RepeatStatement**

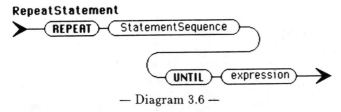

— Diagram 3.6 —

It is up to the programmer to choose either a WHILE loop or a RE-PEAT loop by deciding whether a leading or trailing condition is most appropriate, and whether the StatementSequence should be executed at least once. For example, it is awkward to rewrite the first WHILE loop (Example 3.6) as a REPEAT loop.

                                                    (* Example 3.9 *)

```
MODULE Filter1;
FROM Subs IMPORT ReadLine, eof, ProcessLine;

BEGIN
    ReadLine;
    IF NOT eof THEN
        REPEAT
            ProcessLine;
            ReadLine
        UNTIL eof;
    END
END Filter1.
```

However the second WHILE loop (Example 3.7) is probably *best* written as a REPEAT loop.

( * Example 3.10 * )

```
MODULE Toss1;
FROM Flip IMPORT flip;
FROM InOut IMPORT WriteCard, WriteLn;

VAR
    HeadCnt, Attempts : CARDINAL;

BEGIN
    HeadCnt := 0;
    Attempts := 0;
    REPEAT
        INC(Attempts);
        IF flip() THEN
            INC(HeadCnt)
        ELSE
            HeadCnt := 0
        END
    UNTIL HeadCnt = 5;
    WriteCard(Attempts,5); WriteLn;
END Toss1.
```

**Exercise 3.9.** Newton's method for computing the square root of a positive number is the following. (Note: in the following pseudo code n is the positive number, r is the current approximation to its square root, and both n and r are REAL.

1. Make an initial guess. One half of n is suggested.
2. Refine the guess. Make the new guess the *average* of n/r and r.
3. Explore the *relative* error. $(x/r-r) < (1.E-5*r)$ implies about five digits of accuracy.
4. Return to step 2 if the relative error is too large.

Write a loop to compute the square roots of positive REAL numbers using Newtons method.
□

## 3.5. The FOR Statement

The FOR statement is a specialized loop. In many loops, a certain variable attains a succession of values, such as the succession of values an index variable attains during a table search. Modula–2 uses FOR loops for this control structure.

**ForStatement**

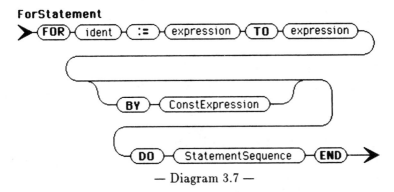

— Diagram 3.7 —

The *identifier* mentioned in the syntax diagram is usually called the *control variable*. The expressions are the *bounds* of the control variable and they must be compatible with the TYPE of the control variable. The ConstExpression is the *increment* that is added to the control variable at the end of each repetition of the loop. If the "BY ConstExpression" phrase is omitted, an increment of 1 is assumed. The increment can be a positive or negative INTEGER or CARDINAL *constant.*

In a FOR loop, the StatementSequence is executed once for each value of the control variable. In the usual case, the first expression is less than the second and the control variable attains every value in that range. The following program sums the numbers from one to 100.

```
                                         (* Example 3.11 *)
MODULE CentSum;
FROM InOut IMPORT WriteCard, WriteLn;

VAR
    sum, i : CARDINAL;

BEGIN
    sum := 0;
    FOR i := 1 TO 100 DO
        sum := sum + i
    END;
    WriteCard(sum,5); WriteLn;
END CentSum.
```

You should obey the following rules when you use FOR loops:
1. The bounds expressions should not depend on anything in the body of the loop.
2. It is forbidden to alter the value of the control variable within the body of the loop.
3. The value of the control variable should be considered *undefined* after the loop terminates.
4. The control variable can *not* be
   • An imported variable
   • A PROCEDURE parameter
   • A member of a RECORD, an ARRAY, or a SET

It is easy to violate these rules. Some violations will be rejected by the compiler, others may be accepted even though they lead to incorrect programs. Use WHILE or REPEAT loops in situations that require unusual flexibility. Programs that violate these rules will not be portable or predictable.

**Exercise 3.10.** Rewrite the CentSum program to sum the numbers from one to 100 starting from 100 and progressing down to one.
□

**Exercise 3.11.** Rewrite the CentSum program to sum the even numbers from one to 100.
□

**Exercise 3.12.** Rewrite the CentSum program using a WHILE loop.
□

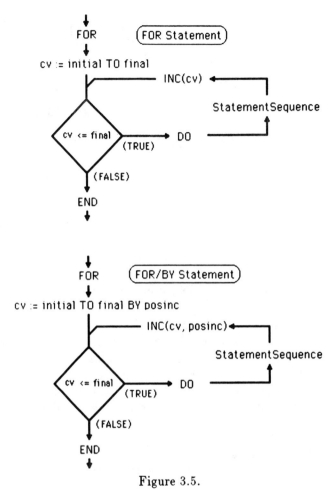

Figure 3.5.

**Exercise 3.13.** Write FOR loops that violate each of the first three rules.

☐

**Exercise 3.14.** Write a program to compute (approximately) the value of the transcendental number e (2.71828...). Compute the first ten terms of the formula

$$e = \frac{1}{0!} + \frac{1}{1!} + \frac{1}{2!} + \ldots$$

N! (N factorial) is N*( (N–1)! ) and 0! is 1.

☐

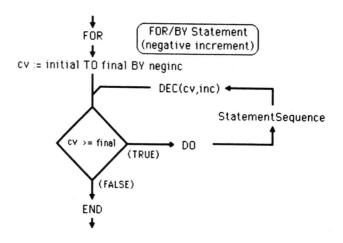

Figure 3.5. (Continued)

## 3.6. The LOOP and EXIT Statements

REPEAT, WHILE, and FOR loops are familiar Pascal control structures. Modula-2's new control structure is the LOOP structure. The
LOOP statement allows a programmer greater control over program loops. REPEAT, WHILE, and FOR loops are stereotypical —
they exist because those types of loops are commonly necessary.
The LOOP statement is Modula-2's most general iterative statement.

**LoopStatement**

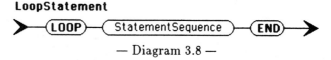

— Diagram 3.8 —

Modula-2 LOOPS appear to be infinite. The LOOP statement itself
does not indicate when the loop terminates. The termination of a
LOOP statement is caused by the EXIT statement. Whenever the
EXIT is encountered the enclosing LOOP statement terminates. A
LOOP without an EXIT statement somewhere in the body of the
LOOP is truly an infinite loop; an EXIT anywhere but in the body of
a LOOP StatementSequence is an error. Note that an EXIT statement inside of several nested LOOP statements will only terminate
the innermost LOOP statement.

Let's rewrite the original example of a WHILE loop (Example 3.6)
using the Modula-2 LOOP statement.

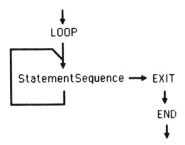

Figure 3.6.

(* Example 3.12 *)

```
MODULE Filter2;
FROM Subs IMPORT ReadLine, eof, ProcessLine;

BEGIN
  LOOP
    ReadLine;
    IF eof THEN EXIT END;
    ProcessLine
  END
END Filter2.
```

This version has some advantages over the original. The ReadLine call only appears once, and ReadLine and ProcessLine are in their natural order. The reverse order in the original example was necessary because (presumably) ProcessLine doesn't know how to process a line when ReadLine encounters the end of file.

Probably the major advantage of the LOOP statement over Modula–2's other iterative statements is *multiple* exit conditions. Wherever possible it's best to code loops that have just a single exit point because they are easier to understand. However occasional loops cannot be conveniently expressed with a single exit point. I believe that multiple exit points are preferable to overly complex controlling expressions. However loops with multiple exit points should be used sparingly.

Another reason to use the LOOP statement in preference to Modula–2's more regimented looping constructs is to have an exit point in the middle of a loop. Although this requirement is not common, it does occur and it is easily solved with a LOOP statement.

Some people have criticized the Modula–2 LOOP statement because it allows multiple exit points. Note that Modula–2's iterative statements do obey the "rule" that structured statements should have only one entrance point. The "suggestion" that structured statements have only one exit point is violated in Modula–2 for flexibility. Multiple exit points should be used carefully. Use WHILE and REPEAT loops where appropriate because they explicitly show the termination conditions. Use the LOOP statement when WHILE, REPEAT or FOR loops are inappropriate.

The string utilities MODULE in Section 8.2 is a good example of using the LOOP statement with multiple exit points. In several of the string manipulation subroutines there are several different exit criteria that may occur. Trying to express all the exit conditions in the control expression of a WHILE or REPEAT loop is too awkward. (Try it!) The LOOP statement with multiple embedded EXIT statements is, in my opinion, a better alternative.

Let's expand our previous example of a LOOP statement to demonstrate multiple exit points. Consider some command language where commands are entered in a two step process — first the command is entered on one line and then any parameters are entered on another line.

(* Example 3.13 *)

```
MODULE Filter3;
FROM Subs IMPORT ReadLine, eof,
     ProcessCommand, ProcessParams;

BEGIN
  LOOP
     ReadLine;
     IF eof THEN EXIT END;
     ProcessCommand;
     ReadLine;
     IF eof THEN EXIT END;
     ProcessParams
  END
END Filter3.
```

**Exercise 3.15.** Use a Modula–2 LOOP statement to sum the even numbers from two to 100. Is this a better program than the one you wrote for Exercise 3.11.
□

**Exercise 3.16.** Rewrite the following as a LOOP statement.

```
WHILE p DO
  ss
END;
```

Is the Modula–2 LOOP construct an improvement in this case?
□

**Exercise 3.17.** Rewrite the following as a LOOP statement.

```
REPEAT
  ss
UNTIL p
```

Is the Modula–2 LOOP construct an improvement in this case?
□

**Exercise 3.18.** Rewrite the following FOR loops using LOOP statements.

```
FOR i := 1 TO 10 DO
  ss
END;
FOR i := 10 TO 0 BY -2 DO
  ss
END;
```

□

**Exercise 3.19.** Modula–2 FOR loops ordinarily operate for a fixed number of iterations. One way to break out prematurely from a FOR loop is to use a RETURN statement — See Section 4.5. How could you use the LOOP/EXIT statements to break out prematurely from a FOR loop? Apply your solution to the following FOR loop so that it terminates when the BOOLEAN variable Err becomes TRUE.

```
FOR i := 1 TO 100 DO
  ss1;
  IF Err THEN (* terminate *) ... END;
  ss2
END
```

Do you think your method is reliable? Is your technique recommended practice, or an aberration that shouldn't be used?
□

**Exercise 3.20.** Modula–2 does not contain a goto statement. Do you think that the control structures that are provided in Modula–2 are adequate? Does the lack of a goto in Modula–2 lead to overuse of the LOOP statement?

# Chapter 4

# Procedures

Your first hurdle in learning to program is getting your first small program to work correctly. As you become more skilled your programs will naturally become larger and more sophisticated. For a large program, managing complexity means dividing a large problem into smaller, more understandable units.

Modula–2 has several facilities for partitioning a program. At one level there are the control structures and PROCEDURES, which allow you to structure your program into small pieces that perform simple chores. At another level there is Modula–2's MODULE structure, which allows you to partition the complexity of a problem into smaller, more manageable units.

PROCEDURES are important facilities in most programming languages. They allow you bundle a group of statements that perform a single chore. A PROCEDURE can be called from various places in a program, it can return computed results, and it can be passed information that it uses to perform its computations. Modula–2 might be complemented for its clean implementation of PROCEDURES. However MODULES, not PROCEDURES, are Modula–2's major contribution.

MODULES and PROCEDURES both allow a programmer to manage the complexity that arises in most non–trivial programs. The ideas behind PROCEDURES are discussed in this chapter. MODULES are discussed more fully in Part II.

## 4.1. MODULES and PROCEDURES

An informal distinction between MODULES and PROCEDURES is easy. PROCEDURES usually perform a specific operation whereas MODULES usually embody several related services. For example there is the sin PROCEDURE that computes the trigonometric sine of an angle and there is the MathLib0 MODULE that contains eight PROCEDURES for computing mathematical functions. The sin PROCEDURE is contained in the MathLib0 MODULE.

A PROCEDURE is active. It does something. In order to get a PROCEDURE to do something it must be *called* or *activated*. MODULES aren't active and you can't call or activate a MODULE. Rather a MODULE is a grouping of PROCEDURES and data. The PROCEDURES contained within a MODULE can be called, but not the MODULE itself.

In Modula–2 there are four main levels that you must understand:
  The Program
  The MODULE
  The PROCEDURE
  The Statement

A *program* is a complete entity. In most computers the programs are the only entities that can be executed to perform some useful task. A Modula–2 program is composed of MODULES. Every program contains at least one MODULE, the *program* MODULE. Most program MODULES are combined with other MODULES, called *global* MODULES to form a complete program.

MODULES contain data structures, PROCEDURES, and possibly a short statement sequence. Data within a MODULE is static — it exists for the entire time that the program is running (except for local MODULES).

PROCEDURES are made of statements, local data items, and other PROCEDURES. Local variables only exist while the enclosing PROCEDURE is running. Local data is created automatically when the PROCEDURE starts to run and it vanishes as soon as the PROCEDURE returns.

*Statements* are the individual active entities of a Modula–2 program. They are the finest level of detail that a programmer can control in a high level programming language such as Modula–2.

## 4.2. PROCEDURES

A PROCEDURE is a collection of local declarations and statements. When a PROCEDURE is *called* (activated) its local variables are created and then control is passed to its first statement. The statements in a PROCEDURE can refer to its local data (constants and variables) or any data visible in the MODULE or PROCEDURE that contains the PROCEDURE.

It is possible to pass *parameters* to a PROCEDURE when it is activated. You might like to think of parameters as *initialized local variables*. (Note that *none* of the true local variables are automatically initialized. Their initialization is the programmer's responsibility.) We have already seen numerous examples of parameters, such as the parameters that are supplied to the routines from InOut.

A PROCEDURE call must provide all the parameters that are listed in a PROCEDURE definition.

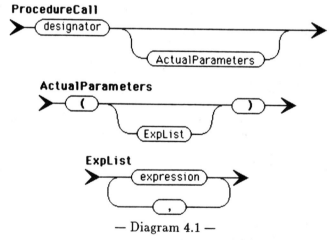

— Diagram 4.1 —

In Modula-2 a PROCEDURE is defined by a *declaration*. PROCEDURES can be part of the declaration part of a MODULE or the declaration part of another PROCEDURE. Remember that the declaration of a variable specifies the name of the variable and its TYPE. Similarly the declaration of a constant specifies its name, its value, and by implication its TYPE. The declaration for a PROCEDURE specifies its name, its own local declarations, the operations that the PROCEDURE performs, the parameters that must be supplied, and for function PROCEDURES (Section 4.4) the TYPE of the value that is returned.

PROCEDURE declarations, like constant declarations and variable declarations, are placed above the BEGIN block of the surrounding MODULE or PROCEDURE. Since declarations aren't ordered in Modula–2, PROCEDURE declarations can be freely intermixed with other types of declarations.

**ProcedureDeclaration**

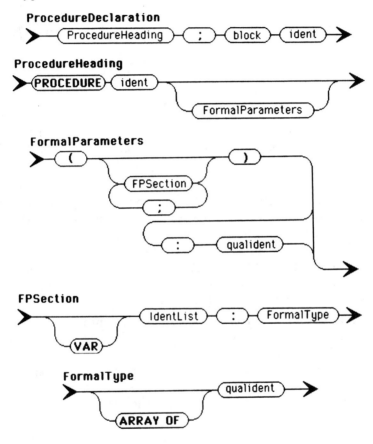

**block**

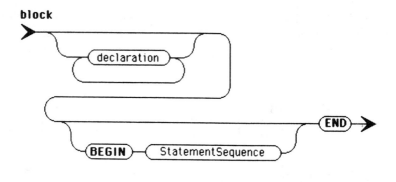

— Diagram 4.2 —

When you *declare* a PROCEDURE you mention by name its *formal parameters*. Formal parameters are placeholders for the *actual parameters* that are supplied when you actually use the PROCEDURE.

In Modula–2 the correspondence between actual parameters and formal parameters is based on their *order* in the PROCEDURE heading. Many PROCEDURES have several parameters. It is your responsibility to make sure that the parameters that you supply when you use a PROCEDURE (the actual parameters) match its formal parameters. The compiler can only check for obvious problems — the wrong number of parameters or the wrong TYPES.

Let's start with a simple example. To debug a program it is usually helpful to know the values of some of the key variables in the program. The standard Modula–2 I/O MODULE InOut contains PROCEDURES to output numbers and character strings but it lacks a PROCEDURE to output a BOOLEAN. Let's remedy this shortcoming by writing a PROCEDURE to output the value of a BOOLEAN.

To output the value of a BOOLEAN we obviously need a PROCEDURE with a BOOLEAN parameter. When we call the PROCEDURE we can supply any variable, constant, or expression that is a BOOLEAN and the WriteBool PROCEDURE will output the corresponding message.

(* Example 4.1 *)

```
PROCEDURE WriteBool (p : BOOLEAN);
BEGIN
  IF p THEN
     WriteString('True')
  ELSE
     WriteString('False')
  END
END WriteBool;
```

We can test this PROCEDURE by embedding it in a testbed
MODULE. Notice that we need to import the WriteString and
WriteLn I/O PROCEDURES from the ubiquitous InOut MODULE.

(* Example 4.2 *)

```
MODULE ProcDemo;
FROM InOut IMPORT WriteString, WriteLn;

CONST
      True = TRUE;
      False = FALSE;
      release = 103;
      Verbose = release<=105;
      DEBUG = True;
      CondDebug = DEBUG AND NOT Verbose;

PROCEDURE WriteBool ( p : BOOLEAN );
BEGIN
  IF p THEN
    WriteString('True')
  ELSE
    WriteString('False')
  END
END WriteBool;

BEGIN
  WriteString('True = ');
  WriteBool(True); WriteLn;
  WriteString('False = ');
  WriteBool(False); WriteLn;
  WriteString('Verbose = ');
  WriteBool(Verbose); WriteLn;
  WriteString('DEBUG = ');
  WriteBool(DEBUG); WriteLn;
```

```
   WriteString('CondDebug = ');
   WriteBool(CondDebug);WriteLn;
END ProcDemo.
```

First take a look at the structure of this program. It is the first program in this book containing a program body (the last seven lines) plus a PROCEDURE. Notice that the PROCEDURE appears above the BEGIN statement that marks the beginning of the program's body. Even though the WriteBool PROCEDURE is placed before the program body (in the program text), it isn't executed until it is explicitly called from within the program body. The program's execution starts with the statement following the keyword BEGIN on line thirteen. Thus the first action in the program is the call to WriteString on line fourteen. Any number of PROCEDURES may be declared above the program body.

The *formal* parameter for WriteBool is named p. The *actual* parameters that are supplied in this testbed program are named True, False, Verbose, DEBUG, and CondDebug.

I got the following results when I ran the program:

```
True = True
False = False
Verbose = True
DEBUG = True
CondDebug = False
```

## 4.3. Variable and Value Parameters

There are two types of parameters in Modula-2: *value* parameters and *variable* parameters. Value parameters pass information to a PROCEDURE, variable parameters have the additional ability to pass information from a PROCEDURE back to the caller. Let's discuss value parameters first because they are simpler.

A value parameter acts like an ordinary local variable except that it is initialized with the value of the corresponding actual parameter. The parameter p in the WriteBool PROCEDURE is an example of a value parameter. When WriteBool starts to execute, p acts like any other local variable and it has the value that was passed to WriteBool. You indicate that a parameter is a *value* parameter in the heading of a PROCEDURE by simply mentioning the name of the parameter followed by its TYPE. The actual parameter that is supplied when the PROCEDURE is called must be *assignment* compatible with the declared TYPE in the heading of the

PROCEDURE.

Any changes to a value parameter are only effective within the PROCEDURE; the outside world is unaware of the changes. This mimics the behavior of other local variables. Compilers usually implement value parameters by making a copy of the actual parameter's value — the called PROCEDURE is unable to access the original parameter. The phrase *call by value* is often used to describe this mechanism.

One advantage of value parameters is safety. One can safely pass information as value parameters to a PROCEDURE without fear that it will be unwittingly modified. The following example is a deranged version of WriteBool that contains a grievous bug, it incorrectly modifies its parameter. First let's see what happens using value parameters.

(* Example 4.3 *)

```
MODULE ValueParams;
FROM InOut IMPORT WriteString, WriteLn;

PROCEDURE WriteBool (p : BOOLEAN);
BEGIN
    IF p THEN
      WriteString('True')
    ELSE
      WriteString('False')
    END;
    p := TRUE;
END WriteBool;

VAR
    tf : BOOLEAN;

BEGIN
    tf := FALSE;
    WriteBool(tf); WriteLn;
    WriteBool(tf); WriteLn
END ValueParams.
```

What appears to happen is that the buggy version of WriteBool inadvertently modifies the variable named tf. Actually, since WriteBool uses a value parameter, it only changes its *local* copy and the variable tf (the *actual* parameter) is unchanged.

When executed, the ValueParams program produced the following messages:

```
False
False
```

It is perfectly legal and acceptable to modify a value parameter within a PROCEDURE. You merely change the local copy of the information, which often is exactly what you want to do. However, intentionally modifying a value parameter is a subtle technique and you should usually provide a comment that explains your actions.

The primary purpose of *variable* parameters is to pass results from a PROCEDURE back to the outside world. Variable parameters are usually implemented so that the called PROCEDURE accesses the actual parameter itself. Otherwise, variable parameters act as initialized local variables. Variable parameters are indicated in the heading of a PROCEDURE by placing the keyword VAR in front of the phrase that defines the formal parameter. The phrase *call by reference* is often used to describe variable parameters because the called PROCEDURE references the actual parameter. The TYPE of the actual parameter must be the same as the TYPE that is declared in the PROCEDURE heading. (This rule is relaxed for systems programming, see Section 16.2 and Section 16.3.)

Here is the previous example modified so that WriteBool contains two grievous errors, it uselessly uses variable parameters and then wantonly modifies its parameters.

(* Example 4.4 *)

```
MODULE VarParams;
FROM InOut IMPORT WriteString, WriteLn;

(* VAR parameter and spurious assignment to p *)
PROCEDURE WriteBool (VAR p : BOOLEAN);
BEGIN
   IF p THEN
     WriteString('True')
   ELSE
     WriteString('False')
   END;
   p := TRUE;
END WriteBool;

VAR
   tf : BOOLEAN;

BEGIN
```

```
    tf := FALSE;
    WriteBool(tf); WriteLn;
    WriteBool(tf); WriteLn
END VarParams.
```

In this example our collection of errors leads to the following output

```
False
True
```

Notice that the actual parameter tf is modified by this PRO-CEDURE call.

A secondary reason for using variable parameters is efficiency. When you are passing large data structures, such as large ARRAYS or large RECORDS there is usually a gain in execution speed from using variable parameters because the information in the data structures does not have to be copied when the PROCEDURE is called. This efficiency difference is only important when a data structure occupies hundreds or thousands of storage locations and you should *avoid* using variable parameters for efficiency except in those *rare* instances where important efficiency gains are possible.

When you are using *value* parameters you may supply any value as the actual parameter. The actual parameter may be a constant, a variable, a PROCEDURE returning a value (See Section 4.4), or an expression containing any and all of these. The TYPE of the formal value parameter must be *assignment compatible* with the TYPE of the actual parameter. Since formal and actual *value* parameters are *assignment* compatible, you can pass INTEGERS or CARDINALS to a PROCEDURE expecting a CARDINAL value and you can pass CARDINALS or INTEGERS to a PROCEDURE expecting an INTEGER value.

With *variable* parameters you must actually supply a variable (*not* a constant or an expression) as the *actual* parameter. This restriction makes sense because it is permissible to assign values to a variable parameter — naturally it is not permissible to assign values to constants or expressions. The TYPE of a formal variable parameter and the TYPE of the variable that is supplied as the actual parameter must be identical. Thus a third reason for using variable parameters emerges — variable parameters incorporate stricter TYPE checking than value parameters.

## 4.4. Ordinary and Function PROCEDURES

There are two types of PROCEDURES, *ordinary* PROCEDURES and *function* PROCEDURES. An *ordinary* PROCEDURE *performs some task.* Values (results) are returned from ordinary PROCEDURES using variable parameters or by modifying variables in the surrounding scope (See Section 4.7).

*Function* PROCEDURES are used to *compute a result.* The result can then be used in expressions. For example the sin PROCEDURE returns the trigonometric sine of its argument, and it might be used within an assignment statement such as the following. (Sin returns a REAL value and a, b, d, and alpha are REALS.)

```
d := 2.0 * a * b * sin(alpha)
```

In this book the term PROCEDURE used by itself usually refers to both types of PROCEDURES.

You will soon become accustomed to this pair of simple rules:
- *Ordinary* PROCEDURES *cannot* be used in expressions.
- *Function* PROCEDURES *must* be used in expressions.
- *Function* PROCEDURES can not compute one of Modula–2's three structured data TYPES: RECORDS, ARRAYS, or SETS.

In the heading of a PROCEDURE declaration, a function PROCEDURE is indicated by mentioning the TYPE of the value that is returned. The TYPE is mentioned following the parameter list. (See syntax Diagram 4.2.) If a structured TYPE must be altered by a PROCEDURE, it must either be in the PROCEDURE'S surroundings or it must be passed as a variable parameter.

The heading of the sin PROCEDURE in MathLib0 is

```
PROCEDURE sin (angle : REAL) : REAL;
```

This heading states that the sin PROCEDURE expects a REAL parameter and that it is a function PROCEDURE returning a REAL result.

A function PROCEDURE without parameters must be called using an empty parameter list. Thus a PROCEDURE that calculates the value of Pi (3.14159...) must be invoked as

```
Pi := CalcPi()
```

As a general rule, PROCEDURES that compute a single numerical, mathematical, or BOOLEAN result are usually written as *function* PROCEDURES. PROCEDURES that return several results are usually written as *ordinary* PROCEDURES with several *variable* parameters. The choice depends on how the PROCEDURE is actually used in the program. PROCEDURES that don't compute results, such as the WriteBool PROCEDURE must be written as ordinary PROCEDURES.

## 4.5. The RETURN Statement

The RETURN statement is used to terminate function PROCEDURES, ordinary PROCEDURES and MODULE bodies. These three uses of RETURN are slightly different, and I will discuss them separately.

Results are returned from *function* PROCEDURES using the RETURN statement. Every function PROCEDURE contains at least one RETURN statement, there may be several. The RETURN statement in a function PROCEDURE is followed by an expression whose value is passed back to the caller when the RETURN statement is encountered.

Encountering a RETURN statement causes a PROCEDURE to return immediately. If there are several RETURN statements in a PROCEDURE only one of them will be executed each time the PROCEDURE is activated. The value returned by a function PROCEDURE must be *assignment* compatible with the TYPE declared in the PROCEDURE heading. It is wrong to terminate a function PROCEDURE by running off the end.

In *ordinary* PROCEDURES the RETURN statement is used without a following expression simply to terminate the PROCEDURE. If a ordinary PROCEDURE doesn't have a RETURN statement then it terminates automatically after the last statement in the PROCEDURE is executed.

RETURN statements are also allowed in the body of a MODULE. In a global or local MODULE the RETURN statement simply terminates execution of the MODULE body. However executing a RETURN statement in a program MODULE terminates the program. MODULE bodies are executed as if they were ordinary, parameterless PROCEDURES. The MODULE body is automatically invoked when the surrounding scope of the MODULE is activated. This point will be discussed more in Section 6.1.

## 4.6. N Factorial

This section contains examples that illustrate value and variable
PROCEDURE parameters, ordinary and function PROCEDURES, and
the RETURN statement. All these examples compute N! (N factorial). N factorial is defined as 1 for N = 1 and as N times (N−1) factorial for N > 1. Two factorial is 2*1, three factorial is 3*2*1, four
factorial is 4*3*2*1, etc.

The first program contains an *ordinary* PROCEDURE that uses a
variable parameter to pass back the value of N!.

```
                                           (* Example 4.5 *)
MODULE FactDemo;
FROM InOut IMPORT WriteCard, WriteLn;

(* true PROCEDURE to compute N! *)
PROCEDURE Factorial
                (n : CARDINAL; VAR nfact : CARDINAL);
BEGIN
  IF n > 12 THEN nfact := 0; RETURN END;
  nfact := 1;
  FOR n := n TO 1 BY -1 DO
       nfact := nfact * n
  END
END Factorial;

VAR
    i, f : CARDINAL;

BEGIN
  FOR i := 0 TO 12 DO
     Factorial(i,f);
     WriteCard(i,3);
     WriteCard(f,12);
     WriteLn;
  END
END FactDemo.
```

(The three and the twelve in the WriteCard PROCEDURE specify
the printed width of the numbers.)

The second example program contains a *function* PROCEDURE for
computing N!. This second approach is probably best in this case
because N! is a single computed value.

(* Example 4.6 *)

```
MODULE FuncFactDemo;
FROM InOut IMPORT WriteCard, WriteLn;

(* function PROCEDURE to compute N! *)
PROCEDURE FuncFactorial (n : CARDINAL) : CARDINAL;
VAR nfact: CARDINAL;
BEGIN
  IF n > 12 THEN RETURN 0 END;
  nfact := 1;
  FOR n := n TO 1 BY -1 DO
     nfact:= nfact * n
  END;
  RETURN nfact;
END FuncFactorial;

VAR
    i : CARDINAL;

BEGIN
  FOR i := 0 TO 12 DO
     WriteCard(i,3);
     WriteCard(FuncFactorial(i),12);
     WriteLn
  END
END FuncFactDemo.
```

Notice that the declaration for the variable named nfact is inside the PROCEDURE definition. A variable declared inside a PROCEDURE is called a *local variable*. The variable named nfact is created when the PROCEDURE is called and then it vanishes when the PROCEDURE terminates. Even more importantly, nfact is private to the FuncFact PROCEDURE. The outside environment is unaware of its existence; thus it can't be modified from outside.

Local variables are used when a private variable is needed only while a PROCEDURE is executing. It is important to use local variables because they *decouple* PROCEDURES from their surroundings. The alternative to local variables is to use (or even more unfortunately to *reuse*) variables from the surrounding context.

**Exercise 4.1.** In the ASCII character set, a given CHAR is a numeral if it is greater than or equal to '0' and less than or equal to '9'. Write a *function* PROCEDURE to determine if a CHAR parameter is a numeral and then write a *ordinary* PROCEDURE

with a variable BOOLEAN parameter to perform the same task.
Which approach do you prefer?
□

**Exercise 4.2.** Write a function PROCEDURE returning a REAL
that computes the value of N!. Determine empirically how large N
can be to compute N! successfully.
□

**Exercise 4.3.** The power series expansion of $e^x$ is

$$\frac{x^0}{0!} + \frac{x^1}{1!} + \frac{x^2}{2!} + \frac{x^3}{3!} + \cdots$$

Write a PROCEDURE that calculates $e^x$ using the factorial PRO-
CEDURE from the previous exercise. Terminate the computation
when N! can no longer be computed accurately or when the relative error is less than 1 part in 10000. (*Note* — there are better
formulas for calculating $e^x$.)
□

**Exercise 4.4.** Compute $e^x$ by calculating each new term from
the previous term. Note that the $i^{th}$ term in the series is

$$e^x = \sum_i t_i$$

where

$$t_i = \frac{x^i}{i!} = t_{i-1} * \frac{x}{i}$$

Which method is more efficient, and which is more accurate
   a. For large $x$?
   b. For small $x$?

How do your results compare with results from the exp function of
MathLib0?
□

**Exercise 4.5.** Write a PROCEDURE to read in the text representation of REAL numbers (like the ReadReal routine from RealI-
nOut). Your PROCEDURE should convert the text into a Modula-2
REAL number and return that number.
□

**Exercise 4.6.** Write a PROCEDURE to calculate square roots using Newton's method. (Exercise 3.9.) Be sure to include checks for
negative parameters. Are there any other parameter values that
might cause trouble?
□

**Exercise 4.7.** Modify the `FuncFact` PROCEDURE so that it automatically adapts to a thirty–two bit machine or to a sixteen bit machine.

□

## 4.7. PROCEDURE Scope

An *identifier* is a name for something. We use identifiers in Modula–2 to name constants, variables, PROCEDURES, MODULES, and TYPES. The *scope* of an identifier is the portion of a program where it can be used. We often say that an identifier is *visible* from a certain part of a program if it can be used at that point. Two structures in Modula–2 have a profound influence on the scope of identifiers, MODULES and PROCEDURES. A discussion of MODULE scope is deferred until Chapter 6, for now we will concentrate on PROCEDURE scope.

In the previous section I presented three related PROCEDURES. The PROCEDURES `FuncFactorial` and `Factorial` both compute factorials and the PROCEDURE `ShowFactorial` calls them to produce a table of factorials. There are several ways that these three PROCEDURES could be combined into a MODULE. Perhaps this is the simplest organization.

(* Example 4.7 *)

```
MODULE factorial;
FROM InOut IMPORT WriteCard, WriteString, WriteLn;

PROCEDURE Factorial
                (n : CARDINAL; VAR nfact : CARDINAL);
BEGIN
  (* ... *)
END Factorial;

PROCEDURE FuncFactorial (n : CARDINAL) : CARDINAL;
VAR f : CARDINAL;
BEGIN
  (* ... *)
  RETURN f
END FuncFactorial;

PROCEDURE ShowFactorials;
VAR n,nfact : CARDINAL;
BEGIN
```

```
     (* ... *)
     END ShowFactorials;

     BEGIN
       ShowFactorials
     END factorial.
```

The statement sequences of the three PROCEDURES are not shown
to make the structure clearer. To compile and run this program
you would have to replace the missing statement sequences. Anything visible from the BEGIN block of the MODULE is said to be at
the MODULE or *outer level*. In this case the three PROCEDURES are
all at the MODULE level. Two of the PROCEDURES (FuncFactorial, ShowFactorials) have local variables. These local variables
(f, n, nfact) are not visible outside the PROCEDURES hence they
are *not* at the MODULE level. Thus a PROCEDURE creates a new
environment, an environment that can not be perturbed (or even
seen) from the surrounding context.

This brings up the question of what is visible from within a PRO-
CEDURE? Two rules apply.

> All identifiers defined *within* the PROCEDURE are visible.

> All identifiers from the surrounding context are visible if
> their names are different from the names created within the
> PROCEDURE. When there is a conflict, only the inside
> identifier is visible.

One other rule is important:

> From the surrounding scope of a PROCEDURE its local
> identifiers are *never* visible.

In the absence of name conflicts, it is possible to see the outside
world from within a PROCEDURE, but it is *never* possible to peer
into a PROCEDURE from outside. (Notice that a PROCEDURE is
visible from within itself. Why?) Standard identifiers are automatically imported into all MODULES and they cannot be
redefined in the outer block of a MODULE. The standard identifiers
can be reused within PROCEDURES although this is poor practice..

Modula–2 allows one PROCEDURE to be nested within another.
Let's try this by organizing the previous example differently. Since
FuncFactorial and Factorial are only referenced from within
the ShowFactorials PROCEDURE, it might be preferable to nest
them inside ShowFactorials.

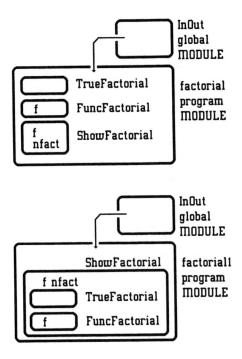

Figure 4.1. These organizational diagrams depict two alternative ways to organize the factorial program. In the first, all three PROCEDURES are at the outer level of the MODULE. In the second scheme, the two PROCEDURES to calculate factorials are nested inside the ShowFactorial PROCEDURE.

```
                                                  ( * Example 4.8 * )
MODULE factorial1;
FROM InOut IMPORT WriteCard, WriteString, WriteLn;

PROCEDURE ShowFactorials;

    PROCEDURE TrueFactorial
                    (n : CARDINAL; VAR f : CARDINAL);
    BEGIN
```

```
    (* ... *)
  END TrueFactorial;

  PROCEDURE FuncFactorial (n : CARDINAL) : CARDINAL;
  VAR f : CARDINAL;
  BEGIN
    (* ... *)
    RETURN f
  END FuncFactorial;

VAR (* ShowFactorials local VARs *)
  n, nfact : CARDINAL;

BEGIN (* ShowFactorials *)
  (* ... *)
END ShowFactorials;

BEGIN
  ShowFactorials
END factoriall.
```

In this version of the `factorial` MODULE, only the `ShowFactori-als` PROCEDURE is visible from the outer level. Within `ShowFac-torials` the variables n and nfact are visible along with the `Fac-torial`, `FuncFactorial` and `ShowFactorials` PROCEDURES. Inside `FuncFactorial` the following are visible:

The local variable `f`
The local variables `nfact` from `ShowFactorials`
The `Factorial`, `FuncFactorial`
        and `ShowFactorials` PROCEDURES

Inside `FuncFactorial` the local variable n from `ShowFactorials` is hidden.

Example 4.10 illustrates the complexity that quickly arises when nesting gets too deep. Local MODULES can be used to reduce the complexity, see Chapter 6. You should usually avoid deep nesting except when the structure of the problem pushes you *strongly* towards a nested solution. Many programs are only nested one deep.

**Exercise 4.8.** In Modula–2 it is easy for a PROCEDURE to peer into its surrounding scope. One problem with this occurs when you forget to insert necessary declarations in a nested PROCEDURE. What does the following program print?

(* Example 4.9 *)

```
MODULE Side;
FROM InOut IMPORT WriteInt, WriteLn;

PROCEDURE SumEm(limit : INTEGER) : INTEGER;
VAR
   sum : INTEGER;
BEGIN
   sum := 0;
   FOR i := 0 TO limit DO
       sum := sum + i
   END;
   RETURN sum
END SumEm;

VAR
   i : INTEGER;

BEGIN (* side program *)
   FOR i := 0 TO 100 DO
       WriteInt(i,5); WriteInt(SumEm(i),5); WriteLn;
   END
END Side.
```

Is this a predictable Modula–2 program? What is wrong with this
program? Do you think that the control variables for FOR loops
should be limited to local variables? If you were designing a programming language, would you allow programs like this?
□

**Exercise 4.9.** Here is a deliberately obscure program. What does
it print?

(* Example 4.10 *)

```
MODULE Scope;
FROM InOut IMPORT Write, WriteLn;

CONST
    Greeting = 'M';
    Greet0 = '2';
    Greet3 = '1';

PROCEDURE Outer;
CONST
    Greeting = 'o';
    Greet1 = '-';

PROCEDURE Middle;
CONST
    Greeting = 'd';
    Greet2 = 'a';

PROCEDURE Inner;
CONST
    Greeting = 'u';
BEGIN (*Inner*)
   Write(Greeting);
   Write(Greet3)
END Inner;

BEGIN (*Middle*)
   Write(Greeting);
   Inner;
   Write(Greet2)
END Middle;

BEGIN (*Outer*)
   Write(Greeting);
   Middle;
   Write(Greet1)
END Outer;

BEGIN (*Scope*)
   Write(Greeting);
   Outer;
   Write(Greet0);
```

```
    WriteLn
  END Scope.
```

□

**Exercise 4.10.** Make a table showing what identifiers are visible from within the Middle PROCEDURE in the previous problem.
□

**Exercise 4.11.** What does the following program print?

(* Example 4.11 *)

```
MODULE Deep;
FROM InOut IMPORT Write, WriteLn;

VAR c : CHAR;

PROCEDURE A;
VAR b : CHAR;

PROCEDURE B;
VAR a : CHAR;

PROCEDURE C;
BEGIN
   Write(c);
   c := b;
   Write(a)
END C;

BEGIN (* B *)
   a := 'e';
   C;
   Write(a)
END B;

BEGIN (* A *)
   b := 'p';
   B
END A;

BEGIN (* Deep *)
   c := 'd';
   A;
   Write(c);
   WriteLn
```

END Deep.

☐

**Exercise 4.12.** Make a table showing what identifiers are visible from within A, B, and C PROCEDURES of the Deep MODULE (Exercise 4.11).
☐

**Exercise 4.13.** Modify the Deep MODULE so that it prints the message "weed".
☐


## 4.8. Recursion

*Recursion* is a simple and powerful technique. There are two forms of recursion:

> *Direct Recursion* means that a PROCEDURE calls itself.
>
> *Indirect recursion* means one PROCEDURE calls some other PROCEDURE that in turn leads to a call of the original PROCEDURE.

Recursion should only be used when the problem naturally lends itself to a recursive solution. Any problem that can be solved recursively can also be solved without recursion. Recursion often simplifies the solution but it is never the only solution.

The definition of N! given in the previous section was stated recursively. N! equals N times (N−1)!. Here is an easy recursive solution to this problem.

```
                                              (* Example 4.12 *)
MODULE Rfact;
FROM InOut IMPORT WriteCard, WriteLn;

PROCEDURE RecursiveFact (n : CARDINAL) : CARDINAL;
BEGIN
  IF n <= 1 THEN RETURN 1
  ELSIF n > 12 THEN RETURN 0 (* error *)
  ELSE RETURN n * RecursiveFact(n-1)
  END
END RecursiveFact;

VAR
    i : CARDINAL;

BEGIN
```

```
    FOR i := 0 TO 12 DO
      WriteCard(i,5);
      WriteCard(RecursiveFact(i),12);
      WriteLn
    END
  END Rfact.
```

In any recursive problem, there must be some condition that leads to an eventual end to the recursion. In this example the recursion terminates when 1! is encountered. Notice that this method for computing factorials is shorter than the other two, but it doesn't really offer any major decrease in complexity. The examples in the following section illustrate recursive techniques in a more appropriate situation, and they lead to a major decrease in complexity compared to a non–recursive solution.

**Exercise 4.14.** Write a recursive factorial program that doesn't use *function* PROCEDURES.
□

**Exercise 4.15.** What visibility rule implies that a PROCEDURE is visible from within itself? Does this make recursion seem more natural?
□

**Exercise 4.16.** What output do you expect from the following program?

```
                                              (* Example 4.13 *)
  MODULE huh;
  FROM InOut IMPORT WriteCard, WriteLn;

  PROCEDURE fact(VAR n : CARDINAL):CARDINAL;
  BEGIN
    IF n = 1 THEN
      RETURN 1
    ELSE
      n := n-1;
      RETURN(n+1*fact(n))
    END
  END fact;

  VAR
      i : CARDINAL;

  BEGIN
    FOR i := 1 TO 3 DO
```

```
      WriteCard(fact(i),8)
   END;
   WriteLn
END huh.
```

What is wrong with this program? Do you think that this is a
predictable Modula–2 program? (Why?) Does the recursion ever
terminate? Is this a portable program?
□

## 4.9. Example — A Desk Calculator

The final section of this chapter details a larger example of PRO-
CEDURES. The goal is to write a program that works somewhat like
a four function numerical calculator. Most hand calculators perform operations as they are keyed in. For example if you key in

```
5 + 2 * 3 =
```

most hand calculators will respond 21 because they evaluate expressions strictly left to right. (A reasonable choice for a machine
that only displays one number at a time.) Our goal is to write a
program that performs calculations and that understands simple
*operator precedence*. If the previous example is performed with
operator precedence in mind, the multiplication is performed before the addition leading to the answer eleven. In our program
parentheses will be allowed to control the order of evaluation.

You might think that this is a hard problem because we want to
be able to handle any expression, from simple addition to complicated formulas with dozens of terms. Actually the solution is quite
easy if we use a technique called *recursive descent*. The idea is to
define our desk calculator language using syntax diagrams. Then
we can write PROCEDURES that perform the required tasks. Here
are the syntax diagrams for our desk calculator. Notice that our
desk calculator will accept a stripped down version of ordinary
Modula–2 expressions. (We don't allow variables, named constants, SETS, BOOLEANS, etc.)

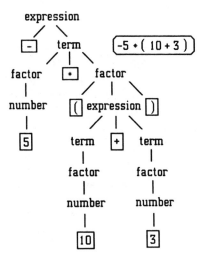

Figure 4.2. Arithmetic expressions can be analyzed in terms of expressions (the addition or subtraction of terms), terms (the multiplication or division of factors), factors (numbers or parenthesized expressions).

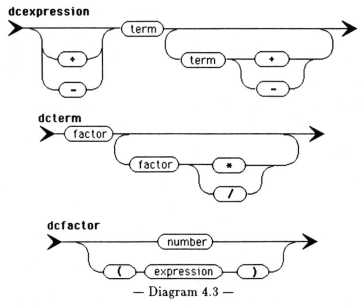

— Diagram 4.3 —

Note that this syntax is *not* part of Modula-2, it is merely the syntax that is recognized by our desk calculator example program. We will write PROCEDURES to handle expressions, terms, factors, and numbers. In this version, a number is simply a sequence of digits representing a base ten integer.

Notice the syntax diagrams that are the "design spec" for this program are recursive. This is the aspect of the problem that makes recursion an appropriate solution. In a program like this, our best assurance of correct operation for all conceivable inputs is to have a clearly written program whose structure mimics the structure of the design specification. This program, like many programs, cannot be tested for all inputs.

The only subtlety of the calculator program is a thorny issue called *look ahead*. Let's suppose that the term PROCEDURE has just finished reading a factor. If the next character is a MulOp then term should read another factor. However if the next character isn't a MulOp then term is finished. Look ahead implies that term should be able to examine the next character without actually gobbling it up irretrievably.

If you carefully examine the syntax, you will see that a single character will always determine the course of events. This means that the individual PROCEDURES will never have to read more than one character too far. The solution is to jam a character back into the input stream. I have written two PROCEDURES to accomplish this. The ungetc PROCEDURE returns a character to the input stream and the getc PROCEDURE returns the next non-blank character, either a character returned to the input stream by ungetc or the next (unread) character.

Here is the pseudo code version of our getc PROCEDURE

> If there is a saved character then
>> Mark the saved character as "used up"
>> Return that character
>
> Otherwise read a character and return that character

The ungetc PROCEDURE saves a character. Its pseudo code is also simple:

> If there is a saved character then print an error message
> Put the character in a safe place

A BOOLEAN flag variable indicates the presence of a valid saved character and a CHAR variable contains the saved character.

The higher level routines in this desk calculator program don't want to worry about the exact form of the input. They would prefer to recognize the higher level objects such as numbers and operators, and forget about the details of spacing, etc. Therefore it's best to supply a routine that skips spaces and tabs, and returns

the next significant character. I've called this PROCEDURE
nextch. Nextch should interface with getc and ungetc so that
look ahead works with both systems. Here is the pseudo code for
the nextch PROCEDURE.

> Keep getting a character from getc until
> it's neither a blank nor a tab.
> Return that character

Note that getc and nextch are both function PROCEDURES that
don't have any parameters. Ungetc is a ordinary PROCEDURE
with a single parameter, the character to be tucked away.

The calculator program has been implemented with INTEGER arithmetic. (Extending the program to work with REALS is left as an
exercise.) Originally I thought I could use the ReadInt standard
PROCEDURE from the InOut MODULE to read the numbers. It
turned out that ReadInt wouldn't work in the calculator program
because of the way it handles the minus sign. Whenever InOut's
ReadInt encounters a minus sign it assumes that it is the first
character of a number. In the calculator syntax minus signs can
also be used in front of parenthesized expressions. Therefore I
wrote the ReadNumber PROCEDURE to handle the minus sign specially. ReadNumber simply reads a digit sequence. It leaves the
handling of minus signs to other PROCEDURES. This is a good example of how unexpected interactions between PROCEDURES can
lead to subtle problems.

The strategy in ReadNumber is simple. First let's admit that
ReadNumber is always going to read one character past the end of
the number. Obviously the final thing that ReadNumber must do
is ungetc this extra character so that it isn't lost forever. In the
ASCII character set you can turn a numerical digit '0' through '9'
into the corresponding number by subtracting the ordinal value of
'0'. This is half of the trick for turning a text string into a number.
The other half of the trick is to realize that the computer will encounter the text digits of the number from left to right. Thus each
time a digit is recognized the following steps are performed: (1)
the previous result is multiplied by ten, (2) the text of the current
digit is converted to a number, and (3) the current digit is added
into the result. These three steps are repeated for as many digits
as the number contains. Here is the pseudo code for the Read-
Number PROCEDURE

> Set the result to zero
> Set the numeric flag to false
> Get a character from `nextch`
> If it's a numeral then
>> Set the numeric flag to true
>> Set the result to the numeric value of the digit
>> Get another character from `nextch`
>> While the current character is a numeral
>>> Multiply the result by ten
>>> Add the numeric value of the current character to the result
>> Push back the extra character

I chose to make `ReadNumber` a ordinary PROCEDURE with two variable parameters: the result and the "I've encountered a number" flag.

The "meat" of the desk calculator program resides in three PROCEDURES: `term`, `factor`, and `expression`. Although these PROCEDURES may look intimidating at first glance, they actually are easy. Each one strictly follows the plan laid out in the syntax diagram, our "design spec."

Since all three of these PROCEDURES are founded on the same principle, it will suffice to present the pseudo code for one of them. Since it appears to be the most complicated, let's examine the `expression` PROCEDURE. An expression is the highest level of syntax that is recognized by the calculator program. An expression starts with an *optional* leading plus/minus sign, followed by the first term. After that there *may* be several trailing terms. Each trailing term is preceded by either a plus or minus sign.

The coding in this PROCEDURE is the embodiment of recursive descent analysis. Since this is a new idea to many people, I'll try to go slowly. Here is the "broad overview" pseudo code for the `expression` PROCEDURE.

> Handle the optional leading plus or minus sign
> Call the `term` PROCEDURE to handle the first term
> While the next character is a plus or minus sign
>> Call `term` to handle the trailing term
>> Add or subtract the value from `term` to the running sum

We can deal with the optional leading plus/minus by calling `nextch` to read a character. If the letter is a minus, record that fact, if it's a plus, do nothing, otherwise push back the character. Almost the same technique can be used in a loop that handles the trailing terms. Here is the more detail oriented pseudo code for the expression PROCEDURE.

    Set the negative flag to false

    Read in a character
    If it's a minus sign then set the negative flag to true
    If it's a plus sign then ignore it
    Otherwise push it back using ungetch

    Set the result to the value returned by the term PROCEDURE
    If the negative flag is set then negate the result

    Repeat forever
      Read in a character using nextch
      If it's a plus add the value returned by term to the result
      If it's a minus subtract the value returned by term to the result
      Otherwise
        Push back the character using ungetc
        Return the result

Finally, here is the desk calculator program.

```
                                          (* Example 4.14 *)
MODULE calc; (* an algebraic calculator *)
FROM InOut IMPORT Write, WriteInt, WriteLn,
    Read, WriteString, EOL, Done;

CONST
    SPACE = ' ';
    TAB = 011C;
    LocalEOF = 0C;

VAR
    savech : CHAR;
    validsavech : BOOLEAN;

(* Get a char, either from savech or from Read *)
PROCEDURE getc() : CHAR;
VAR
   ch : CHAR;
BEGIN
   IF validsavech THEN
      validsavech := FALSE;
      RETURN savech
   ELSE
```

```
      Read(ch);
      IF NOT Done THEN ch := LocalEOF END;
      RETURN ch
   END (* IF *)
END getc;

(* save a char so it can be getc'd again *)
PROCEDURE ungetc(ch : CHAR);
BEGIN
   IF validsavech THEN
     WriteString('error in ungetc.')
   END;
   savech := ch; validsavech := TRUE
END ungetc;

(* get the next non blank char by calling getc *)
PROCEDURE nextch() : CHAR;
VAR
   ch : CHAR;
BEGIN
   REPEAT
     ch := getc()
   UNTIL (ch # SPACE)  AND (ch # TAB);
   RETURN ch
END nextch;

(* READ A NUMBER *)
PROCEDURE ReadNumber
            (VAR x : INTEGER; VAR IsNum : BOOLEAN);
VAR
   ch : CHAR;
BEGIN
   IsNum := FALSE;
   ch := nextch();
   IF (ch >= '0') AND (ch <= '9') THEN
      IsNum := TRUE;
      x := VAL(INTEGER,ORD(ch) - ORD('0'));
      ch := getc();
      WHILE (ch >= '0') AND (ch <= '9') DO
        x := 10*x + VAL(INTEGER,ORD(ch) - ORD('0'));
        ch := getc()
      END (* WHILE *)
   END; (* IF *)
   ungetc(ch)
```

```
   END ReadNumber;

   (*
    * factor = number | "(" expr ")".
    *)
   PROCEDURE factor() : INTEGER;
   VAR
      t : INTEGER;
     IsNum : BOOLEAN;
     ch : CHAR;
   BEGIN
      ReadNumber(t,IsNum);
      IF IsNum THEN RETURN t END;
      ch := nextch();
      IF ch = '(' THEN
         t := expression();
         ch := nextch();
         IF ch # ')' THEN
           ungetc(ch);
           WriteString('Unbalanced Parentheses');
           WriteLn
         END;
        RETURN t
      ELSIF (ch = EOL) OR (ch = OC) THEN
         ungetc(ch)
      ELSE
         WriteString('Error in factor.  Expected a ');
         WriteString('number but encountered: ');
         Write(ch); WriteLn
      END; (* IF *)
      RETURN 0 (* error return *)
   END factor;

   (*
    * term = factor { ("*"|"/") factor}.
    *)
   PROCEDURE term() : INTEGER;
   VAR
      t, u : INTEGER;
     ch : CHAR;
   BEGIN
      t := factor();
      LOOP
        ch := nextch();
```

```
        IF ch = '*' THEN
           t := t * factor()
        ELSIF ch = '/' THEN
            u := factor();
            IF u # 0 THEN
               t := t DIV u
            ELSE
               WriteString('Divide by zero ');
               t:= 0
            END
        ELSE ungetc(ch); RETURN t
        END (* IF *)
      END (* LOOP *)
END term;

(*
 expression = [ ("+"|"-") ] term { ("+"|"-") term }.
 *)
PROCEDURE expression() : INTEGER;
VAR
    t : INTEGER;
   ch : CHAR;
   neg : BOOLEAN;
BEGIN
   neg := FALSE;
   ch := nextch();
   IF ch = '-' THEN
      neg := TRUE
   ELSIF ch = '+' THEN
      (* do nothing *)
   ELSE
      ungetc(ch)
   END;
   t := term();
   IF neg THEN t := -t END;
   LOOP
      ch := nextch();
      IF ch = '+' THEN
         t := t + term()
      ELSIF ch = '-' THEN
         t := t - term()
      ELSE
         ungetc(ch);
         RETURN t
```

```
            END (* IF *)
      END (* LOOP *)
   END expression;

   VAR
      ch : CHAR;

   BEGIN
      WriteString('calc-> ');
      validsavech := FALSE;
      LOOP
         WriteInt(expression(),6); WriteLn;
         ch := nextch();
         IF ch = LocalEOF THEN
               EXIT
         ELSIF ch = EOL THEN
               WriteString('calc-> ')
         ELSE
               ungetc(ch)
         END
      END (* LOOP *)
   END calc.
```

**Exercise 4.17.** The input to the calc program is naturally divided into lines. How is this fact recognized in the calc program? When does the calc program print prompts? Can you think of a better scheme? Might the program have been better designed if the line oriented nature of the input were recognized in the syntax diagram "design spec?"

□

**Exercise 4.18.** Modify the calc program to work with REALS instead of INTEGERS.

□

**Exercise 4.19.** Modify the calc program to work with either REALS or INTEGERS, depending upon which is most appropriate for a given calculation. For example if the user typed 5*(7−2) your program should perform the calculations for INTEGERS and print an INTEGER result. However if the user types 0.5*(7−2) you should perform REAL calculations and print a REAL result. Settle the following two issues before you start to work. (1) Exactly what criteria should you use to determine which number system is most appropriate for a given input? (2) How can you maintain results for both number systems simultaneously?

□

# Chapter 5

# ARRAYS

A *data structure* is a way to package data, so that data can be bound together into a single unit. The hallmark of a structured TYPE is the idea of *components* (elements). Data TYPES that lack components are called *simple* TYPES because each variable contains a single value.

There are three structured data TYPES in Modula–2:

An ARRAY is a group of indexed elements that all have the same TYPE.

A RECORD is a group of named elements that may have different TYPES.

A SET is a group of members.

(RECORDS are discussed in Chapter 13, SETS are discussed in Chapter 12.)

People with a mathematical background might prefer to use the term *vector*; others might prefer to think of an ARRAY as a *table*

VAR X : ARRAY [ 1 .. 6 ] OF CARDINAL;

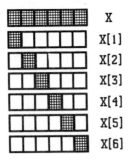

Figure 5.1. An ARRAY is composed of elements, each of which can be selected using an index expression.

(or list) of values.

ARRAYS are used in situations where some standard processing has to be performed on a collection of values. Examples might be

- Storing lists of points to be displayed on a graph
- Storing lists of numbers to be averaged
- Storing the coefficients of a matrix
- Storing lists of characters that are valid command codes
- Storing the status (white piece, black piece, or free) of the squares of a checkerboard.

The second major use of ARRAYS is handling text. Words and sentences are made up of individual characters. Text is stored in a special type of ARRAY called a variable *string*.

The declaration of an ARRAY must mention (at least) two TYPES: the TYPE of the *elements* of the ARRAY and the TYPE(S)(s) of the *index(es)* of the ARRAY. An ARRAY declaration must also define the *lower* and *upper bounds* of the index(es).

Here is a simple declaration that creates two ARRAYS.

                                                    ( * Example 5.1 * )
    VAR
        Gchars, Xchars : ARRAY [1 .. 100] OF CHAR;

Gchars and Xchars are ARRAYS of 100 CHAR elements. The lower bound of the index is one and the upper bound is 100. The *implied* TYPE of the index is CARDINAL because the lower bound is non–negative.

An individual element of Gchars is selected by mentioning the name Gchars followed by an index expression. In Modula–2 the index expression is set off by square braces.

(* Example 5.2 *)

```
Gchars[10] := 0C
```

This assignments moves the value 0C into the tenth member of Gchars.

Many operations involving ARRAYS deal with one element at a time as shown in the expression above. In addition Modula–2 allows one entire ARRAY to be assigned to another.

(* Example 5.3 *)

```
Gchars := Xchars
```

This assignment transfers all one hundred members of Xchars into the corresponding members of Gchars.

There are only two operations in Modula–2 that work with ARRAYS as a whole.
- Assigning one ARRAY to another of the same TYPE.
- Passing ARRAYS as parameters to PROCEDURES.

It is not permissible in Modula–2 to:
- Compare two arrays.
- Return an ARRAY as the value of a function PROCEDURE.
- Add one ARRAY to another.

The *elements* of an ARRAY may be any Modula–2 data TYPE. However, the *index(es)* of an ARRAY must be one of the following:

INTEGER CARDINAL CHAR BOOLEAN Enumeration Subrange

The following Modula–2 data TYPES are *unacceptable* ARRAY indices:

REAL   ARRAY   RECORD   SET   POINTER   PROCEDURE

The actual index expression used to select an ARRAY element must be *compatible* with the TYPE of the index in the ARRAY declaration. If the lower bound of a subrange is non–negative (e.g. Gchars and Xchars) then the ARRAY indices must be compatible with CARDINALS. Similarly if the lower bound of a subrange is negative then the index expression must be compatible with INTEGERS.

I am going to implement several simple statistical operations to demonstrate simple ARRAY usage. This trivial statistics package will operate on an ARRAY named StatData defined by the following:

(* Example 5.4 *)

```
CONST
    MaxIndex = 99;
VAR
    StatData : ARRAY [0..MaxIndex] OF REAL;
```

Here are the PROCEDURES to find the minimum and average of the StatData ARRAY.

(* Example 5.5 *)

```
PROCEDURE min () : REAL;
(* Return the smallest element of StatData *)

VAR
    i : CARDINAL;
    minval : REAL;

BEGIN
    minval := StatData[0];
    FOR i := 1 TO MaxIndex DO
        IF StatData[i] < minval THEN
          minval := StatData[i]
        END
    END;
    RETURN(minval)
END min;
```

(* Example 5.6 *)
```
(* Return the average of the elements of StatData *)
PROCEDURE ave () : REAL;

VAR
    i : CARDINAL;
    sum : REAL;

BEGIN
    sum := 0.;
    FOR i := 0 TO MaxIndex DO
      sum := sum + StatData [i]
    END;
```

```
        RETURN(sum / FLOAT(MaxIndex + 1))
    END ave;
```

The FOR loop is appropriate for processing ARRAYS when every
element of the ARRAY must be processed. However some ARRAY
applications don't require processing of the entire ARRAY. For example, the following PROCEDURE searches through an ARRAY for a
particular value.

```
                                              (* Example 5.7 *)
    (*
     * Return TRUE if an element of StatData
     *      is equal to val
     *)
    PROCEDURE lsearch (val : REAL) : BOOLEAN;

    VAR
        i : CARDINAL;

    BEGIN
        i := 0;
        WHILE (i <= MaxIndex) AND (StatData[i] <> val) DO
            INC(i)
        END;
        RETURN( NOT(i > MaxIndex) )
    END lsearch;
```

There is one interesting aspect of the lsearch PROCEDURE that
we need to explore. In Section 2.2.1 I mentioned that BOOLEAN
expressions in Modula–2 feature *short circuit* evaluation. BOOLE-
AN expressions are evaluated from left to right just far enough to
determine whether the expression is TRUE or FALSE.

In Example 5.7 short circuit expression evaluation assures us that
the ARRAY element StatData[i] will not be evaluated when the
variable i becomes greater than MaxIndex. If the first part of the
while condition (i <= MaxIndex) evaluates to FALSE then the
second part is *not* evaluated. Note that the WHILE loop condition
in Example 5.7 could *not* be written as

```
                                              (* Example 5.8 *)
    WHILE (StatData[i] <> val) AND (i <= MaxIndex) DO
```

because StatData[i] is not defined for i > MaxIndex.

**Exercise 5.1.** How would you express the WHILE loop in Example 5.7 if Modula–2 didn't *guarantee* short circuit evaluation of
BOOLEAN expressions.

□

**Exercise 5.2.** Rewrite the 1search PROCEDURE to use a FOR loop to search through the ARRAY, and use a RETURN statement embedded in the FOR loop to return TRUE when the value is found. This rewrite makes the loop contain *multiple* exit conditions. Do you think this is an example of poor programming style?

□

**Exercise 5.3.** In Exercise 3.6 I presented a program using a CASE statement that detected a particular series of (simulated) coin tosses. The same effect can be attained using an ARRAY to store the state information.

(* Example 5.9 *)

```
MODULE AStates;
FROM Flip IMPORT flip;
FROM InOut IMPORT WriteCard, WriteLn;

VAR
    State, Attempts : CARDINAL;
    Pattern : ARRAY [0..4] OF BOOLEAN;

BEGIN
    State := 0;
    Attempts := 0;
    Pattern[0] := TRUE; Pattern[1] := TRUE;
    Pattern[2] := FALSE; Pattern[3] := TRUE;
    Pattern[4] := FALSE;
    WHILE State # 5 DO
      INC(Attempts);
      IF Pattern[State] = flip() THEN
          INC(State)
      ELSIF Pattern[State] # Pattern[0] THEN
          State := 1
      ELSE
          State := 0
      END
    END; (* WHILE *)
    WriteCard(Attempts,5); WriteLn;
  END AStates.
```

Which version is simpler? Which version would be more appropriate if there were a thousand or more states?

Detecting a given pattern of coin tosses is a relatively simple problem. In many programs the state transitions are the result of much
more sophisticated decision making. If transitions from one state
to another were more involved that testing a single value, which
version would you prefer?

□

## 5.1. TYPE Declarations

Chapter 2 of this book discussed the basic Modula–2 data TYPES:
INTEGERS, CARDINALS, and REALS for storing numbers, CHARS for
storing character data, and BOOLEANS for storing truth values.
These basic data TYPES are found in most programming languages
and they are adequate for writing many useful programs. However
some problems require (or are programmed more effectively) using
more sophisticated data structures.

Modula–2's basic data TYPES are built into the language. To use
them all you have to do is use the name of the data TYPE (e.g. the
word INTEGER) in a variable declaration. However most of the
more sophisticated data TYPES have to be partly defined by you
(the programmer). For example Modula–2 knows that ARRAYS are
lists of elements, but to declare an ARRAY you must define the
TYPE of the *elements*, define the TYPE of the *index*, and define the
upper and lower *bounds* of the index. Although Modula–2 understands the general idea of ARRAYS, the programmer must fill in the
definition each time a new TYPE of ARRAY is declared.

The ARRAY StatData (Example 5.4) from the previous section is
an ARRAY of one hundred REAL elements. The variable StatData
is an *anonymous* TYPE because it has no TYPE name. A Modula–2
TYPE declaration specifies a new data TYPE and gives a name to
the new TYPE.

                                                    (* Example 5.10 *)
     TYPE
          Statistic = ARRAY [0..MaxIndex] OF REAL;

This declaration doesn't declare an ARRAY variable, instead it
serves to *name* and *define* a new data TYPE.

Once we have declared a new data TYPE we can use the name of
the data TYPE just as we can use the names of the built–in data
TYPES. For example we can declare a variable of TYPE Statistic
as

(* Example 5.11 *)

```
VAR
    StatData : Statistic;
```

The syntax diagram for TYPE declarations is

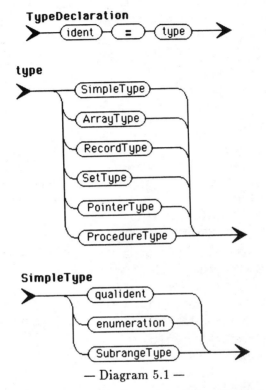

— Diagram 5.1 —

Modula–2 TYPES are generally incompatible unless the TYPES are declared as equivalent. If we define a new TYPE as

(* Example 5.12 *)

```
TYPE
    MathValues = Statistic;
```

then variables declared as TYPE Statistic will be *compatible* with variables declared as TYPE MathValues. However if we were to declare the MathValues TYPE as

(* Example 5.13 *)

```
TYPE
    MathValues = ARRAY [0..MaxIndex] OF REAL;
```

then variables declared as TYPE Statistic will be *incompatible* with variables declared as TYPE MathValues. Although the characteristics of Statistics and MathValues are identical, Modula-2 makes them incompatible if they are declared separately.

There are many reasons to use named TYPES in preference to anonymous TYPES. One reason is that anonymous TYPES that are declared in separate declarations are *always* incompatible. Let's introduce the following variable declarations:

(* Example 5.14 *)

```
VAR
    a, b, c : ARRAY CHAR OF BOOLEAN;
    x, y, z : ARRAY CHAR OF BOOLEAN;
```

The variables a, b, and c are compatible (with each other) because they are declared in a single declaration. (Notice that their TYPE is anonymous.) Similarly the variables x, y, and z are compatible. However a and x are incompatible (even though the declarations are identical) because they are declared in separate declarations. If you want to declare compatible variables at several places in a program, then you need to use TYPE declarations.

Similarly if you want to pass a programmer defined TYPE to a PROCEDURE you need to use TYPE declarations so that the name of the parameter's TYPE can be mentioned in the heading of the PROCEDURE. Also if you want to export a TYPE from a MODULE you must use a TYPE declaration to provide a name for the TYPE.

Example 5.14 also shows that the bounds expression in an ARRAY declaration doesn't need to mention the upper and lower bounds. In Example 5.14, the lower bound of the ARRAY is MIN(CHAR) and the upper bound is MAX(CHAR). Note that the ARRAY declaration

(* Example 5.15 *)

```
VAR
    huge : ARRAY CARDINAL OF BOOLEAN;
```

wouldn't work on many computers because there wouldn't be enough space to store such a huge ARRAY. This illustrates a limitation of most current computer hardware technology, not a limitation of the Modula-2 language.

## 5.2. ARRAYS as PROCEDURE Parameters

In the first part of this chapter I defined three PROCEDURES that operated on an ARRAY OF REALS called StatData. The problem with these PROCEDURES is their lack of generality. It would be useful to have a PROCEDURE to compute the average (or minimum or whatever) of several different ARRAYS, not just the StatData ARRAY. The following example shows how TYPE declarations enable you to generalize the ave program.

(* Example 5.16 *)

```
CONST
    MaxIndex = 99;

TYPE
    Statistic = ARRAY [0..MaxIndex] OF REAL;

(* Return the average of the elements of A *)
PROCEDURE Ave (A : Statistic) : REAL;
VAR
    i : CARDINAL;
    sum : REAL;
BEGIN
    sum := 0.;
    FOR i := 0 TO MaxIndex DO sum := sum + A[i] END;
    RETURN (sum / FLOAT(MaxIndex + 1))
END Ave;
```

**Exercise 5.4.** Rewrite the lsearch PROCEDURE (Example 5.7) so that it is passed a value to search for and *any* ARRAY of TYPE Statistic.
□

**Exercise 5.5.** One of the fastest ways to search an *ordered* ARRAY of values is called the *binary search*. The binary search is efficient because the area of the search is (typically) cut in half during each repetition of the search loop. The active area of the search is delimited by two indices, which I will call high and low. An ARRAY index that I will call mid indicates a point about halfway between high and low. Each pass through the loop determines whether the desired element (key) is above or below mid, and then the reduced portion of the ARRAY is searched on the next iteration. Here is the algorithm (in pseudo-code) for the binary search technique.

Set found to false
Set low to the lower ARRAY bound
Set high to the upper ARRAY bound
Repeat the following
    Set mid to the average of high and low
    If key equals the element indicated by mid
        Then set found to true
    If key is less than element indicated by mid
        Then set high to the larger of low, mid minus one
    Else set low to mid
While low is less than high

Write a binary search PROCEDURE. It should accept two parameters: the key (the element to search for) and an ARRAY to search through. Your bsearch PROCEDURE should return TRUE if the element is found. Note: a more useful binary search PROCEDURE would also return the index of the found element.
□

**Exercise 5.6.** In the binary search, actually finding the item occurs only once in many passes through the loop. Also, you are much more likely to find the item during a late pass through the loop than during an early pass. Is it more efficient to exit immediately from the loop when the element is found? Write both versions. Which version is easier to understand? Which version is simpler, hence more likely to be correct? Concoct some test data and measure the speed of the two versions.
□

I can't avoid the subject of efficiency during this discussion of ARRAYS. As a general rule, the more advanced data TYPES are less efficient than the simpler data TYPES. Even though StatData[i] and val (from Example 5.7) are both REALS, using StatData[i] involves somewhat more overhead than using val. This slight difference is usually negligible, and should be ignored altogether when ARRAYS are necessary.

A more important efficiency concern is passing ARRAYS as parameters to PROCEDURES. Typically an ARRAY passed as a *value* parameter must be entirely duplicated each time it is passed to a PROCEDURE. For large ARRAYS, such as an ARRAY of one thousand REALS, this is a considerable overhead. Imagine the overhead of passing a large ARRAY as a value parameter to a series of deeply nested PROCEDURES, or to a deeply recursive PROCEDURE.

Another problem with value ARRAY parameters occurs on comput-ers with limited memory capacities. There may not be enough space to make a copy of a large ARRAY. Using variable parameters instead of value parameters requires less overhead since the entire ARRAY does not have to be copied. My inclination is to try to use variable parameters only in situations where I want the PRO-CEDURE to modify the original copy. However there are rare situa-tions where it is necessary (for the sake of efficiency or to allow a program to fit into available memory) to sacrifice this principle.

In a program with numerous small ARRAYS, such as a text process-ing application, it makes sense to write a body of generic PRO-CEDURES and to pass the individual ARRAYS to the PROCEDURES as necessary. When there is one enormous ARRAY, such as the symbol table of a compiler program, it is usually best to make the ARRAY a global variable and write PROCEDURES that reference the ARRAY without having it passed as a parameter.

As always, you should make efficiency and storage concerns secon-dary. Correctness should be your primary goal. Once you have a correct program you should, if necessary, worry about efficiency.

## 5.3. Open ARRAY Parameters

For the most part Modula–2 scrupulously checks your programs to make sure that you use each PROCEDURE correctly. Modula–2 forces you to supply the correct TYPES of parameters, and it makes sure that you use the returned value (if any) correctly. It is an *er-ror* to call the Ave PROCEDURE from Example 5.16 without sup-plying an ARRAY to average.

```
                                              (* Example 5.17 *)
    result := Ave( );   (*ERROR*)
```

The *correct* invocation of Ave requires one parameter, and the parameter must be the correct TYPE.

```
                                              (* Example 5.18 *)
    result := Ave(dvalues);
```

(Examples 5.17 and 5.18 assume that result is a REAL variable and that dvalues is declared to have the Statistic TYPE as defined in Example 5.16.)

The Ave PROCEDURE in Example 5.16 includes an ARRAY of *known* dimensions as a parameter. In is often overly restrictive to require an ARRAY parameters to have a *fixed* size. Programs that handle text often use ARRAYS OF CHARS of varying lengths to hold words, phrases, sentences, paragraphs, etc. A PROCEDURE to average REALS should be able to work with an ARRAY OF REALS of any length.

Modula–2 has *open* ARRAY *parameters* so that PROCEDURES can handle ARRAYS of varying length. This flexibility is used in many applications, including text processing and systems programming.

Let's rewrite the Ave PROCEDURE to handle any ARRAY OF REALS. Instead of declaring the ARRAY parameter as Statistic, declare it to be an ARRAY OF REAL. Notice that the ARRAY bounds aren't mentioned in the PROCEDURE parameter declaration.

*Inside* the PROCEDURE you should use these two simple rules for open ARRAY bounds:

1. The *lower bound* of the ARRAY is zero.
2. The *upper bound* is determined using the built in function HIGH.

HIGH is a function PROCEDURE that takes the name of an ARRAY variable as its argument. It RETURNS the upper bound of that ARRAY. Note, the number of elements in an open ARRAY named x is HIGH(x) plus one.

Remember that *outside* the PROCEDURE the ARRAY bounds are the values mentioned in the ARRAY's declaration. The two rules mentioned above only apply *inside* a PROCEDURE that is passed an open ARRAY parameter.

Here is the generalized version of Ave using open ARRAY parameters.

```
                                          (* Example 5.19 *)
    (*
     * Return the average of the elements
     *      of an ARRAY of REALs
     *)
    PROCEDURE AVE (x : ARRAY OF REAL) : REAL;
    VAR
        i : CARDINAL;
        sum : REAL;
    BEGIN
        sum := 0.;
        FOR i := 0 TO HIGH(x) DO sum := sum + x[i] END;
        RETURN (sum / FLOAT(HIGH(x) + 1))
    END AVE;
```

In Example 5.1 I defined Gchars to be an ARRAY OF CHARS with bounds one to one hundred. How do open ARRAY parameters work when the *lower* bound of the actual parameter isn't zero? If Gchars is passed to a PROCEDURE expecting an ARRAY OF CHARS, the bounds of the formal PROCEDURE parameter will be mapped into the range zero to ninety nine. Open ARRAY parameters always range from zero to HIGH(FormalParameter). These two forms are illustrated in the following two PROCEDURES, which count the number of blanks in a CHAR ARRAY.

```
                                          (* Example 5.20 *)
TYPE
    Cvector = ARRAY [64..96] OF CHAR;


CONST
    SPACE = 40C;
                                          (* Example 5.21 *)
(* count the number of blanks in a Cvector *)
PROCEDURE blanks ( ch : Cvector ) : CARDINAL;
VAR
    i,cnt : CARDINAL;
BEGIN
    cnt := 0;
    FOR i := 64 TO 96 DO
        IF ch[i] = 0C THEN RETURN cnt END;
        IF ch[i] = SPACE THEN INC(cnt) END
    END;
    RETURN cnt
END blanks;
                                          (* Example 5.22 *)
(* count the number of blanks in an ARRAY OF CHAR *)
PROCEDURE blanks1 ( ch : ARRAY OF CHAR ) : CARDINAL;
(* Note: open array parameters *)
VAR
    i,cnt : CARDINAL;
BEGIN
    cnt := 0;
    FOR i := 0 TO HIGH(ch) DO
        IF ch[i] = 0C THEN RETURN cnt END;
        IF ch[i] = SPACE THEN INC(cnt) END
    END;
    RETURN cnt
END blanks1;
```

When a PROCEDURE contains a parameter that is declared to be a named ARRAY TYPE the bounds of the ARRAY inside the PRO-

CEDURE are identical to the bounds in the ARRAY's declaration. If however a PROCEDURE is passed an open ARRAY parameter then within the PROCEDURE the bounds of the ARRAY are mapped into the range 0 to HIGH of the ARRAY parameter. The HIGH function can also be used on ARRAYS other than open ARRAY parameters to determine the final index of the ARRAY.

Several restrictions apply to open ARRAY parameters. Remember that it's legal to assign one ordinary ARRAY to another (provided their TYPES are compatible). However it is not permissible to assign one open ARRAY to another. (Because their sizes aren't known beforehand.) Actually there are only two ways that open ARRAY parameters can be used.

1. The individual elements of the ARRAY can be accessed.
2. The ARRAY can be passed to another PROCEDURE that expects open ARRAY parameters.

The following short example illustrates an *incorrect* use of open ARRAY parameters.

```
                                              (* Example 5.23 *)
PROCEDURE Ident(VAR s : ARRAY OF CHAR);
BEGIN
   s := 'Version 3.31, Copyright 1984'
END Ident;
```

The Ident PROCEDURE is incorrect because the ARRAY is accessed as a whole — only *elementwise* operations are allowed on open ARRAY parameters.

**Exercise 5.7.** A technique called the *insertion sort* is often used to sort *small* ARRAYS. The insertion sort is not efficient, but it is easy to program and it is adequate for short ARRAYS. The quick-sort (Section 15.1, Section 16.5) is a better technique for large ARRAYS. Here is a pseudo–code description of the insertion sort algorithm:

> Set top to upper bound
> While top is greater than lower bound
> > For each ARRAY element e from lower to one less than top
> > > If e is greater than top element
> > > > Then swap the two elements
> > Subtract one from top

Write a PROCEDURE to perform insertion sorts. For testing (and learning) you might want to print out the entire ARRAY after the inner loop to watch the sort process.
□

## 5.4. Multiple ARRAY Dimensions

An ARRAY of a simple TYPE, such as an ARRAY OF CHARS, is a *one* dimensional entity. It is also possible to form ARRAYS of structured TYPES, such as an ARRAY OF ARRAYS. This allows us to create *multi*–dimensional data structures.

There are several methods for declaring multi–dimensional ARRAYS. Probably the most obvious is to mention the ARRAYS explicitly.

(* Example 5.24 *)

```
VAR
    x : ARRAY [0..9] OF ARRAY [0..99] OF CHAR;
```

This ARRAY could also be declared as

(* Example 5.25 *)

```
TYPE
    CHarray = ARRAY [0..99] OF CHAR;
VAR
    x : ARRAY [0..9] OF CHarray;
```

Both of these declarations specifies that the variable x is a two–dimensional ARRAY. x is an ARRAY of ten ARRAYS of one hundred CHARS. A particular element of x can be accessed using double subscript notation.

(* Example 5.26 *)

```
x[5][50] := 'a'
```

This notation for declarations and indexing is obvious, but bulky. Let's look at the syntax diagram for ARRAYS to discover a simpler method for declaring and indexing multi–dimensional ARRAYS.

**ArrayType**

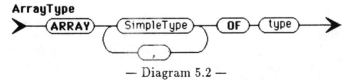

— Diagram 5.2 —

There are several restriction on the *SimpleType* in an ARRAY de–

claration. It must either be
- An explicit subrange.
- An explicit enumeration.
- An identifier indicating a subrange TYPE.
- An identifier indicating an enumeration TYPE.
- The built-in CHAR or BOOLEAN TYPE .

An element of an ARRAY is referenced using a designator.

**designator**

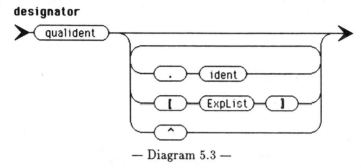

— Diagram 5.3 —

A simpler way to declare the ARRAY x from Examples 5.24 and
5.25 is

(* Example 5.27 *)

```
VAR
    x : ARRAY [0..9],[0..99] OF CHAR;
```

and a simpler way to reference a single element of x is

(* Example 5.28 *)

```
x[5,50] := 'a'
```

Notice that x[5] is itself an ARRAY. Since it permissible to assign
one ARRAY to another, Modula-2 allows the expression

(* Example 5.29 *)

```
x[0] := x[3]
```

This assignment copies all one hundred of the values in the x[3]
ARRAY into the x[0] ARRAY. Also notice that x is itself an AR-
RAY. If there were an ARRAY named y that was declared along
with x in Example 5.27, we could even perform the assignment

(* Example 5.30 *)

```
y := x
```

This innocuous looking assignment transfers all 1000 elements of x
into y.

**Exercise 5.8.** Modula–2 doesn't contain any two dimensional open ARRAY parameters. Thus the PROCEDURE heading

(* Example 5.31 *)
```
PROCEDURE Q ( x : ARRAY OF ARRAY OF CHAR );
```

is illegal. However it is possible to have an open ARRAY of a structured TYPE. Write a PROCEDURE that finds the largest element in an ARRAY of Statistic ARRAYS (See Example 5.10).
□

## 5.5. Subranges

A subrange is a TYPE that can only attain a limited range of values of a full range data TYPE. Subranges are useful because limiting the range of a variable provides an additional layer of automatic program verification, and because they make it easier to understand a program. Subranges are also important because their notation is often used to declare the bounds of ARRAY subscripts.

A subrange is presumed to be an INTEGER subrange if its lower bound is negative; it is presumed to be a CARDINAL subrange otherwise. For example a subrange variable whose range is minus ten to ten is an INTEGER subrange whereas a variable with the range 1 to 100 is assumed to be a CARDINAL subrange. We have already seen that a range is written by mentioning the extremes of the range separated by a pair of dots.

The range minus ten to ten is written as

```
-10 .. 10
```

We can declare a TYPE with this subrange as

(* Example 5.32 *)
```
TYPE
    R = [ -10 .. 10 ];
```

and we can declare variables with this restricted range as

(* Example 5.33 *)
```
VAR
    i, j, k : R;
```

An *anonymous* declaration doesn't reference a named TYPE. Here is an anonymous declaration that creates three variables with the range minus ten to ten.

(* Example 5.34 *)

```
VAR
    l, m, n : [ -10 .. 10 ];
```

Using a named TYPE in the declaration of i, j, and k means that they will be compatible with variables declared elsewhere in the program whose TYPE is R. The anonymous declaration of l, m, and n means that they will be compatible only with each other.

You should also notice that only a single connected range is possible. It is impossible to declare a subrange variable that has a range of zero to ten and 1200 to 1300.

The syntax diagram for a subrange is

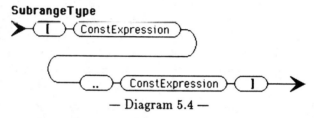

— Diagram 5.4 —

The optional identifier in front of the opening brace can be used to identify the base TYPE of the subrange. For example the declaration

(* Example 5.35 *)

```
VAR
    s : LONGINT[0..100];
```

means that s is a subrange TYPE whose base TYPE is LONGINT. Without the base TYPE specifier, the base TYPE of s would be assumed to be CARDINAL (because the lower bound is non-negative).

In Modula–2 it is possible to declare a subrange of
- INTEGERS or LONGINTS
- CARDINALS or LONGCARDS
- CHARS
- Enumerations

Subrange TYPES are often used in ARRAY declarations. For example we can declare the subranges

(* Example 5.36 *)

```
TYPE
    Xrange = [0..9];
    Yrange = [0..99];
```

and then use those declarations to declare an ARRAY variable.

(* Example 5.37 *)

```
VAR
    d : ARRAY Xrange, Yrange OF CHAR;
```

One advantage of using a named subrange TYPE to declare the AR-RAY is the ease of declaring compatible subscripts.

A subrange TYPE is always compatible with its base TYPE, thus the R TYPE from above is compatible with INTEGERS. Similarly two subranges of a given TYPE are compatible with each other. However compatibility between two TYPES doesn't necessarily mean that all operations between those TYPES are legal. For example if a variable named xsub is declared as

```
VAR
    xsub : Xrange;
```

then the assignment

(* Example 5.38 *)

```
xsub := 200;
```

is out of bounds. Since 200 is a constant, the compiler will probably object to such an obvious blunder.

It is possible to construct more devious value errors. Suppose Q is an INTEGER. Thus it is assignment compatible with a Xrange TYPE variable named xsub. The following code fragment also assigns an out of bounds value to xsub, but this one is much harder to notice during *compilation*.

(* Example 5.39 *)

```
Q := 200;
    . . . (* intervening code doesn't modify Q *)
xsub := Q;
```

Some compilers offer optional checking of assignments during *execution* to detect (among other things) illegal subrange assignments. Bounds checking is very useful during program development, even though it introduces a small execution overhead.

**Exercise 5.9.** Complete the following subrange TYPE declarations.

a.   TYPE LowerCaseLetters = _____ ;
b.   TYPE UpperCaseLetters = _____ ;
c.   TYPE Numerals = _____ ;
d.   TYPE ControlChars = _____ ;
e.   TYPE ASCII = _____ ;
     TYPE Months = (Jan, Feb, Mar, Apr, May, Jun,
          Jul, Aug, Sep, Oct, Nov, Dec );
f.   TYPE Summer = _____ ;
g.   TYPE Fall = _____ ;
h.   TYPE DayOfMonth = _____ ;

□

**Exercise 5.10.** Rewrite the CalcVariables MODULE from the Calc2 program (Example 10.2) using subranges.
□

## 5.6. String Variables

Most programs need to handle text. Today text is the interface between people and computers. A simple use of text might be to output instructions to the person operating a program. Most programs must display results on the output terminal or on a printer. In either case the output is text.

Programs often read text input. In a simple application a program might read in a series of numbers or keywords from the terminal. A more difficult application is deciphering an intricate command language, such as a database querry language or a programming language.

A *string* is a sequence of characters delimited by single or double quotes. The pair of quotes must match. As a special case a string that is one character long is compatible with the CHAR TYPE. Strings delimited by double quotes can contain single quotes and vice versus. A single string can't contain both types of quote, and strings can't contain ASCII control codes. It is possible to *construct* variable strings containing control characters by writing code to combine constant strings with the control characters. Embedded blanks are allowed within strings, but strings must not extend past the end of the line.

The following are valid Modula-2 strings:

```
"The quick brown fox."
"Don't rain on my parade."
'He said "Get out of town in a hurry."'
"."
'raisins'
'NIH'
"NIH"
```

The following are examples of *incorrect* Modula–2 strings:

```
'abc"
bye'
'hello
'Don't rain on my parade.'
```

The first is incorrect because it starts with a single quote and ends with a double quote — the start and the end quote must be the same. The second and third are wrong because one of the quotes is missing, and the fourth is wrong because a string delimited by single quotes can't contain a single quote.

The following is *not* a legal Modula–2 string because it tries to span two lines:

```
"Take the Money and Run -
   a film by Woody Allen"
```

Variables whose TYPE is ARRAY OF CHAR are sometimes loosely referred to as "strings" although we usually mean constant strings when we use the term strings.

In general it is impossible to assign one ARRAY variable to another unless they are the same TYPE, and ARRAYS of the same TYPE are always the same length. This ruled is relaxed to make it acceptable to assign a constant string to an ARRAY OF CHAR variable if the variable long enough to hold the string.

When a constant string is assigned to a longer ARRAY OF CHAR variable it's important to keep track of how much of the ARRAY variable is used. In some languages the "unused" tail end of the ARRAY is filled in with the ASCII space character (20C). Unfortunately this technique changes the meaning of string constants that contain trailing spaces! Modula–2 uses a better technique — the end of the valid text in a string variable is marked with the special ASCII value called *null* whose value is 0C. The positions in the ARRAY past the terminating null are undefined.

For example if cstrin has been declared to be an ARRAY of eighty CHARS, then the assignment

(* Example 5.40 *)

    cstrin := 'abc'

will set the first element of cstrin to 'a', the second to 'b', the third to 'c', and the fourth to 0C. The final seventy–six elements are undefined.

It is legal to assign constant strings to ARRAY OF CHAR variables because this flexibility is often necessary. PROCEDURES that use ARRAY OF CHAR arguments should be able to handle embedded nulls marking the end of the valid portion.

**Exercise 5.11.** Write your own version of the ReadString PROCEDURE. Your PROCEDURE should obtain input from the Read PROCEDURE in InOut, you should accept a variable ARRAY OF CHAR as a parameter, and then you should put as much of an input string into the ARRAY as you can. Strings are delimited by white space and control characters, so your PROCEDURE should skip leading white space and control characters, then read letters, digits and punctuation into the string. You should stop filling the string when white space or control characters are encountered, or when the string is full. If the string isn't full you should delimit the active part of the string with a trailing 0C.
□

**Exercise 5.12.** In Exercise 5.3 an ARRAY OF BOOLEANS was used to represent a series of states. Unfortunately that solution was somewhat cluttered because an ARRAY OF BOOLEANS cannot be initialized by assigning it a constant value. Instead five individual assignment statements were used. One value of strings in Modula–2 is the availability of string constants that can simplify initialization of ARRAYS. Rewrite the program in Exercise 5.3 using an ARRAY OF CHARS to store the state sequence.

The complication of this version of the program is the conversion of the value returned by the flip PROCEDURE into a character. Which version of the program do you prefer and why?
□

## 5.7. Example — Long Arithmetic

Computers work internally in binary because the logic elements
that form the basis of computing are two state devices, on or off.
Binary arithmetic is efficient because it is the native ability of the
machine. However there are certain applications where the native
binary arithmetic of a computer is unsuitable. For example, consider a problem in the area of banking and foreign currency exchange.

International bankers often perform calculations involving large
numbers (e.g. a trillion lira) where round–off is completely unacceptable. REAL numbers are unsuitable for this application because
on most computers they have only a limited number of digits of
accuracy, and certain common fractions cannot be expressed exactly as REAL numbers. (INTEGERS or CARDINALS) are also unsuitable because they have a limited range. LONGCARDS or LONGINTS
might be suitable for some applications, but they aren't available
in all Modula–2 implementations.

Sometimes the best solution is to write a new set of arithmetic
operations for a particular application. Just as there is no such
thing as the "best" computer, there is no "best" arithmetic system. The arithmetic that is built into Modula–2 is suitable for
many applications, but it must be extended or enhanced for others.

The following example is an implementation of an arithmetic system with ten digit precision. For now I will ignore negative
numbers, or numbers with fractional parts and concentrate on a
simple arithmetic package for (possibly large) positive whole
numbers.

The first decision we must make is how we will *represent* our
numbers. Probably the easiest way is simply to use an ARRAY with
one position for each digit in the number. Let's store the character
"0" in a digit whose value is zero, etc. We must define an ARRAY
TYPE called LONG that can store ten digit numbers. The individual
elements of a LONG are DIGITS, single characters between zero and
nine. (See Section 5.5.)

( * Example 5.41 * )

```
CONST
    MSDigit = 9;
TYPE
    DIGIT = [ '0' .. '9' ];
    LONG = ARRAY[ 0 .. MSDigit ] OF DIGIT;
```

This representation of LONG numbers is an example of making tradeoffs in the design of software. Our LONG data TYPE is not particularly efficient or compact. There are better ways to represent large whole numbers. The only advantage of this system is *simplicity*. The routines to manipulate LONG numbers are simple exercises in getting the subscripts right. LONG arithmetic shouldn't be used for "number crunching" because it is too slow. Our LONGs package is merely useful for extending the range of arithmetic for some applications. Example 12.10 demonstrates LONG arithmetic in a program that searches for prime numbers.

In our LONG number system the zeroeth element of the ARRAY is the least significant digit of the number. (Note that this is the reverse of how a number is stored in a character string. In a string the least significant digit stored in the highest element of the string.)

The first PROCEDURE outputs a LONG number. Thus WriteLong does for LONGs what WriteCard does for CARDINALS. The first parameter to WriteLong is the number, the second specifies the minimum field width. The strategy in WriteLong is simple, although it is easy to get the subscripts jumbled. The first chore is to determine the length of the active digit sequence. This avoids printing batches of leading zeroes. Once we have computed the length of the active digit sequence we can print leading spaces (to pad to the minimum width), and then we print the digit sequence. The printed number is always proceeded by at least one blank.

Here is the pseudo–code for WriteLong:

> Set i to the number of non–zero digits, or at least 1
> Write (width-i) leading blanks, but at least one
> Write digit sequence

Most of the work of translating this pseudo–code is getting the subscripts to work correctly. Notice that the WHILE loop in Write-Long depends on Modula-2's short circuit evaluation.

```
                                          (* Example 5.42 *)
PROCEDURE WriteLong(x : LONG; n : INTEGER);
VAR
    i : INTEGER;
BEGIN
    (* Find first non-zero digit in the number *)
    i := MSDigit;
    WHILE (i > 0) AND (x[i] = '0') DO
        DEC(i)
    END;
    (* left pad with (at least one) space(s) *)
    REPEAT
        Write(' ');
        DEC(n)
    UNTIL n <= (i+1);
    (* output the digit sequence *)
    REPEAT
        Write(x[i]);
        DEC(i)
    UNTIL i < 0;
END WriteLong;
```

**Exercise 5.13.** Write a program that tests the WriteLong PRO-CEDURE.
□

**Exercise 5.14.** Modify the WriteLong PROCEDURE to insert commas between each millenia to make large numbers more legible.
□

**Exercise 5.15.** What happens if WriteLong is passed a minimum field width of 0?
□

**Exercise 5.16.** Why is it better to use a CHAR subrange TYPE for DIGIT rather than to use an ordinary CHAR TYPE?
□

**Exercise 5.17.** How would WriteLong's behavior change if the second loop in the PROCEDURE were changed to the following?

```
WHILE n > (i+1) DO
    Write(' ');
    DEC(n)
END;
```

□

Adding a pair of LONG numbers involves adding a sequence of individual elements. Let's simplify our addition routine by isolating the code for adding two digits into a separate PROCEDURE. Our AddDigit PROCEDURE will accept two DIGITs and a carry flag and will return the sum of the two DIGITs. If there is a carry the carry parameter will be set accordingly.

Here is the pseudo code for adding two digits:

> Set temp to the sum of the two digits
> Add 1 to temp if the carry flag is set
> If temp is above nine Then
> > subtact ten from temp
> > set the carry flag
> Otherwise clear the carry flag

The Modula–2 code for adding a pair of digits is

```
                                              (* Example 5.43 *)
PROCEDURE AddDigit
        (a, b: DIGIT; VAR carry : BOOLEAN) : DIGIT;
VAR
    temp : CHAR;
BEGIN
    temp := CHR(ORD(a) + ORD(b) - ORD('0'));
    IF carry THEN INC(temp) END;
    IF temp > '9' THEN
        temp := CHR(ORD(temp) - 10);
        carry := TRUE
    ELSE
        carry := FALSE
    END;
    RETURN temp
END AddDigit;
```

Let's start with incrementing a LONG before tackling addition. The key idea behind incrementing a LONG is to add one to the least significant digit. If there is a carry, then we must add one to the next digit, and so on. Here is the pseudo–code for IncLong:

> Start at the least significant digit
> Set carry to one
> For each digit in the number
> > Add the carry to the digit

IncLong expressed in Modula–2 is

```
                                                    (* Example 5.44 *)
PROCEDURE IncLong(VAR x : LONG);
VAR
    i : INTEGER;
    carry : BOOLEAN;
BEGIN
    carry := TRUE;
    FOR i := 0 TO MSDigit DO
        x[i] := AddDigit(x[i],'0',carry)
    END
END IncLong;
```

Notice that IncLong is extremely simple because most of the work is done in AddDigit.

**Exercise 5.18.** Notice that in IncLong we only need to continue the loop until there isn't a carry to bring forward. Modify Inc-Long so that the loop terminates as soon as the carry becomes FALSE. What is the "worst case" test for your program? Does your loop have one exit condition or two?
□

Addition is just slightly harder than incrementing. Here is the pseudo code for a PROCEDURE to add two LONG numbers:

> Start at the least significant digit
> Clear the carry
> For each digit
>     Add the input digits and put result in output digit

Here is the Modula–2 code for adding two LONG numbers.

```
                                                    (* Example 5.45 *)
PROCEDURE AddLong(x,y : LONG; VAR result : LONG);
VAR
    i : INTEGER;
    carry : BOOLEAN;
BEGIN
    carry := FALSE;
    FOR i := 0 TO MSDigit DO
        result[i] := AddDigit(x[i],y[i],carry)
    END;
END AddLong;
```

**Exercise 5.19.** Write the IncLong PROCEDURE to call AddLong instead of AddDigit. Notice the limitation imposed by Modula-2's lack of ARRAY constants (except for string constants).
□

**Exercise 5.20.** Write a PROCEDURE to subtract two LONGs. Since our LONG arithmetic system doesn't have negative numbers, it is an error to subtract a larger number from a smaller.
□

**Exercise 5.21.** Write a PROCEDURE to compare two LONGs. Return −1 if the first is less than the second, 0 if they are equal, and +1 if the first is larger than the second.
□

**Exercise 5.22.** Write a PROCEDURE to translate a LONG to a CARDINAL. Obviously this will only work if the LONG has a value less than MAX(CARDINAL).
□

**Exercise 5.23.** Write a program that compares the arithmetic performance of LONG arithmetic to the performance of Modula-2's built in CARDINAL arithmetic and to the performance of REAL arithmetic. For example, write a program to measure the execution time of ten thousand LONG additions, ten thousand CARDINAL additions, and ten thousand REAL additions. How much slower is LONG addition than CARDINAL addition, than REAL addition?
□

# Part II

# MODULES

MODULES are obviously the most important new feature of Modula-2. They are an *organizational* structure. Each MODULE creates a new environment — an empty palette to suit the needs of the programmer. Global MODULES allow you to divide a large program into several pieces that can be worked on and compiled separately. They also allow you to create libraries that contain generally useful MODULES.

A MODULE organizes a program much as cells organize biological tissues. A cell is an environment that supports the vital activities within the cell. I might even stretch the analogy by noting that cells have cell membranes that only allow particular substances to pass into (or out of) the cell. MODULES have a similar import, export control system.

The major role of a MODULE in Modula-2 is to create a known environment in which a collection of PROCEDURES and data structures can thrive. MODULES use IMPORT lists to control what outside items are accessible from within.

Local MODULES are MODULES that are nested within another MODULE — they are discussed in Chapter 6. Global MODULES come in two parts, DEFINITION MODULES, which list and define the visible services and IMPLEMENTATION MODULES, which implement

the services. DEFINITION MODULES are discussed in Chapter 7, IM-
PLEMENTATION MODULES in Chapter 8. Most Modula–2 systems
contain several common global MODULES that are discussed in
Chapter 9. An example of partitioning a program into MODULES
appears in Chapter 10.

# Chapter 6

# Local MODULES

A *local* MODULE is a MODULE that is nested within another. (Occasionally a local MODULE is nested within a PROCEDURE.) Improving the organization of a program is the most common reason for using a local MODULE. They are also used to protect critical regions of code (Section 17.2) and to provide for static variables (Appendix VII). Placing several related PROCEDURES and data structures into a local MODULE *binds* them together and *segregates* them from the outer MODULE.

A local MODULE creates a new environment that is isolated from the surrounding environment. As in any MODULE, items from outside cannot be referenced from within unless they are *imported* into the local MODULE. Similarly items inside a local MODULE cannot be accessed from outside unless they are exported from the local MODULE.

Local MODULES can only import items from their *immediate* surroundings (usually another MODULE). Therefore anything that a local MODULE needs from a *global* MODULE must first be imported into the surrounding scope of the local MODULE and then imported into the local MODULE itself.

Items inside a local MODULE are made available to the surrounding environment using an EXPORT list. Only those items mentioned in an EXPORT list are visible in the surrounding scope — all other items are hidden by the wall that separates a local MODULE from its surroundings. EXPORT lists are present only in local MODULES.

**export**

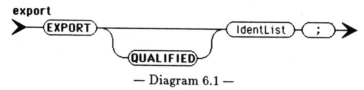

— Diagram 6.1 —

The word QUALIFIED in an export list means that the exported items must be referenced using qualified identifiers in the surrounding environment. Omitting the QUALIFIED phrase means the exported items are referenced from outside using their short names, and it means that it is the programmer's responsibility to avoid name collisions.

Local MODULES are most often used to create a new, nested environment that is isolated from the surrounding environment. For example the following program contains a local MODULE named hide that contains three private variables: q, r and s. The surrounding MODULE in this example also contains three variables: p, q, and r.

```
                                           (* Example 6.1 *)
MODULE show;
VAR
   p, q, r : CARDINAL;

MODULE hide;
VAR
   q, r, s : CARDINAL;
      (* Visible: q, r, and s *)
      (* Hidden: p, q, and r from outside *)
END hide;

BEGIN
   (* Visible: p, q, and r *)
   (* Hidden: q, r, and s from hide *)
END show.
```

Notice that show is a program MODULE, the local MODULE in this example is hide.

Local MODULES often are designed with hidden variables and exported PROCEDURES that use the hidden variables. Exporting

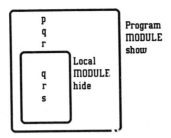

Figure 6.1. The organization of the show program.

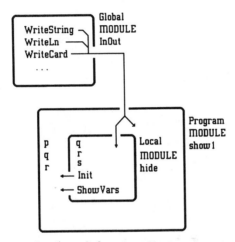

Figure 6.2. The organization of the show1 program.

PROCEDURES that operate on hidden data is usually safer than making the data universally accessible. The following example exports two PROCEDURES from the hide local MODULE.

(* Example 6.2 *)

```
MODULE show1;
FROM InOut IMPORT WriteString, WriteLn, WriteCard;

MODULE hide;
IMPORT WriteString, WriteLn, WriteCard;
EXPORT Init, ShowVars;

VAR
   q, r, s : CARDINAL;

PROCEDURE Init;
BEGIN
   q := 10; r := 20; s := 30
END Init;

PROCEDURE ShowVars;
BEGIN
    WriteString('q, r, and s from ');
    WriteString('local module hide: ');
    WriteCard(q,4);
    WriteCard(r,4);
    WriteCard(s,4);
    WriteLn
END ShowVars;

END hide; (* MODULE *)

VAR
   p, q, r : CARDINAL;

BEGIN
   p := 0; q := 1; r := 2;
   Init;
   ShowVars;
   WriteString('p, q, and r from ');
   WriteString('program module show1: ');
   WriteCard(p,4);
   WriteCard(q,4);
   WriteCard(r,4);
   WriteLn
END show1.
```

This program produced the following messages when it was executed:

```
q, r, and s from local module hide:    10  20  30
p, q, and r from program module show:   0   1   2
```

The local MODULE hide in this example uses *un*QUALIFIED export for the Init and ShowVars PROCEDURES. These two PROCEDURES can be used in the surrounding MODULE by simply mentioning their name. In Section 1.3 I outlined the rules for QUALIFIED EXPORT, an alternative form of EXPORT. When a local MODULE uses QUALIFIED EXPORT, the exported items are referenced from outside using *qualified identifiers*.

QUALIFIED EXPORT is used to avoid name collisions since qualified identifiers are *always* unique. Qualified identifiers clearly show where something originates so they sometimes make a program easier to understand. The QUALIFIED attribute applies to *everything* that is exported because local MODULES can only have one EXPORT list.

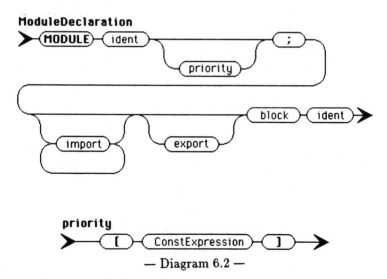

— Diagram 6.2 —

The following example shows how QUALIFIED EXPORT can avoid name collisions.

(* Example 6.3 *)

```
MODULE Collision;
VAR
    oranges, bananas : CARDINAL;

MODULE fruits; (* local module *)

(* public citrus *)
EXPORT QUALIFIED oranges, grapefruit;

VAR
    oranges, grapefruit, grapes, bananas : CARDINAL;
    (* only the local variables are visible here *)
END fruits; (* MODULE *)

BEGIN
    (*
     * Visible here:
     *     oranges, bananas,
     *     fruits.oranges, fruits.grapefruit
     *)
    (* oranges from program MODULE *)
    oranges := 0;
    (* oranges from fruits MODULE *)
    fruits.oranges := 100;
END Collision.
```

QUALIFIED EXPORT is mandatory in this example because of the oranges name collision.

Something that is exported from a local MODULE is placed into the surrounding environment. Thus it can be picked up from another local MODULE by importing as illustrated in  the following:

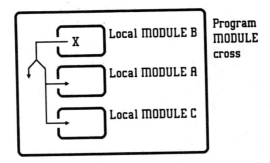

Figure 6.3. The organization of the cross program.

(* Example 6.4 *)

```
MODULE Cross;

MODULE A;
IMPORT x;
   (* x is visible here *)
END A;

MODULE B;
EXPORT x;
VAR
   x : CARDINAL;
   (* x is defined here *)
END B;

MODULE C;
IMPORT B; (* import all of the exports from B *)
   (* B.x is visible here *)
END C;

BEGIN (* cross *)
   (* x is visible here *)
END Cross.
```

In Section 1.3 we examined *un*qualifying import in program MODULES. The same facility is also available in local MODULES by using the FROM phrase in an IMPORT list.

One restriction of an IMPORT or EXPORT list is that it can *only* contain identifiers, qualidents are not allowed. A local MODULE that needs to import the QUALIFIED EXPORTS of another local MODULE must either import the entire MODULE or to use the FROM phrase in the IMPORT list.

(* Example 6.5 *)
```
MODULE Cross2;

MODULE A;
FROM B IMPORT x; (* UNqualifying import *)
   (* x is visible here *)
END A;

MODULE B;
EXPORT QUALIFIED x; (* qualified export *)
VAR
   x : CARDINAL;
   (* x is defined here *)
END B;

MODULE C;
IMPORT B; (* import all of the exports from B *)
   (* B.x is visible here *)
END C;

BEGIN (* cross *)
   (* B.x is visible here *)
END Cross2.
```

# 6.1. Local MODULE Bodies

The *body* of a MODULE is a statement sequence bracketed by BE-GIN and END that follows the declarations in the MODULE. The local MODULES in Examples 6.1 through 6.5 don't contain MODULE bodies. In general a MODULE may or may not contain a MODULE body. The body of a local MODULE is often used for initializing its variables, although more general applications are certainly possible.

Statement sequences in local MODULES are executed *before* the statement sequence for the surrounding MODULE. If there are several local MODULES embedded in a surrounding MODULE, the statement sequences from the local MODULES are executed in the order of the local MODULES before the statement sequence of the surrounding MODULE.

The following example illustrates these rules.

(* Example 6.6 *)

```
MODULE order;
FROM InOut IMPORT WriteString, WriteLn;

MODULE A;
IMPORT WriteString, WriteLn;
BEGIN (* MODULE A's statement sequence *)
   WriteString('Statement sequence from ');
   WriteString('module A executing.');
   WriteLn
END A;

MODULE B;
IMPORT WriteString, WriteLn;
BEGIN (* MODULE B's statement sequence *)
   WriteString('Statement sequence from ');
   WriteString('module B executing.');
   WriteLn
END B;

BEGIN (* order *)
   WriteString('Statement sequence from ');
   WriteString('order executing.');
   WriteLn
END order.
```

When this program was executed, it produced the following output:

```
Statement sequence from module A executing.
Statement sequence from module B executing.
Statement sequence from order executing.
```

Notice that there weren't any *explicit* calls to the local modules, the execution of their MODULE bodies is automatic. You should be careful when programs contain several local MODULES. Since the services of a local MODULE probably won't operate correctly until its body has executed, the body of one local MODULE should not rely on the services of a *following* local MODULE.

The RETURN statement may be used within a MODULE body just as it may be used within a PROCEDURE to terminate execution. It's not possible to return a value from a MODULE body. Thus MODULE bodies are somewhat like parameterless true PROCEDURES. The difference is that MODULE bodies are activated automatically when their surrounding context starts to execute.

**Exercise 6.1.** Rewrite the order program (Example 6.6) so that a new MODULE named C is nested inside MODULE B. The body of C should print a identifying message. What output do you expect?
□

Example 6.2 used a PROCEDURE named Init to initialize the variables in a local MODULE. A better method is to place the initialization within the body of the MODULE.

```
                                          (* Example 6.7 *)
MODULE show2;
FROM InOut IMPORT WriteString, WriteLn, WriteCard;

MODULE hide;
IMPORT WriteString, WriteLn, WriteCard, p;
EXPORT ShowVars, s;

VAR
   q, r, s : CARDINAL;

PROCEDURE ShowVars;
BEGIN
   WriteString('q, r, and s from ');
   WriteString('local MODULE hide: ');
   WriteCard(q,4);
   WriteCard(r,4);
   WriteCard(s,4);
   WriteLn
END ShowVars;

BEGIN (* hide module body *)
   p := 0;
   q := 10;
   r := 20;
   s := 30
END hide; (* local module *)

VAR
   p, q, r : CARDINAL;

BEGIN  (* show2 module body *)
   p := 10;
   q := 20;
   r := 30;
```

```
      s := 40;
      ShowVars;
      WriteString('p, q, and r from ');
      WriteString('program MODULE show: ');
      WriteCard(p,4);
      WriteCard(q,4);
      WriteCard(r,4);
      WriteLn
   END show2.
```

**Exercise 6.2.** What does the show2 program print?
□

**Exercise 6.3.** The following program is a puzzle.

(* Example 6.8 *)

```
MODULE DeepMod;
FROM InOut IMPORT Write, WriteLn;

VAR
   c : CHAR;

PROCEDURE A;
VAR
   b : CHAR;

MODULE B;
IMPORT c, Write;
VAR
   a : CHAR;

PROCEDURE C (c : CHAR) : CHAR;
BEGIN (* procedure C *)
   Write(c);
   INC(a);
   c := a;
   INC(c);
   RETURN c
END C;

BEGIN (* module body B *)
   a := 'M';
   Write(C(a));
   c := a;
   DEC(c)
```

```
   END B;

   BEGIN (* procedure A *)
      Write('D')
   END A;

   BEGIN A;
      Write('U');
      DEC(c);
      Write(c);
      Write('A');
      WriteLn
   END DeepMod.
```

What does this puzzle print?

□

**Exercise 6.4.** Make a list of the items that are visible within each of the two MODULES and two PROCEDURES in DeepMod.

□

## 6.2. Static Variables

In Chapter 4 I discussed variables declared within PROCEDURES. These variables are often described as *local* to emphasize that they aren't visible in the surrounding scope of the PROCEDURE. It is also possible to take a different vantage point and describe them as *dynamic* or *automatic* to emphasize that they are created when the PROCEDURE starts to execute and that they cease to exist when the PROCEDURE exits.

The local variables of a MODULE obey a slightly different set of rules. One difference is that variables within a MODULE may be exported so that they become visible in the surrounding context. Variables local to a PROCEDURE are *never* visible outside the PRO-CEDURE.

Another difference is that variables within a MODULE are created when the *surrounding scope* of a MODULE starts to execute. Local MODULES are usually declared within program MODULE or IMPLE-MENTATION MODULES. The surrounding context for these local MODULES is the program itself, which means that their variables exist throughout the life of the program. Hence the variables in a MODULE are often called *static* (as opposed to dynamic) because they are not created and destroyed each time the PROCEDURE is called.

It is possible for a local MODULE to be nested inside a PROCEDURE.
Then the variables in the MODULE are created when the surrounding PROCEDURE starts to execute and they vanish when it finishes.
If a MODULE nested within a PROCEDURE contains a MODULE
body, the MODULE body is executed before the body of the surrounding PROCEDURE.

Here is the outline of a PROCEDURE that contains both a local
MODULE and another PROCEDURE. In this hypothetical case the
MODULE is used to hide some of the local data of the outer PRO-
CEDURE from the nested PROCEDURE.

(* Example 6.9 *)

```
PROCEDURE X;
VAR
     a, b, c : CARDINAL;

MODULE Y;    (* nested inside X *)
EXPORT   . . . ;
VAR
     q, r, s : CARDINAL; (* private *)
  . . .
END Y;

PROCEDURE Z; (* nested inside X *)
  (* a, b, and c from X are visible here *)
  (* q, r, and s from Y are not visible here *)
END Z;

BEGIN
  (* a, b, c, X and Z are visible here *)
  . . .
END X;
```

Variables in Modula-2 have two major characteristics, their TYPE
and their *lifetime*. From earlier chapters you should recall that
the TYPE of a variable indicates what operations apply to that
variable and how much storage it occupies. The lifetime of a variable is important: dynamic variables only exist while their surrounding PROCEDURE is executing, static variables exist
throughout the execution of the program. One copy of a
PROCEDURE's local variables is created for each activation, thus
for a recursive PROCEDURE there can be multiple copies of the
dynamic variables.

Here is the skeleton of a program that takes advantage of static variables.

(* Example 6.10 *)

```
MODULE ShowStatic;

MODULE Stats;
EXPORT Fn;
VAR
    (* static, private to the Stats MODULE *)
    firstime : BOOLEAN;

PROCEDURE Fn;
VAR
        . . .   (* dynamic, private to the Fn PROCEDURE *)
BEGIN
IF firstime THEN
    firstime := FALSE;
    . . .
ELSE
    . . .
END
END Fn;

BEGIN (* Stats MODULE body *)
  firstime := TRUE
END Stats;

BEGIN (* ShowStatic MODULE body *)
    . . .
END ShowStatic.
```

In this skeleton example the variable named firstime in the Stats MODULE exists for the lifetime of the program, but it is a private variable. It is created once, initialized automatically by the MODULE body of Stats, and then it exists for the life of the program. Like the local variables of the Fn PROCEDURE, it can't be seen or altered from outside. (Technically, firstime has a slightly different scope from the local variables of Stats, but in a practical sense its scope is the same.)

Scope control systems as elaborate as the two shown above are unusual, but occasionally the need does arise. Control of scope is one of the most important uses of local MODULES.

## 6.3. Example — The Sieve of Eratosthenes

As an example I am going to show a local MODULE named WriteMod that paginates and columnates output. WriteMod exports a PROCEDURE named WRITECARD that is called to output a CARDINAL. The WriteMod MODULE uses static variables to keep track of the line number and the column number. Each time a number is output WriteMod checks to see if it is necessary to advance to the next line, or to provide several blank lines to advance to the next page. I am placing the WriteMod local MODULE in a program that prints a table of prime numbers using the sieve of Eratosthenes method.

Before you look at the actual code for the sieve MODULE, look at Figure 6.4, which shows the organization of the program. Whenever you look at a long program, it might help you to construct a mental diagram showing the relationships between the MODULES.

```
                                         (* Example 6.11 *)
MODULE Sieve;
FROM InOut IMPORT WriteCard, WriteLn, WriteString;

MODULE WriteMod;
IMPORT WriteCard, WriteLn;
EXPORT WRITECARD;

CONST
    PageLength = 66;

VAR
    line, col: CARDINAL; (* static *)

PROCEDURE WRITECARD(x : CARDINAL);
BEGIN
    WriteCard(x,7);
    INC(col);
    IF col = 10 THEN col := 0; WRITELN END;
END WRITECARD;

PROCEDURE WRITELN;
VAR
    i : CARDINAL; (* dynamic *)
BEGIN
    INC(line);
    WriteLn;
```

```
      IF line = (PageLength - 4) THEN
          FOR i := 1 TO 7 DO WRITELN END;
      ELSIF line = PageLength THEN
          line := 0;
      END;
  END WRITELN;

  BEGIN (* WriteMod *)
     col := 0;
     line := 0;
     WRITELN;
     WRITELN;
     WRITELN
  END WriteMod;

  CONST
     Last = 20000;

  VAR
     flags : ARRAY [0..Last] OF BOOLEAN;
     suspect, convicted, prime : CARDINAL;

  BEGIN    (* Sieve of Eratosthenes *)
     (* Init flags array *)
     FOR suspect := 0 TO Last DO
         flags[suspect] := TRUE
     END; (* FOR *)
     (*
      * Suspect - a possible prime
      * If suspect is TRUE
      *   then calculate prime and rule out multiples
      *)
     FOR suspect := 0 TO Last DO (* search *)
         IF flags[suspect] THEN (* found one *)
            prime := suspect + suspect + 3;
            WRITECARD(prime);
            convicted := prime + suspect;
            WHILE convicted <= Last DO
               (* rule out multiples of known prime *)
               flags[convicted] := FALSE;
               convicted := convicted + prime;
            END (* WHILE *)
         END (* IF *)
     END; (* FOR *)
```

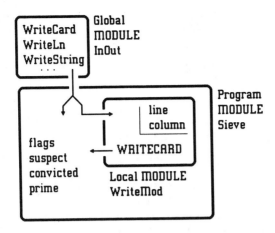

Figure 6.4. In this version of the Sieve of Eratosthenes a local MODULE named WriteMod manages the details of columnating and paginating the table of prime numbers. WriteMod hides its own state variables, line and column, and it exports the WRITECARD routine.

```
    WriteLn
END Sieve.
```

The purpose of WriteMod is to isolate the page formatting function from the search for primes. Notice that this "busywork" consumes nearly as many lines of code as the search for primes. WriteMod hides the WRITELN PROCEDURE and it hides the static variables named col and line. The operation of WriteMod should be obvious and I won't discuss it further.

Unlike the page formatting algorithms, Eratosthenes' sieve algorithm (named after the Greek mathematician and astronomer 276? – 195? B.C.) is not very obvious. The basic idea of Eratosthenes is simple. Start with a list of numbers from 2 to whatever. All the numbers on the list are either prime or non prime. We work forward from the beginning of the list, starting with 2. We can strike out multiples of two because they are non prime. Next examine the number 3. Since it hasn't been crossed out, it must be prime and we proceed to cross out its multiples. The number 4 is crossed out so we can ignore it. 5 isn't crossed out so it is prime and we must cross out its multiples. By the time we get to the end of the list we have crossed out all the non primes.

Eratosthenes method as programmed above uses an ARRAY OF BOOLEANS to represent the numbers on the list. To save space, I only put odd numbers on the list since we know that the even numbers aren't prime. The variable flags[0] corresponds to the

| flags<br>Index | Corresponding<br>Number |
|:---:|:---:|
| 0 | 3 |
| 1 | 5 |
| 2 | 7 |
| 3 | 9 |
| 4 | 11 |
| 5 | 13 |
| 6 | 15 |
| 7 | 17 |
| 8 | 19 |

Figure 6.5. The correspondence between elements of the flags ARRAY and odd numbers explains why

    prime := suspect + suspect + 3;

For example flags[5] corresponds to the number 13 because 5+5+3 is 13.

number 3, flags[1] corresponds to 5, and so on (Figure 6.5). We can locate multiples of a prime by repeatedly adding the value of the prime to the ARRAY index of the prime. For the prime number 7 (flags[2]) we rule out 21 (flags[2+7]), 35 (flags[2+7+7]), 49 (flags[2+7+7+7]), etc.

**Exercise 6.5.** Rewrite the WRITELN PROCEDURE so that it isn't recursive.
□

**Exercise 6.6.** The most obvious way to search for primes is to look at the remainder of dividing a prospective prime by 2, 3, etc. If the remainder is zero then the prospective prime is not a prime. Modify the prime number program (Example 6.11) to use this more obvious method.
□

| Ruling Out Multiples of Five | | |
|---|---|---|
| | flags Index | Corresponding Number |
| | 0 | 3 |
| | 1 | 5 | Prime |
| | 2 | 7 |
| | 3 | 9 |
| | 4 | 11 |
| | 5 | 13 |
| 1 + 5 | 6 | 15 | 5 * 3 |
| | 7 | 17 |
| | 8 | 19 |
| | 9 | 21 |
| | 10 | 23 |
| 1 + 5 + 5 | 11 | 25 | 5 * 5 |
| | 12 | 27 |

Figure 6.6. Repeatedly adding a prime number to its index in the flags ARRAY produces an index that corresponds to a multiple of the prime. For example 5, whose index is 1, is a prime. flags[1+5], flags[1+5+5], and flags[1+5+5+5] correspond to multiples of 5. The inner loop of the Sieve rules out multiples (non–primes) using this technique.

# Chapter 7

# Definition Modules

The major feature that distinguishes Modula–2 from Pascal is the MODULE. The assumption that underlies Pascal is that many useful programs can be written on a few pages. This is sufficient for student projects or simple programs. One new idea of Modula–2 is that many programs are so complicated that they must be divided into smaller pieces so that they can be understood. Thus Modula–2 works wherever Pascal does, but it also is an ideal language for larger projects.

A *program* MODULE is the main body of a program. Most Modula–2 program MODULES are combined with other MODULES to form a complete program. For example most programs are combined with standard MODULES for Input/Output, mathematical functions, and other commonly used services. Many large programs are designed as several separate MODULES. Thus large programs are usually assembled from numerous pieces.

*Global* (sometimes called an *external*) MODULES have two parts, the publicly visible DEFINITION part and the private IMPLEMENTATION part. DEFINITION MODULES serve as an interface. They announce and define the services of the MODULE, but they don't have any role in actually implementing the services. The two parts of a global MODULE are worked on separately, stored in separate files, and *compiled* separately. The parts share the same MODULE name, and naturally the two parts must correspond.

Everything that is defined within a DEFINITION MODULE is automatically exported. These exports are thrown out into the "world," out into an unpredictable sea of names. Thus the automatic exports acts as if it were a QUALIFIED EXPORT. When a global MODULE'S wares are imported, the FROM phrase can be used to unqualify the names.

The function of a MODULE is to hide a body of details. We don't have to understand precisely how to convert a CARDINAL number's internal binary representation into a text representation to use the WriteCard PROCEDURE from the InOut global MODULE. What we do have to understand about the InOut MODULE is

What capabilities it provides.

How to use the capabilities.

This information is found in the DEFINITION MODULE for InOut (Section 9.1). It informs us that there is a PROCEDURE named WriteCard, that the first parameter for WriteCard is a CARDINAL number to be output, and the second parameter for WriteCard is the minimum width of the output text. This is all we need to use WriteCard.

DEFINITION MODULES have two roles. One role is to describe the MODULE to interested programmers. Comments are often used in a DEFINITION MODULE to explain the usage of the defined items. In addition most Modula–2 implementations document the supplied global MODULES in a manual. The second role of a DEFINITION MODULE is to describe the MODULE interface to the Modula–2 *compiler*. Thus a DEFINITION MODULE, like any other MODULE, has two masters.

The Modula–2 compiler isn't interested in what the MODULE accomplishes, instead it is interested in checking the interface to make sure that the services are accessed according to the rules of Modula–2. For example the WriteCard PROCEDURE expects two CARDINAL parameters. The compiler will complain if you try to use WriteCard without supplying exactly two parameters, or if you supply a BOOLEAN in place of a CARDINAL, etc. The TYPE checking of Modula–2 applies across MODULE boundaries, and except for the rules of visibility, TYPE checking applies as if the contents of the global MODULES were all part of the program MODULE.

Occasionally the information in a DEFINITION MODULE is inadequate. If possible, you can refer to the IMPLEMENTATION MODULE to see how it really works. However commercial Modula–2 systems are often supplied without the source code for the IMPLE-MENTATION MODULES. I needed to understand the inner mechanics of a MODULE while I was working on the first version of the desk calculator program (Example 4.14). I originally read in numbers using the ReadInt PROCEDURE from the InOut MODULE. Unfortunately leading plus and minus signs seemed to be disappearing from the front of parenthesized expressions. Examination of the InOut IMPLEMENTATION MODULE revealed the problem, and suggested a solution that became the ReadNumber PROCEDURE in the Calc program.

MODULES simplify programs by dividing large problems into simpler pieces. The goal is to make the MODULES independent, so that you don't have to worry about the internal details of one MODULE while you are struggling with the details of another. Thus one important job of a MODULE is to hide the implementation details of one aspect of a solution.

The two main ingredients of any program are algorithms and data. Naturally a MODULE can be used to hide the details of algorithms or of data structures. The InOut MODULE and the MathLib0 MODULE both hide algorithms. The Streams MODULE is a example of hiding the details of a data structure. A stream is a data structure, of indefinite extent, that can be read or written. It is similar to an ARRAY because it is a sequence of elements, but it isn't known in advance how many elements exist (or can be written) and only one element is available at a time. Streams are discussed more completely in Section 9.4.

The distinction between hiding the details of algorithms and the details of data structures is often academic. For example the Streams MODULE implements the stream data structure by using several PROCEDURES as well as a the buffer for the stream. Conceptually the Streams MODULE hides a data structure, but examining the code reveals the hidden algorithms that are an important part of creating a stream.

Although the main role of a DEFINITION MODULE is managing exports, occasionally it is necessary to import something in a DEFINITION MODULE. The most common example is a DEFINITION MODULE that needs to import a TYPE from another MODULE so that it can export variables of that TYPE.

Any variable, constant, or TYPE that is defined within a DEFINITION MODULE is automatically made a part of the corresponding IMPLEMENTATION MODULE. On the other hand, something that is imported into a DEFINITION MODULE is *not* automatically made

| Relationships between the parts of a global MODULE. | |
| DEFINITION MODULE | IMPLEMENTATION MODULE |
| --- | --- |
| Imported items. | Not automatically available. They must be explicitly imported as necessary. |
| Declared Constants. | Automatically available. |
| Declared Variables. | Automatically available. |
| Transparent TYPES. | Automatically available. |
| Opaque TYPES. | Must be fully declared. (Either a subrange or POINTER) |
| PROCEDURE Definitions. | Must be fully declared. |

Figure 7.1.

available within the corresponding IMPLEMENTATION MODULE. If something imported into a DEFINITION MODULE is also required within the corresponding IMPLEMENTATION MODULE it must be explicitly imported in both MODULES. You should only import items in a DEFINITION MODULE that are required for defining the exports. All other imports should be handled by the IMPLEMENTATION MODULE. (IMPLEMENTATION MODULES are allowed to import, but not to export.)

## 7.1. Definitions

We programmers would be satisfied with DEFINITION MODULES that merely contained comments indicating what services were available in the corresponding IMPLEMENTATION MODULE. All we really want to know is how we can use the IMPLEMENTATION MODULE's services. However the compiler requires *definitions* explaining exactly what PROCEDURES, TYPES, variables, and constants are exported. The purpose of including rigorous definitions is to allow the compiler to check the *usage* of the exported items.

As you have probably guessed, the major role of a DEFINITION MODULE is to define the public elements of the MODULE. The syntax diagram for a DEFINITION MODULE is

**DefinitionModule**

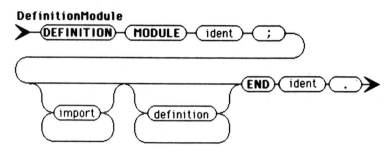

— Diagram 7.1 —

The *definitions* define the properties of the exports entities.

**definition**

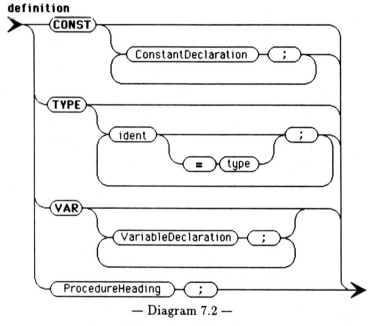

— Diagram 7.2 —

For constants, and variables the definition is identical to a declaration. For PROCEDURES the definition consists of the PROCEDURE heading, and for TYPE the definition consists of the TYPE name possibly followed by a description of the TYPE. The next three subsections provide more information about definitions.

## 7.1.1. Constant and Variable Definitions

Constants and variables can be exported from a MODULE. Exporting a constant broadcasts a value to the client MODULES. This allows the client MODULE to adapt to slightly different versions of a MODULE, or to adapt to different environments. For example the InOut MODULE exports a constant named eolc whose value indicates the current line termination character. Since the value of eolc varies from system to system, broadcasting its value makes programs more portable.

Exporting a variable makes it available to client MODULES. Exported variables usually should not be changed by the client MODULES. Note that there is no enforcement of this in Modula-2. Occasionally a MODULE exports a variable that clients are expected to alter. For example the InOut global MODULE exports a BOOLEAN variable named Done that indicates the success or failure of an I/O operation.

The definitions for constants and variables are shown in Diagram 7.2. Constant and variable definitions are identical to declarations. These declarations act as if they were part of the outer level declarations of the corresponding IMPLEMENTATION MODULE. Thus the constant and variable definitions in a DEFINITION MODULE should *not* be repeated in the corresponding IMPLEMENTATION MODULE.

Here is a simple DEFINITION MODULE that exports one constant and one variable.

```
                                          (* Example 7.1 *)
DEFINITION MODULE demo1;

CONST
   c = 25;

VAR
   v : INTEGER;

END demo1.
```

Let's also show the corresponding IMPLEMENTATION MODULE. Unlike most global MODULES, this pair doesn't serve any useful purpose except to show how a constant or variable defined in a DEFINITION MODULE is automatically available (without explicit import) in the corresponding IMPLEMENTATION MODULE.

```
                                              (* Example 7.2 *)
IMPLEMENTATION MODULE demo1;
FROM InOut IMPORT WriteInt, WriteLn;

BEGIN
    WriteInt(c,5);
    v := c + c;
    WriteInt(v,5);
    WriteLn;
END demo1.
```

Notice that c and v aren't declared in the demo1 IMPLEMENTATION
MODULE.

## 7.1.2. TYPE Definitions

TYPES are exported so that TYPES defined in one MODULE can be
used in client MODULES. This facility is often used when a group of
MODULES are designed to work together in a large program.

There are two forms of TYPE export, transparent and opaque. In
transparent export the TYPE is fully declared in the DEFINITION
MODULE and the TYPE declaration should *not* be repeated in the
IMPLEMENTATION MODULE. A client MODULE that imports a transparent TYPE has access to the full details of the TYPE.

An opaque TYPE DEFINITION simply consists of a TYPE name.
The full details of an opaque TYPE must be declared in the
corresponding IMPLEMENTATION MODULE. A client MODULE that
imports an opaque TYPE is unaware of the details of the TYPE.
Opaque export is limited to subranges of the standard TYPES and
POINTERS. Opaque export of subranges may be subject to implementation restrictions. (CARDINALS and INTEGERS can be exported opaquely in some Modula–2 implementations as they can be
considered improper subranges.)

Opaque TYPE export lets the host MODULE exercise more control
over that TYPE. A client MODULE that imports an opaque TYPE
can only
  • Declare variables of the opaque TYPE.
  • Assign one variable to another.
  • Pass variables of that TYPE to PROCEDURES.
  • Test two variables for equality or inequality.

No other operations are available.

Opaque TYPES should not be confused with hidden (private)
TYPES. A hidden TYPE is completely hidden from a client MODULE.

Opaque TYPES are public, but their details are hidden and their usage is restricted.

The following DEFINITION MODULE exports two TYPES, one opaque and one transparent.

(* Example 7.3 *)
```
DEFINITION MODULE TranspOpaque;

TYPE
    PBunit = ARRAY [0..15] OF BITSET; (* Transp. *)
    PBptr; (* Opaque *)
END TranspOpaque.
```

Notice that the following IMPLEMENTATION MODULE supplies a declaration for the PBptr TYPE because it is exported opaquely in the DEFINITION MODULE. (PBptr is a POINTER TYPE, discussed fully in Chapter 14.) Notice that PBunit is automatically available within the IMPLEMENTATION MODULE.

(* Example 7.4 *)
```
IMPLEMENTATION MODULE TranspOpaque;

TYPE
    (* Here is the full declaration of PBptr *)
    PBptr = POINTER TO PBunit;

VAR
    (* PBunit is available automatically *)
    a,b,c : PBunit;

BEGIN
    (* ... *)
END TranspOpaque.
```

Completeness requires a brief explanation of transparently exported RECORD and enumeration TYPES. Although these two data TYPES won't be covered until Chapter 13 and Chapter 11 it's appropriate to mention their export behavior at this point. When a RECORD is exported all its field names are automatically exported. If a field in a RECORD is a locally defined TYPE then that TYPE must be exported separately. When an enumeration TYPE is exported all the enumeration's identifiers are automatically exported.

## 7.1.3. PROCEDURE Definitions

PROCEDURES are exported so that one MODULE may perform services for another. PROCEDURES are the most common bond between two MODULES. There are two reasons for this. First, most MODULES have a host/client relationship. The host usually performs services for the clients, and the best way to perform most services is to export a PROCEDURE. TYPES, constants and variables are also exported as part of a MODULE'S services, but they are exported less often than PROCEDURES in most cases.

The second reason that PROCEDURE export is preferred is safety. If a MODULE exports a variable it can be modified by the client. However the interface to a PROCEDURE can be carefully controlled. The Modula–2 compiler makes sure that PROCEDURE parameters are the correct TYPE and that the correct number of parameters are actually supplied. Then inside the PROCEDURE it is possible to check the values of the parameters. Thus PROCEDURES allow a very controlled interface.

Every PROCEDURE in a global MODULE is either *visible* or *hidden* (sometimes called public and private). PROCEDURES mentioned in the DEFINITION part of a global MODULE are visible, all others are hidden. For *visible* PROCEDURES only the *interface* (the heading) is published in the DEFINITION MODULE; the *body* of the PROCEDURE is hidden in the IMPLEMENTATION MODULE.

The definition of a PROCEDURE in a DEFINITION MODULE consists simply of the PROCEDURE *heading* (See Section 4.2). The heading defines the parameters for the PROCEDURE and it also defines the result TYPE for function PROCEDURES. The complete PROCEDURE declaration (the heading together with the body) must be supplied in the IMPLEMENTATION MODULE. Obviously the PROCEDURE heading in the DEFINITION MODULE must *agree* with the complete PROCEDURE declaration in the IMPLEMENTATION MODULE. If the parameters (or result) of an exported PROCEDURE are locally defined TYPES then those TYPES must be exported separately.

Examples of PROCEDURE definitions are in the following two sections, which show complete examples of useful DEFINITION MODULES. The corresponding IMPLEMENTATION MODULES are shown in the next chapter.

## 7.2. Hiding PROCEDURES — String Utilities Definition

Manipulating variable character strings is a common programming requirement. None of these facilities are built into Modula–2, instead they must be supplied in a global MODULE. Programs often need to find the length of a string, compare two strings to see if they are equal, append one string to the end of another, see if one string is a substring of another, etc.

The following DEFINITION MODULE implements several common operations on strings. Working with Modula–2 strings is complicated because a string may completely fill up an ARRAY OF CHAR, or there may be a null (0C) somewhere in a variable string to delimit the active part of the string. Open ARRAY parameters are used throughout these PROCEDURES so that they can handle strings of any length.

(* Example 7.5 *)

```
DEFINITION MODULE Strings;

CONST
    StrSize = 80;

TYPE
    String = ARRAY [ 0 .. StrSize-1 ] OF CHAR;

(* How long is the active part of a string? *)
PROCEDURE StrLen(s : ARRAY OF CHAR) : CARDINAL;

(* How much free space is at the end of a string *)
PROCEDURE StrSpace(s : ARRAY OF CHAR) : CARDINAL;

(* Move a string from src to dest *)
PROCEDURE StrCopy
    (src : ARRAY OF CHAR; VAR dest : ARRAY OF CHAR);

(* Move one string to the end of another *)
PROCEDURE StrCat
    (src : ARRAY OF CHAR; VAR dest : ARRAY OF CHAR);

(* Is sub in str? If so RETURN TRUE and set loc *)
PROCEDURE SubStr (sub, str : ARRAY OF CHAR;
                    VAR loc : CARDINAL) : BOOLEAN;
```

```
    (* Note, returned loc assumes lower bound
     *    of str is zero *)

(* Compare two strings:
 *      RETURN 0 if they are equal
 *      RETURN -1 if a < b
 *      RETURN +1 if a > b  *)
PROCEDURE StrCmp(a, b : ARRAY OF CHAR) : INTEGER;

END Strings.
```

The String ARRAY TYPE and the StrSize constant are exported
so that client MODULES can conveniently declare 80 character
string variables. All PROCEDURES in Strings are careful to work
with any length of string, the String TYPE is simply a conveni-
ence.

# 7.3. Hiding Data — A Circular Buffer

*Buffering* is used to store data temporarily. Often a task that
produces data needs a method to synchronize with a task that
consumes data. For example data may be produced infrequently
in bursts but consumed regularly in small chunks. Buffering allows producers and consumers to interact easily.

A *circular buffer* is similar to a secretary's circular cardfile. In
software it is easily implemented using an ARRAY. Since an AR-
RAY is a *linear* data structure a small amount of logic is required
to make it appear to be a *circular* structure.

Programs interact with the circular buffer using two PROCEDURES,
a constant, and a variable:

- Deposit places a character into the buffer.
- Withdraw removes a character from the buffer.
- The constant BufSize indicates how many characters can be
  stored in the buffer.
- The variable cnt indicates how many characters are in the
  buffer.

Notice that the buffer itself is hidden. This has two advantages.
The first advantage is complexity — hiding the buffer makes it
easier for clients to use it without worrying about the details. The
second reason is reliability — the buffer logic can't be broken by
an errant client.

The cnt variable shouldn't be modified by the clients. It could be completely protected by encapsulating it in a PROCEDURE, but this would be inefficient and it doesn't seem to be necessary. The program that uses a buffer shouldn't attempt to put an element into a full buffer or to withdraw an element from an empty buffer. Illegal operations cause warning messages to be printed, but the buffer itself continues to function and the host program continues to operate.

The following DEFINITION MODULE is the interface to a circular buffer for CHAR data.

(* Example 7.6 *)

```
DEFINITION MODULE OneBuffer;

CONST
    BufSize = 128;

PROCEDURE deposit (c : CHAR);

PROCEDURE withdraw() : CHAR;

VAR
    cnt : CARDINAL;

END OneBuffer.
```

**Exercise 7.1.** Write a DEFINITION MODULE to advertise LONG arithmetic PROCEDURES (Chapter 11). You should include definitions for:
- The LONG data TYPE.
- PROCEDURES to increment and decrement LONGs.
- PROCEDURES to add, subtract, and compare LONGS.
- A PROCEDURE to convert a LONG (less than MAX(CARDINAL)) to a CARDINAL.

□

**Exercise 7.2.** Write a DEFINITION MODULE to advertise the following operations on three by three matrices:
- Multiplication of a matrix by a scalar.
- Matrix Multiplication.
- Computation of the determinant of a matrix.

□

# Chapter 8

# IMPLEMENTATION MODULES

An IMPLEMENTATION MODULE is the hidden part of a global MODULE. It is where the services of a global MODULE are actually performed, unlike the DEFINITION MODULE, which publicizes those services. The heading of an IMPLEMENTATION MODULE starts with the word IMPLEMENTATION. Otherwise an IMPLEMENTATION MODULE is constructed like a program MODULE.

An IMPLEMENTATION MODULE must be constructed in accordance with its corresponding DEFINITION MODULE. The constants, variables, and transparent TYPES that are declared in the DEFINITION part are automatically available with the IMPLEMENTATION part of a global MODULE. The opaque TYPES and PROCEDURES that are alluded to in the DEFINITION part must be further declared within the IMPLEMENTATION part.

There are two aspects to implementing the services advertised in a DEFINITION MODULE. First the IMPLEMENTATION MODULE must *agree* with the definitions defined in the DEFINITION MODULE:

- The PROCEDURE declarations in the IMPLEMENTATION MODULE must agree with the PROCEDURE definitions in the DEFINITION MODULE.

- The opaque TYPES from the DEFINITION MODULE must be declared in the IMPLEMENTATION MODULE.
- The constants, variables, and TYPES declared in the DEFINITION MODULE must be used appropriately in the IMPLEMENTATION MODULE.

The compiler has adequate information to perform these checks.

The second aspect of implementing the services of a DEFINITION MODULE can't be checked by the compiler. The implementation must faithfully perform the advertised services. Sometimes a service in an IMPLEMENTATION MODULE will have a subtle error. For example the StrLen PROCEDURE (Section 7.2) might return a length that is always one too large, or a math routine such as the sin function might not perform an accurate calculation. Another possibility is that the services might be wildly incorrect, such as the StrLen PROCEDURE actually returning the length of the unused space in a string variable rather than the length of the active part.

IMPLEMENTATION MODULES may have MODULE bodies. These bodies will always be executed before the body of the program MODULE. If one global MODULE imports another, the MODULE body of the second will be executed first. If there are circular references between global MODULES, then the order of execution of the global MODULE bodies is undefined.

Comments in a DEFINITION MODULE often explain what actions are performed by MODULE. Sometimes the IMPLEMENTATION MODULE is changed without updating the comments in the DEFINITION MODULE. Sometimes the comments in a DEFINITION MODULE tell too much — they detail a side effect or some other hidden matter that clients shouldn't rely on. These sorts of inconsistencies can be subtle and you should be careful.

## 8.1. Compilation

*Compilation* is the translation of a program from text form to an executable form. Compiling is simple in pure Pascal because it happens in one fell swoop. Things are more complicated in Modula–2 because compilation usually occurs several stages. Because MODULE–to–MODULE connections in Modula–2 are well defined, the compiler is able to make sure that compilation is performed in a reasonable *order*.

Separate compilation means that the parts of a program are compiled at different times. It also means that the compiler performs consistency checks so obvious inter–module problems are discovered. Separate compilation is better than independent compilation because independently compiled program pieces aren't checked.

A *compilation unit* is a text file that can be submitted to the compiler for compilation. Modula–2 contains the following types of compilation units.

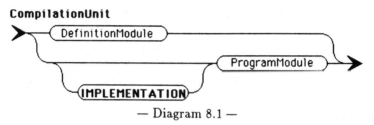

CompilationUnit

— Diagram 8.1 —

PROCEDURES and local MODULES are not compilation units.

Once all the parts of a program have been compiled they must be *linked* together to form a complete program. In some systems the linking happens automatically as part of the compilation of a *program* MODULE. On other systems linkage is a separate task and it must be done as the final step in creating an executable program.

Modula–2 compilation units must be submitted to the compiler in the correct order. The rules for ordering compilation are straightforward and they are presented in the following paragraphs. The Modula–2 compiler in most implementations is able to keep track of the (perhaps relative) time at which compilations are performed and thus most Modula–2 systems will enforce the following rules.

The first rule is that the DEFINITION part of a global MODULE must always be compiled before the IMPLEMENTATION part. You should remember that items declared within or imported into a DEFINITION MODULE are available in the corresponding IMPLEMENTATION MODULE. It would be useless to compile the IMPLEMENTATION MODULE before the DEFINITION MODULE because some of the pieces would be missing.

The second rule is similar. If MODULE A imports something from MODULE B, then the DEFINITION MODULE for B must be compiled before A is compiled. Obviously DEFINITION MODULES should be compiled early on because it is impossible to work on IMPLEMEN-

| Recompilation Rules | |
| --- | --- |
| If You | You Must |
| Recompile a DEFINITION MODULE | 1. Update and recompile its IMPLEMENTATION MODULE.<br><br>2. Update and recompile all MODULES that import its exports.<br><br>3. Relink all programs that import it. |
| Recompile an IMPLEMENTATION MODULE | 1. Relink all programs that import it. |
| Recompile a Program MODULE. | 1. Relink the program. |

Figure 8.1.

TATION MODULES until the DEFINITION MODULES are compiled.

In the normal course of events, the only errors in a DEFINITION MODULE are syntactical, or they are errors of design. DEFINITION MODULES don't embody algorithms and they aren't usually the source of bugs (errors). In a large project, the highest level design partitions the problem into separate tasks and the interfaces between the tasks are designed. Then these interfaces are translated into DEFINITION MODULES and compiled towards the beginning of the project. These DEFINITION MODULES may be poorly designed or inadequate, but they probably don't contain subtle bugs that will only show up long after the principal program authors have moved on to greener pastures.

During the middle and later stages of a large project the IMPLEMENTATION MODULES are designed, built, and tested. IMPLEMENTATION MODULES are the home of most errors, and they are the site of most work in a programming project. Normally an IMPLEMENTATION MODULE will be changed and recompiled many times without change to its DEFINITION MODULE.

When an IMPLEMENTATION MODULE is corrected and recompiled it isn't necessary to *recompile* the other global MODULES that use its services. However it is necessary to *relink* the MODULE into any *programs* that use it (perhaps by recompiling the relevant program MODULES).

The important fact to notice is that changing an IMPLEMENTATION MODULE doesn't make the other global MODULES obsolete. However changing and recompiling a DEFINITION MODULE often makes many MODULES obsolete. Once a DEFINITION MODULE is changed, any MODULE that imports something from that DEFINITION MODULE may have to be updated and it certainly must be recompiled. Naturally if a DEFINITION MODULE is changed its corresponding IMPLEMENTATION MODULE must also be recompiled.

## 8.2. Strings Implementation

This is the IMPLEMENTATION part of the Strings global MODULE that was introduced in Section 7.2. The six PROCEDURES in the Strings MODULE provide basic operations for handling text.

A *string variable* is an ARRAY OF CHAR variable whose active region is possibly delimited by a special character constant value, 0C. The contents of the string following the delimiter is irrelevant. A completely full string variable doesn't have a 0C delimiter, just as a *string constant* doesn't have a delimiter. Strings are handled using open ARRAY parameters so that the PROCEDURES can discover the lengths of the strings. These routines are designed to work with strings of any length, with or without a delimiting 0C.

Many of these string handling primitives are more complicated than you might expect. Let's look at some of the problems before looking at the Modula–2 code that solves these problems.

*Copying* one string to another is difficult because the two strings may have different lengths. Some of the interesting possibilities are shown in Figure 8.2 s1. String catenation means copying one string onto the end of another. Catenation presents the same problems as copying, except that two index variables must be used instead of one.

*Comparing* strings is difficult because there are so many different ways that strings can be judged equal:
  1. The two strings are the same length and they are equal over that length
  2. The two strings are equal up to terminating 0C markers.
  3. The first part of one string (delimited by 0C) is equal to the entire other string.

These three cases are diagrammed in Figure 8.3. In addition we must handle strings that are identical up to the end of the shorter. Here I made the arbitrary decision that short strings are "less than" long strings, so that

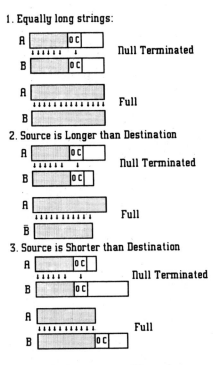

Figure 8.2. There are many cases to consider when copying one Modula-2 string to another.

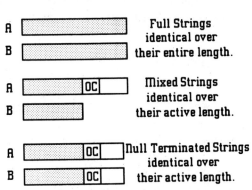

Figure 8.3. Two Modula-2 strings are judged equal if any of these three conditions are met.

```
StrCmp('abc','abcd')
```

indicates that 'abc' is less than 'abcd'. In addition I had to decide
what values would be returned to indicate the results of the comparison. I made the arbitrary decision that the return value from
comparing two strings should be

*Negative*
>if the first string is less than the second.

*Zero*
>if the two strings are equal.

*Positive*
>if the first string is greater than the second.

The most ambitious PROCEDURE in the Strings MODULE determines whether one string is a substring of another. The overall
task is straightforward:

>Start at the beginning of the main string
>See if the substring matches the main string
>If not, move over one place in the main string and try again

In the code, this turns into a pair of loops, an outer loop to course
through the mainstring and inner loop to compare the indexed
part of the mainstring with the substring.

Most of the PROCEDURES in the Strings MODULE use Modula–2
loop statements to perform the repetitive tasks because there are
so many different exit conditions. In my opinion, this is a situation
where the LOOP statement is well used because the more formal
iterative statements (FOR, WHILE, REPEAT) are too rigid.

(* Example 8.1 *)

```
IMPLEMENTATION MODULE Strings;

(* How long is a string *)
PROCEDURE StrLen(s : ARRAY OF CHAR): CARDINAL;
VAR
    i : CARDINAL;
BEGIN
    FOR i := 0 TO HIGH(s) DO
        IF s[i] = 0C THEN RETURN i END
    END;
    RETURN HIGH(s) + 1 (* no delimiter *)
END StrLen;


(* How much space is unused in a string VARiable *)
PROCEDURE StrSpace(s : ARRAY OF CHAR): CARDINAL;
```

```
BEGIN
   RETURN (HIGH(s)+1) - StrLen(s)
END StrSpace;

(* copy src to dest, different lengths ok *)
PROCEDURE StrCopy
     (src : ARRAY OF CHAR; VAR dst : ARRAY OF CHAR);
VAR
   i : CARDINAL;
BEGIN
   i := 0;
   LOOP (* until src or dest is exhausted *)
     IF i>HIGH(dst) THEN
        EXIT
     ELSIF i>HIGH(src) THEN
        dst[i] := 0C;
        EXIT
     END;
     dst[i] := src[i];
     IF src[i] = 0C THEN EXIT END;
     INC(i)
   END
END StrCopy;

(* copy one string to the end of another *)
PROCEDURE StrCat
     (src : ARRAY OF CHAR; VAR dst : ARRAY OF CHAR);
VAR
   si, di : CARDINAL; (* src and dest indexes *)
BEGIN
   si := 0;
   di := StrLen(dst);
   LOOP (* until exhaustion *)
      IF di > HIGH(dst) THEN
         EXIT
      ELSIF si > HIGH(src) THEN
         dst[di] := 0C;
         EXIT
      END;
      dst[di] := src[si];
      IF src[si] = 0C THEN EXIT END;
      INC(si);
      INC(di)
   END
```

```
END StrCat;

(* is sub in str? *)
PROCEDURE SubStr(sub, str : ARRAY OF CHAR;
                        VAR loc : CARDINAL): BOOLEAN;
VAR
   i,j : CARDINAL;
BEGIN
   loc := 0;
   LOOP (* search through str *)
      IF (loc > HIGH(str)) OR (str[loc] = OC) THEN
         RETURN FALSE
      END;
      i := 0; (* index into sub *)
      j := loc; (* index into str *)
      LOOP (* compare with sub *)
         IF sub[i] = OC THEN
            RETURN TRUE
         ELSIF (j > HIGH(str) OR
                           (sub[i] # str[j]) THEN
            EXIT
         ELSIF i = HIGH(sub) THEN
            RETURN TRUE
         END;
         INC(i);
         INC(j)
      END; (* inner LOOP *)
      INC(loc)
   END (* outer LOOP *)
END SubStr;


(* Compare strings a and b:
     RETURN 0 if they are equal
     RETURN +1 if a > b
     RETURN -1 if a < b   *)
PROCEDURE StrCmp(a,b : ARRAY OF CHAR) : INTEGER;
VAR
   i : CARDINAL;
BEGIN
   i := 0;
   LOOP
      IF (i>HIGH(a)) THEN RETURN -1 END;
      IF (i>HIGH(b)) THEN RETURN +1 END;
      IF a[i] < b[i] THEN RETURN -1 END;
```

```
      IF a[i] > b[i] THEN RETURN +1 END;
      IF a[i] = OC THEN RETURN O END;
      IF (i=HIGH(a)) AND (i=HIGH(b)) THEN
        RETURN O
      END;
      IF (i=HIGH(a)) AND (i<HIGH(b)) AND (b[i+1]=OC)
        THEN RETURN O
      END;
      IF (i<HIGH(a)) AND (i=HIGH(b)) AND (a[i+1]=OC)
        THEN RETURN O
      END;
      INC(i)
    END
  END StrCmp;


END Strings.
```

**Exercise 8.1.** Carefully examine the following two lines from strcmp:

```
IF a[i] < b[i] THEN RETURN -1 END;
IF a[i] > b[i] THEN RETURN 1 END;
```

a. Why is it incorrect to replace these two statements with the apparently simpler test

```
IF a[i] # b[i] THEN RETURN a[i]-b[i] END;
```

b. Why is it incorrect to replace the original statements with

```
IF a[i] # b[i] THEN RETURN ORD(a[i])-ORD(b[i]) END;
```

c. Devise a one–statement replacement for the pair of statements given above.
□

**Exercise 8.2.** Notice that the routines StrCat and StrCopy (from Example 8.1) are similar. Rewrite the StrCopy PROCEDURE so that it calls StrCat to do the copying. Is this a more efficient approach? Is it a more reliable approach?
□

**Exercise 8.3.** Could the SubStr PROCEDURE (from Example 8.1) be simplified by using recursion? Write a recursive version. Do you think it's better or worse than the original? How many copies of the strings could be created if the recursive version of SubStr were passed two eighty character strings.
□

**Exercise 8.4.** Think about the overhead of passing strings to recursive PROCEDURES? Write a second recursive version of the SubStr PROCEDURE (Example 8.1) that passes ARRAY indices rather than the ARRAYS themselves as parameters. Is this a good place to use a local MODULE embedded in a PROCEDURE?
□

**Exercise 8.5.** Write a program to provide test cases for the Strings global MODULE. Devise your test cases carefully to explore the behavior of these routines at the limit.
□

**Exercise 8.6.** Which of the PROCEDURES in the Strings global MODULE will operate strangely if the source and destination strings are actually the same string? Rewrite the dubious PROCEDURES to eliminate the problem, or to at least act sensibly in the face of danger.
□

**Exercise 8.7.** Write a version of StrCmp that ignores case distinction when comparing letters of the alphabet.
□

**Exercise 8.8.** Write a version of StrCmp (from Example 8.1) that uses the table lookup technique to compare characters. What are the advantages of using table lookup to compare characters.
□

# 8.3. Circular Buffer Implementation

The previous chapter presented the DEFINITION MODULE for a circular buffering scheme. The following is the corresponding IMPLEMENTATION MODULE. Notice that the constants BufChans and BufSize from the DEFINITION MODULE are automatically available in this MODULE.

The actual buffer structure is defined as a ARRAY. To manage the buffer we also need the head index, the tail index, and the count of the number of items in the buffer. Note that the count was declared in the DEFINITION MODULE and it doesn't need to be redeclared here.

When an item is deposited it is placed into the buffer at the location indexed by the head variable and then head is incremented by one. Head is set back to zero each time the end of the ARRAY is reached. Similarly withdrawing an item causes the variable named tail to be incremented and then the item indexed by tail

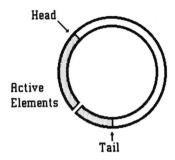

Figure 8.4. A circular buffer is constructed by logically connecting the beginning of an ARRAY to the end. The active part of a circular buffer is delimited by the head and the tail.

is returned. Deposit increments the cnt variable while withdraw decrements cnt.

(* Example 8.2 *)

```
IMPLEMENTATION MODULE OneBuffer;
FROM InOut IMPORT WriteString, WriteLn;

(*
 * Circular buffering.
 *    Deposit places a character into a buffer.
 *    Withdraw removes a character from a buffer.
 *    Cnt contains the current count of chars in the
 *    buffer. It is used to determine if a buffer is
 *    full or empty. Cnt should be considered
 *    "read-only".
 *)

CONST
    BufEnd = BufSize-1;
    EmptyErr = 1; (* Possible errors *)
    FullErr = 2;

VAR
    x : ARRAY [0..BufEnd] OF CHAR;
    head, tail : CARDINAL;

PROCEDURE err(cause : CARDINAL); (* private *)
BEGIN
    CASE cause OF
        EmptyErr : WriteString("You can't withdraw ");
```

```
           WriteString("from an empty buffer") |
         FullErr : WriteString("You can't deposit ");
           WriteString("into a full buffer")
     END; (* CASE *)
     WriteLn
  END err;

  PROCEDURE deposit(ch : CHAR);
  BEGIN
     IF cnt < BufSize THEN
       INC(cnt)
     ELSE
       err(FullErr);
       RETURN
     END;
     x[head] := ch;
     IF head = BufEnd THEN
       head := 0
     ELSE
       INC(head)
     END
  END deposit;

  PROCEDURE withdraw() : CHAR;
  BEGIN
     IF cnt > 0 THEN
       DEC(cnt)
     ELSE
       err(EmptyErr);
       RETURN 0C
     END;
     IF tail = BufEnd THEN
       tail := 0
     ELSE
       INC(tail)
     END;
     RETURN x[tail]
  END withdraw;

  BEGIN (* initialization for Buffer MODULE *)
     head := 0;
     tail := BufEnd;
     cnt := 0;
  END OneBuffer.
```

The body of the Buffer MODULE initializes the three indices for the buffer. These statements must be executed before the buffer will operate properly. Notice that depositing into a full buffer is detected and aborted, and that withdrawing from an empty buffer is detected and the value 0C is returned.

**Exercise 8.9.** Write a program to test the Buffers MODULE.
□

**Exercise 8.10.** Write the IMPLEMENTATION MODULE for the Long arithmetic MODULE (Exercise 7.1).
□

**Exercise 8.11.** Write the IMPLEMENTATION MODULE for the Matrix Operations MODULE (Exercise 7.2).
□

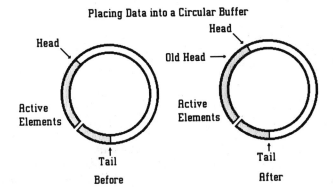

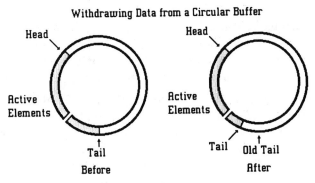

Figure 8.5.

# Chapter 9

# Common Global MODULES

Every implementation of Modula–2 includes a set of global MODULES to round out Modula–2's capabilities. There are no absolute standards for these global MODULES, instead there are suggestions detailing the facilities that should be provided. You should expect minor differences in these MODULES from one system to another.

InOut is probably the most standard global MODULE. It provides Pascal–like I/O facilities that should be available in all implementations of Modula–2. InOut was first mentioned in Section 1.4; it will be discussed further in the first section of this chapter.

InOut performs I/O to either the terminal or to files. In most implementation it does this by importing routines from the MODULES Terminal and Streams. Terminal provides primitives for reading and writing the user's terminal, Streams provides similar primitives for accessing files. Terminal and Streams are both less standardized than InOut because they are more closely related to the host computer.

Programs that rely solely on InOut for I/O should be portable. Unfortunately InOut is limited and many programs will need further flexibility. The first recourse is to use Terminal and Streams. Although these MODULES are less standardized, the ser–

vices provided in them are likely to be available in all Modula–2 installations and programs that rely on them should be portable without undue effort.

Sometimes programs need even more sophisticated services. Most of these services are unique to particular computer systems and most Modula–2 implementations provide MODULES to interface Modula–2 programs to the host environment. These programs will not be portable from one environment to another without effort. Portability is maximized if usage of the less standard I/O MODULES is confined to a few MODULES in the application program.

A global MODULE named Storage is responsible for managing and allocating free space. It is discussed in Chapter 14 rather than this chapter because it is typically used to allocate space for dynamic data structures.

There aren't any mathematical functions built into Modula–2, but a small set of functions is provided in the MODULE MathLib0. The trailing "0" in its name is a clue that many implementations will provide further math support in additional math MODULES.

One final service that is often available is graphics. Although there are many standardization efforts underway, even the basic issues of representing and communicating graphical information are presently undecided. At installations where graphical output devices are available, there may be a global MODULE called LineDrawing that provides graphics primitives.

## 9.1. InOut

In Section 1.4 I mentioned InOut's two major limitations: it only allows one input file and one output file, and it assumes that all I/O is sequential. Many programs fit within this narrow model, and for them InOut may be adequate. Programs that have more elaborate I/O requirements should use the facilities of the lower level I/O MODULES.

Here is a typical InOut DEFINITION MODULE. Although some variation is possible (and likely), the following capabilities should be found in any version of InOut.

```
                                        (* Example 9.1 *)
DEFINITION MODULE InOut;

CONST
   EOL = 12C;

VAR
   Done : BOOLEAN;
   termCH : CHAR;

(*
 * OpenInput
 * Request input file name from the console.
 * ext is used on some systems to supply part of the
 * file name automatically.
 * Done = TRUE means the open was successful.
 *)
PROCEDURE OpenInput(ext : ARRAY OF CHAR);

(* Close input file and reconnect to console *)
PROCEDURE CloseInput;

(*
 * OpenOutput
 * Request output file name from console.
 * ext is used as in OpenInput
 * Done - TRUE means open was successful.
 *)
PROCEDURE OpenOutput(ext : ARRAY OF CHAR);

(* Close output file
 *    and reconnect output to console. *)
PROCEDURE CloseOutput;

(* Read a CHAR from the input connection *)
(* Done = TRUE means a CHAR was read *)
PROCEDURE Read ( VAR ch : CHAR);

(*
 * Read an INTEGER or a CARDINAL
 *   Skip blanks or control chars.
 *   Then read a sequence of digits as an INT or CARD
 *   (INTS can have a leading plus or minus sign)
```

```
 *   termch is the CHAR following the digits.
 *   Done = TRUE means a number was read.
 *)
PROCEDURE ReadInt  ( VAR X : INTEGER );
PROCEDURE ReadCard ( VAR X : CARDINAL );

(*
 * Read a string from the input connection.
 * Leading blanks are skipped, then text is read
 * until a terminating blank or control character
 * is encountered.
 * The terminating character is assigned to termCH.
 * Done becomes FALSE if end of file is encountered.
 *)
PROCEDURE ReadString(VAR s : ARRAY OF CHAR);

(* Write a CHAR to the output connection *)
PROCEDURE Write (ch : CHAR);

(*
 * Write a number to the output connection
 * x is the number, n is the minimum field width.
 * Blanks are prepended if necessary.
 *)
PROCEDURE WriteInt(x : INTEGER; n : CARDINAL);
PROCEDURE WriteCard (x,n : CARDINAL);
PROCEDURE WriteOct (x,n : CARDINAL); (* Base 8 *)
PROCEDURE WriteHex (x,n : CARDINAL); (* Base 16 *)

(* Start a new line *)
PROCEDURE WriteLn;

(* Write a string to the output connection *)
PROCEDURE WriteString (s : ARRAY OF CHAR);

END InOut.
```

In some systems the explicit file open and close routines aren't necessary because those facilities are provided by the operating system.

## 9.2. RealInOut

The RealInOut MODULE provides PROCEDURES to read and write text strings denoting REAL numbers. RealInOut actually performs I/O using the Read and Write PROCEDURES from the InOut MODULE so I/O from RealInOut goes to (and comes from) the same place as InOut's I/O.

```
DEFINITION MODULE RealInOut;

(* Done is TRUE if a number was read *)
VAR
   Done : BOOLEAN;

(* Read a REAL number from the input *)
PROCEDURE ReadReal(VAR x : REAL);

(* Write REAL number x using n characters.
 *  Pad with leading blanks if necessary. *)
PROCEDURE WriteReal(x : REAL; len : CARDINAL);

(* Write REAL number in octal format *)
PROCEDURE WriteRealOct(x : REAL);

END RealInOut.
```

If your program needs to input or output a custom TYPE, you can write a global MODULE analogous to RealInOut for that TYPE.

## 9.3. Terminal

The Terminal MODULE provides PROCEDURES to read and write the user's terminal. These capabilities are oriented towards text and they do not include either simple graphics or terminal-specific operations (e.g. cursor movement). The following is a typical definition for the Terminal MODULE.

```
DEFINITION MODULE Terminal;

(* Read a char from the terminal.
 *  If none avail then wait *)
PROCEDURE Read(VAR ch : CHAR);

(* Read a CHAR from the terminal.
 *  If none avail then
 *   return immediately with 0C as the result *)
PROCEDURE BusyRead(VAR ch : CHAR);

(* Push back the last CHAR that was read so that it
 * will be returned the next time Read is called *)
PROCEDURE ReadAgain;

(* Write a CHAR to the terminal *)
PROCEDURE Write(ch: CHAR);

(* Advance to the next line on the terminal *)
PROCEDURE WriteLn;

(* Write a string to the terminal *)
PROCEDURE WriteString(s : ARRAY OF CHAR);

END Terminal.
```

Read, Write, WriteLn, and WriteString do exactly what you expect and they won't be further discussed. The BusyRead PROCEDURE is used when the program can't wait if a character isn't available immediately. This requirement is common when programs are controlling machines or real–time processes and they can't pause indefinitely waiting for a command.

The ReadAgain PROCEDURE is a simple solution to the read ahead problem that was mentioned in Section 4.9. It is often impossible to know how far to read. For example a PROCEDURE reading a number from the terminal doesn't know in advance how many digits are in the number. It is only when a non–digit is encountered that the PROCEDURE knows it has encountered the end of the number, and by that time it has read too far. The ReadAgain PROCEDURE makes the most recently read character available once again the next time that Read is called.

## 9.4. Streams

A *stream* is a sequential data structure. Streams are a simple approach to working with files. By connecting the abstract idea of a stream with the file system of a host computer, the Streams MODULE makes it possible to write simple (and probably portable) programs that work with files.

The usual problem with writing programs that use files is that different computers use totally different rules for accessing files. These range from elaborate access methods on mainframes to rudimentary file systems on small computers. Some programs make good use of the specific capabilities of particular computers and they sacrifice portability and simplicity for power.

However, it is possible to distill a few simple, common elements from this wide range of possibilities. These common capabilities are embodied by the concept of a *stream*. All computers (with file systems) provide the capability to read existing files and to create and write new files. It is usually possible to start at the beginning and proceed towards the end. Many computers allow files containing elaborate data structures. However for streams we postulate the ability to deal with just two data TYPES: CHARS and WORDS. (WORDS are discussed in Section 16.2. When used as a formal PROCEDURE parameter WORDS are compatible with numerous actual parameter TYPES.)

Let's summarize the key features of streams. A stream is used either for writing or reading a file. Streams pass either CHARS or WORDS, and only one element of a stream can be read (or written) at a time. When a stream is first connected with a file it is positioned at the start of the file. Reading (or writing) an element moves the stream forward to the next position. Some streams include the ability to return to the beginning of the stream, and some even include the ability to move about randomly from one place to another. Both of these "advanced" features are probably less portable than the basic features.

Since there can be several streams open at once we need a way to identify individual streams. The Streams MODULE exports a TYPE (an opaque TYPE named STREAM) that is used to identify individual streams. Each program must declare a variable of this TYPE for each stream that it is going to use.

The InOut MODULE automatically implements two CHAR streams, one for input and one for output. By using the STREAMS MODULE, it is possible to use additional WORD or CHAR streams.

```
DEFINITION MODULE Streams;

EXPORT QUALIFIED
    STREAM,
    eolc, EOS,
    Connect, Disconnect, Reset, EndWrite,
    WriteWord, WriteChar, ReadWord, ReadChar,
    SetPos, GetPos;

TYPE
   STREAM;  (* Opaque Stream TYPE *)

VAR
   eolc : CHAR;     (* The end of line marker *)

(*
 * Connect a stream to an already open file
 * identified by filenum.
 * Set ws parameter TRUE to connect a WORD STREAM
 *)
PROCEDURE Connect
 (VAR s : STREAM; filenum : CARDINAL; ws : BOOLEAN);

(*
 * Disconnect a stream from a file.
 * Set closefile parameter to TRUE to automatically
 *   close the file
 *)
PROCEDURE Disconnect
             (VAR s : STREAM; closefile : BOOLEAN);

(*
 * Are we at the end of a STREAM?
 *   TRUE --> End Of Stream
 *)
PROCEDURE EOS(s : STREAM) : BOOLEAN;
(* Note ReadChar supplies the value 0C to ch
   at End Of Stream *)

(* Retreat to the beginning of the STREAM *)
PROCEDURE Reset(s : STREAM);

(*
```

```
    * Call EndWrite after the last write to a STREAM
    * to write the end marker
    *)
PROCEDURE EndWrite(s : STREAM);

(* The read and write PROCEDUREs *)
PROCEDURE ReadChar(s : STREAM; VAR ch : CHAR);
PROCEDURE ReadWord(s : STREAM; VAR w : WORD);
PROCEDURE WriteChar(s : STREAM; ch : CHAR);
PROCEDURE WriteWord(s : STREAM; w : WORD);

(* Find out where a STREAM is positioned *)
PROCEDURE GetPos
              (s : STREAM; VAR high, low : CARDINAL);

(* Move to a given point in a STREAM *)
PROCEDURE SetPos(s : STREAM; high, low : CARDINAL);
(* Note high and low together form a long card *)

END Streams.
```

Streams are usually used as follows:

1. A file is opened for reading (or writing) using Lookup (or Create) from the Files MODULE. This is the most system dependent aspect of using streams.
2. A STREAM is connected to the file using Connect.
3. Read (or write) operations are performed using ReadChar or ReadWord (WriteChar or WriteWord). Positioning may be performed using Reset, GetPos and SetPos.
3a. EndWrite is called for output streams.
4. Operations on the STREAM are completed by calling Disconnect and the file is closed.

The EOS PROCEDURE is called to detect the end of an input STREAM. In a text STREAM, calls to ReadChar(s,ch) will set ch to 0C once the end of a STREAM is encountered. Therefore EOS isn't strictly necessary with text files, and the character 0C shouldn't be stored in text files.

Different systems use different characters to signal the end of a line. The variable eolc is exported from Streams so that programs can adapt to different environments. Some systems use two characters to separate the lines of a text file. For example on RT11 systems the end of a line is signaled by a carriage return character followed by a line feed character. Accessing text files via STREAM connections compresses the two separators into one. Calling

WriteChar(s,eolc) will write both line terminators. Calling
ReadChar(s,ch) sets ch to eolc at the end of a line even if a pair
of characters is the actual line terminator.

The WORD data TYPE is a special data TYPE that is compatible
with many of the simple Modula-2 data TYPES. The exact assortment of TYPES that are compatible with WORDS is implementation
dependent. WORD parameters are used in the ReadWord and
WriteWord PROCEDURES so that they can be used to read or write
most of the data TYPES that occupy a word of storage. The WORD
data TYPE is described in more detail in Section 16.2.

## 9.5. Files

Different types of computers usually have different methods for
accessing files. In Modula-2 uniformity is attempted within the
Files MODULE, which implements basic operations for accessing
files on a particular computer. Here is a typical DEFINITION
MODULE for Files.

```
DEFINITION MODULE Files;

EXPORT QUALIFIED Create, Lookup, Rename,
    Close, ReadF, WriteF;

(* create a file with the given name *)
PROCEDURE Create (VAR descriptor : CARDINAL;
        name : ARRAY OF CHAR; VAR reply : INTEGER);

(* open a file with the given name *)
PROCEDURE Lookup(VAR descriptor : CARDINAL;
        name : ARRAY OF CHAR; VAR reply : INTEGER);

(* change the name of a file *)
PROCEDURE Rename
    (new, old : ARRAY OF CHAR; VAR reply : INTEGER);

(* Close a file *)
PROCEDURE Close(descriptor : CARDINAL);

(*
 * Read count elements from a file
 *   starting at block
 *)
```

```
PROCEDURE ReadF
   (descriptor : CARDINAL; VAR buf : ARRAY OF WORD;
      block, count : CARDINAL; VAR reply : INTEGER);

(*
 * Write count elements into a file
 *    starting at block
 *)
PROCEDURE WriteF
   (descriptor : CARDINAL; VAR buf : ARRAY OF WORD;
      block, count : CARDINAL; VAR reply : INTEGER);

END Files.
```

Throughout `Files` the `reply` parameter is used to signal success or failure of the operation. In general a negative number indicates failure and a positive number heralds success. Sometimes more specific interpretations can be placed on the value of `reply`, for example a specific negative number may explain exactly why an operation failed. Although `Files` attempts to smooth over the differences between various computer systems, this is a very tricky area. Programmers should be aware that programs that rely on `Files` will need work when they are ported.

## 9.6. MathLib0

`MathLib0` contains several common mathematical functions.

```
DEFINITION MODULE MathLib0;

PROCEDURE sqrt(x: REAL): REAL; (* Square Root *)
PROCEDURE exp(x: REAL): REAL; (* Exponential *)
PROCEDURE ln(x: REAL): REAL;  (* Natural Log *)
PROCEDURE sin(x: REAL): REAL; (* Trig sin *)
PROCEDURE cos(x: REAL): REAL; (* Trig cos *)
PROCEDURE arctan(x: REAL): REAL; (* Trig arctan *)
(* Convert an INTEGER to a REAL *)
PROCEDURE real(x: INTEGER): REAL;
(* Convert a REAL to the largest INTEGER
 * that is not greater than that REAL *)
PROCEDURE entier(x: REAL): INTEGER;
END MathLib0.
```

Additional mathematics libraries are available in many Modula-2 implementations.

## 9.7. LineDrawing

The LineDrawing MODULE provides simple graphics capabilities. It assumes that there is a graphics device (a display or possibly a plotter), which is organized using an x,y coordinate matrix. Each element of the matrix is called a pixel (short for picture element). The *spatial resolution* of the display is roughly measured by the number of individual pixels. On a simple black and white display screen there might be a 256x192 matrix of pixels, with each pixel either turned on or off. A high quality color video display might have somewhat higher spatial resolution combined with many more colors available at each pixel.

Because of the wide variety of graphics displays, the LineDrawing MODULE must export information concerning the display characteristics. In addition the LineDrawing MODULE typically exports PROCEDURES to draw a line, to assign a certain color to a given pixel, and to fill a rectangular area with a given color, and to move a rectangular area from one place to another. Remember that on a black and white display the available colors consist of black and white, or of black, shades of grey, and white.

I'm not going to include a DEFINITION MODULE for LineDrawing because it varies too much from one system to another.

# Chapter 10

# Desk Calculator with Variables and Assignments

The goal of this final chapter in Part III is to learn to partition a large problem into several pieces so that it is easier to manage. Certain things can be proven in computer science, but I doubt that it is possible to prove that a certain program organization is optimal. If you have some programming experience, you may be able to look at a particular program organization and evaluate its merits. Those of us who have tried writing non–trivial program can attest to the difficulty of organizing a large software project. One difficult chore is choosing an organization strategy. Although there are no "laws," there are several factors that should be considered.

The organization of your software should reflect the natural boundaries of the problem. For example a game program might be divided into the display functions, the control functions, and the game logic. Although this organization might work for many games, it is always possible to imagine pathological cases that require a different organization. Sometimes you have to write one version and throw it away before you really understand the issues of a problem.

Another consideration is the number of linkages between the various parts of a program. Ideally there will be only a few logical connections between the various pieces. In Modula-2 the number of connections is measured by the number of imports and exports. Obviously there aren't any firm rules, but as a rough guide you might limit MODULES to a dozen exports. Sometimes more will be appropriate. For example most of Modula-2's common global MODULES have more than a dozen exports. Remember that the global MODULES are written very generally. Although InOut exports about twenty items, in most of my programs I only import three or four of them. In an applications system one tends to program few extraneous features — all the exports from a MODULE will usually be imported by its clients.

The last consideration that I'm going to mention is the size of the various pieces of a program. It makes little sense to partition a job into three pieces if two of the pieces have twenty lines of code and the third piece has ten thousand. However the goal of balancing the load should be taken lightly. Don't feel as if you've failed if one MODULE has 200 lines and another has 600. Sometimes large MODULES must be partitioned even when there isn't an obvious dividing line. Sometimes small MODULES create more clutter than necessary and they need to be combined.

Another consideration is that Modula-2 program MODULES cannot export. Therefore it is impossible to put any routine or data structure in a program MODULE if it is needed by any of the DEFINITION or IMPLEMENTATION MODULES. This rule is built into the language and must be observed.

## 10.1. Adding Variables to the Desk Calculator Program

The desk calculator program was first presented in Section 4.9. The original version was able to calculate the answer to algebraic expressions such as

```
-5 * (9 - 3)
```

This new version is going to include *variables* that can be assigned a value and used in expressions. For example one can enter the statements

```
a = 30
b = 40
a * b * 10
```

and the new desk calculator program will respond with the answer 12000.

The syntax for expressions, terms, and factors are the same as before. The new element that is recognized by this version of the desk calculator program is the statement.

**dcstatement**

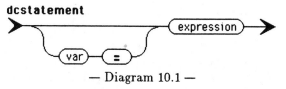

— Diagram 10.1 —

Notice that for this version of the desk calculator I use a simple equals sign to signal assignment rather than the ":=" that is used in Modula-2. A two letter symbol is slightly harder to handle than a one letter symbol, and the program is already long enough.

## 10.2. Organizing the Desk Calculator

Let's consider the various aspects of the problem.

- As in the previous desk calculator program, expressions must be analyzed and the result must be printed. In the earlier version of the calculator there were three PROCEDURES — term, factor, and expression — to perform this chore. This new version of the calculator is going to need an additional PROCEDURE — perhaps called statement — to handle assignment statements.
- Another requirement is to read the input data from the terminal, and to handle the look ahead. (It turns out that look ahead is a thornier problem in this version.) The previous version of the desk calculator used three PROCEDURES — getc, nextch, and ungetc — to perform these chores.
- The new aspect of this desk calculator is variables. We obviously need at least two PROCEDURES — perhaps called GetValue and SetValue — to manage the variables. Some miscellaneous initialization is also required.
- In the previous calculator program the ReadNumber PROCEDURE was conceptually related to the getc crowd, but it operated on a slightly higher level. In this version Read-

Number has an additional chore. It should treat variables transparently so that factor doesn't need to care whether its values are literal numbers or the values of variables. Thus in this version ReadNumber is also a relative of GetValue.

All of these pieces of the problem are candidates for treatment in separate MODULES. In order to get additional guidance, let's make a table showing how some of the major PROCEDURES call each other.

| PROCEDURE | Calls |
|---|---|
| statement | expression, nextch, ungetc SetValue |
| expression | term nextch, ungetc |
| term | factor nextch, ungetc |
| factor | ReadNumber, expression nextch, ungetc |
| ReadNumber | GetValue |
| GetValue | — |
| SetValue | — |
| nextch | getc |
| ungetc | — |
| getc | Read |

Some of the organization is obvious. The statement, expression, term, and factor PROCEDURES are obviously a cohesive group. Similarly GetValue and SetValue belong together, as do nextch, getc, and ungetc. The problem is ReadNumber (which ideally should be imported from InOut).

Let's look carefully at ReadNumber. It is only called from factor, and it only calls getc, nextch, ungetc and GetValue. Since ReadNumber must be placed somewhere, it might as well be in the same MODULE as factor. Logically a number is just a component of a factor, so this placement is reasonable.

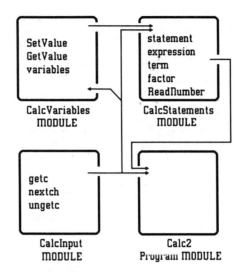

Figure 10.1. The organization of the Calc2 program.

The organization that has emerged suggests the following:

- A global MODULE called CalcStatements to house the statement, expression, term, factor, and ReadNumber PROCEDURES. It exports the statement PROCEDURE and imports SetValue, GetValue, nextch getc, and ungetc. Notice that CalcStatement only exports one of its five major PROCEDURES.

- A global MODULE called CalcVariables to house SetValue and GetValue. CalcVariables exports both SetValue and GetValue. The main role of CalcVariables is to hide the data structure that contains the values of the variables.

- A global MODULE called CalcInput containing getc, nextch, and ungetc. CalcInput will export getc, nextch and ungetc. It will hide the data structure that allows characters to be pushed back onto the input stream.

- A program MODULE called Calc2. Calc2 imports statement from CalcStatements, and nextch and ungetc from CalcInput. The major role of Calc2 is to call statement to perform the expression analysis, and to print the results. In addition Calc2 prints the prompts and exits when the input is exhausted.

Note that all four of these MODULES import various items from InOut.

## 10.3. The CalcVariables MODULE

The simplest way to handle variable names is to allow for twenty six variables, each with a one letter name chosen to be a letter of the alphabet. For simplicity I am going to ignore upper/lower case distinction. These restrictions are easy to relax. Several exercises at the end of this section suggest changes to make this a more flexible MODULE.

The DEFINITION MODULE for CalcVariables is

```
                                    (* Example 10.1 *)
(* 26 integer variables for the desk calculator *)
DEFINITION MODULE CalcVariables;

PROCEDURE SetValue(which : CHAR; x : INTEGER);
PROCEDURE GetValue(which : CHAR) : INTEGER;

END CalcVariables.
```

Implementing these variables is straightforward. I don't think that a pseudo code description is warranted.

```
                                    (* Example 10.2 *)
(* variables named 'A' to 'Z' for calc *)
IMPLEMENTATION MODULE CalcVariables;
FROM InOut IMPORT WriteString, WriteLn;

VAR
    vars : ARRAY ['A'..'Z'] OF INTEGER;

(* test a variable name.  (private) *)
PROCEDURE test(index : CHAR) : CHAR;
BEGIN
    index := CAP(index);
    IF (index > 'Z') OR (index < 'A') THEN
      WriteString('Bad variable name.'); WriteLn;
      RETURN 'A'
    END;
    RETURN index;
END test;

(* Assign a value to a variable *)
PROCEDURE SetValue(which : CHAR; x : INTEGER);
BEGIN
```

```
      vars[test(which)] := x
   END SetValue;

   (* get the value of a variable *)
   PROCEDURE GetValue(which : CHAR) : INTEGER;
   BEGIN
      RETURN vars[test(which)]
   END GetValue;

   VAR
      i : CHAR;

   BEGIN (* CalcVariables Initialization *)
      FOR i := 'A' TO 'Z' DO vars[i] := 0 END
   END CalcVariables.
```

**Exercise 10.1.** Modify `CalcVariables` to allow more descriptive (longer) variable names.
□

**Exercise 10.2.** Modify `CalcVariables` so that the values of its variables can be saved or recovered using a permanent disk file.
□

**Exercise 10.3.** Modify `CalcVariables` so that it includes trigonometric functions, absolute values, logarithms, etc. Is this MODULE a good place to add these functions?
□

**Exercise 10.4.** Modify `SetValue` and `test` so that variable a is not clobbered when an illegal variable name is encountered.
□

## 10.4. The CalcInput MODULE

The role of the `CalcInput` MODULE to isolate the single character input and to provide a "push back" mechanism so that a PROCEDURE that has read too far can return characters to the input stream.

One unfortunate complication of this version of the desk calculator program is look ahead. In the original version (Example 4.14 from Section 4.9) I explained why a single character of "look ahead" was necessary. For example an expression consists of a term possibly followed by an addition operator and another term. Once the first term has been handled, the expression PROCEDURE must read one character further to see if it is an addition operator. If so another term is handled, if not the character must be returned to the input sequence (using the ungetc PROCEDURE).

This new version of the calculator has assignment statements that complicate the "look ahead" issue. Any statement consisting of a variable name followed by an equals sign is an assignment statement, otherwise it is simply an expression. Thus we need to read two symbols (the variable name and the equal sign) before we can know for sure whether something is an assignment, and we need to be able to push two symbols back into the input. The new version of ungetc and getc use a small stack (two elements) and an index variable to handle up to two characters of look ahead.

How could you rearrange the desk calculator program so that we could return to one letter look ahead? In the current version of the desk calculator program each PROCEDURE communicates with the other PROCEDURE using values. The look ahead requirement could be reduced to a single character if the PROCEDURES exchanged TYPE information (expression or simple variable) along with value information.

CalcInput exports just three PROCEDURES.

```
                                        (* Example 10.3 *)
      DEFINITION MODULE CalcInput;

      CONST
         LocalEOF = 0C;

      (* push characters back into the input stream *)
      PROCEDURE ungetc(ch : CHAR);

      (* get the next non blank char from the input *)
      PROCEDURE nextch() : CHAR;

      (* get the next char from the input *)
      PROCEDURE getc() : CHAR;

      END CalcInput.
```

Except for the slight changes for the two character push back, the body of CalcInput is similar to the previous version.

```
                                        (* Example 10.4 *)
(* Input routines for the desk calculator *)
IMPLEMENTATION MODULE CalcInput;
FROM InOut IMPORT Read, WriteString, Done;

CONST
   SPACE = ' ';
   TAB = 011C;
   Max = 2;

VAR
   savech : ARRAY [1..Max] OF CHAR;
   Nchars : CARDINAL;

PROCEDURE getc() : CHAR;
(* Get a char, either from savech or from Read *)
VAR
   ch : CHAR;
BEGIN
   IF Nchars > 0 THEN
     ch := savech[Nchars];
     DEC(Nchars);
     RETURN ch
   ELSE
     Read(ch);
     IF NOT Done THEN ch := LocalEOF END;
     RETURN ch
   END
END getc;

(* save up to Max chars so they can be
 *  getc'd again *)
PROCEDURE ungetc(ch : CHAR);
BEGIN
   IF Nchars > Max-1 THEN
     Nchars := Max-1;
     WriteString('error in ungetc.')
   END;
   INC(Nchars);
   savech[Nchars] := ch
END ungetc;

(* get the next non blank char by calling getc *)
```

```
PROCEDURE nextch() : CHAR;
VAR
   ch : CHAR;
BEGIN
   REPEAT
      ch := getc()
   UNTIL (ch # SPACE)  AND (ch # TAB);
   RETURN ch
END nextch;

BEGIN (* CalcInput *)
   Nchars := 0;
END CalcInput.
```

## 10.5. The CalcStatement MODULE

CalcStatement contains the statement, expression, term, factor, and ReadNumber PROCEDURES. The addition of statements changes the syntax slightly, and the variables complicate the ReadNumber PROCEDURE. The CalcStatement DEFINITION MODULE is surprisingly short.

```
                               (* Example 10.5 *)
(* Analyze an algebraic statement *)
DEFINITION MODULE CalcStatement;

PROCEDURE statement() : INTEGER;

END CalcStatement.
```

Most of the ideas of these PROCEDURES were discussed in Section 4.9. There would be little point in repeating that information. The only new PROCEDURE, named statement, is fundamentally similar to expression or factor and its explanation is left to the reader.

```
                                          (* Example 10.6 *)
IMPLEMENTATION MODULE CalcStatement;
FROM CalcVariables IMPORT GetValue, SetValue;
FROM CalcInput IMPORT nextch, getc, ungetc;
FROM InOut IMPORT Write, WriteString, WriteLn, EOL;

(* Return TRUE if ch is a numeral - private *)
PROCEDURE IsNumeral (ch : CHAR) : BOOLEAN;
BEGIN
   RETURN (ch >= '0') AND (ch <= '9')
END IsNumeral;

(* Return TRUE if ch is a letter (a..z, A..Z) *)
PROCEDURE IsAlpha (ch : CHAR) : BOOLEAN; (*private*)
BEGIN
   RETURN (CAP(ch) >= 'A') AND (CAP(ch) <= 'Z')
END IsAlpha;

(* READ A NUMBER - either a variable or a const *)
PROCEDURE ReadNumber
             (VAR x : INTEGER; VAR IsNum : BOOLEAN);
VAR ch : CHAR;
BEGIN
   IsNum := FALSE;
   ch := nextch();
   IF IsAlpha(ch) THEN
     IsNum := TRUE;
     x := GetValue(ch);
     RETURN
   END;
   IF IsNumeral(ch) THEN
     IsNum := TRUE;
     x := VAL(INTEGER,ORD(ch) - ORD('0'));
     ch := getc();
     WHILE IsNumeral(ch) DO
       x := 10*x + VAL(INTEGER,ORD(ch) - ORD('0'));
       ch := getc()
     END (* WHILE *)
   END; (* IF *)
   ungetc(ch)
END ReadNumber;

(*
```

```
* factor = number | "(" expr ")".
*)
PROCEDURE factor() : INTEGER;
VAR
   t : INTEGER;
   IsNum : BOOLEAN;
   ch : CHAR;
BEGIN
   ReadNumber(t,IsNum);
   IF IsNum THEN RETURN t END;
   ch := nextch();
   IF ch = '(' THEN
      t := expression();
      ch := nextch();
      IF ch # ')' THEN
         ungetc(ch);
         WriteString('Unbalanced Parentheses');
         WriteLn
      END;
      RETURN t
   ELSIF (ch = EOL) OR (ch = OC) THEN
      ungetc(ch)
   ELSE
      WriteString('Error in factor.');
      WriteString('Expected a number but ');
      WriteString('encountered: ');
      Write(ch); WriteLn
   END; (* IF *)
   RETURN 0 (* error return *)
END factor;

(*
 * term = factor { ("*"|"/") factor}.
 *)
PROCEDURE term() : INTEGER;
VAR
   t, u : INTEGER;
   ch : CHAR;
BEGIN
   t := factor();
   LOOP
      ch := nextch();
      IF ch = '*' THEN
         t := t * factor()
```

```
        ELSIF ch = '/' THEN
            u := factor();
            IF u # 0 THEN
                t := t DIV u
            ELSE
                WriteString('Divide by zero ');
                t:= 0
            END
        ELSE
            ungetc(ch);
            RETURN t
        END (* IF *)
    END (* LOOP *)
END term;

(*
 * expression = ["+"|"-"] term { ("+"|"-") term }.
 *)
PROCEDURE expression() : INTEGER;
VAR
    t : INTEGER;
    ch : CHAR;
    neg : BOOLEAN;
BEGIN
    neg := FALSE;
    ch := nextch();
    IF ch = '-' THEN
        neg := TRUE
    ELSIF ch = "+" THEN
        (* do nothing *)
    ELSE
        ungetc(ch)
    END;
    t := term();
    IF neg THEN t := -t END;
    LOOP
        ch := nextch();
        IF ch = '+' THEN
            t := t + term()
        ELSIF ch = '-' THEN
            t := t - term()
        ELSE
            ungetc(ch);
            RETURN t
```

```
        END (* IF *)
    END (* LOOP *)
END expression;

(*
 * statement = [ var "=" ] expression
 *)
PROCEDURE statement() : INTEGER;
VAR
    v, ch : CHAR;
BEGIN
    v := nextch();
    IF NOT IsAlpha(v) THEN (* not an assignment *)
        ungetc(v);
        RETURN expression()
    END;
    (* Maybe an assignment *)
    ch := nextch();
    IF ch = '=' THEN
        SetValue(v,expression());
        RETURN GetValue(v)
    END;
    (* return two chars to ungetc *)
    ungetc(ch); ungetc(v);
    RETURN expression();
END statement;

END CalcStatement.
```

**Exercise 10.5.** Modify `CalcStatement` so that it allows multiple assignment statements such as

```
x = y = z = 30
```

☐

**Exercise 10.6.** When the expression PROCEDURE in Calc-Statement doesn't recognize something, it assumes it has come to the end of an expression. Modify `CalcStatement` so that only a Carriage return or a semicolon are allowed at the end of an expression.

☐

**Exercise 10.7.** Why is it important for `ReadNumber` to call `getc` rather than `nextch` in the midst of a number? Why do the other routines call `nextch` when they want to read another character?

☐

## 10.6. The Calc2 Program

You may have noticed that the desk calculator's "work" has been placed into the three global MODULES. That leaves little work for the main program.

```
                                         (* Example 10.7 *)
(* an algebraic desk calculator with variables *)
MODULE Calc2;

FROM InOut IMPORT WriteLn, WriteString,
     WriteInt, EOL;
FROM CalcInput IMPORT nextch, ungetc, LocalEOF;
FROM CalcStatement IMPORT statement;

VAR
    ch : CHAR;

BEGIN
    WriteString('calc-> ');
    LOOP
       WriteInt(statement(),6); WriteLn;
       ch := nextch();
       IF ch = LocalEOF THEN RETURN END;
       IF ch = EOL THEN
         WriteString('calc-> ')
       ELSE
         ungetc(ch)
       END;
    END (* LOOP *)
END Calc2.
```

Just how good is this organization of the desk calculator program? On the basis of the program following the structure of the prob-lem, the results are encouraging. You may have noticed that the original design of this revised calculator concentrated on organiz-ing the PROCEDURES according to function. On the basis of inter-connections the results are also encouraging. Notice that there are less than a dozen interconnections among the four MODULES.

Our third organizational criteria is "distributing the load" fairly. On this criteria the results are mixed. The CalcStatement MODULE is 141 lines long while CalcInput is only 41, CalcVari-ables is only 34, and the Calc2 program MODULE is only 18 lines long. Clearly the burden is carried by CalcStatement. Partly this extra length is due to ReadNumber, but partly it reflects the fact that the work in this program is analyzing the expressions. The other matters are details. Also keep in mind that the statement, expression, term, and factor routines are essentially similar. Even though the CalcStatement MODULE contains more lines than the other MODULES, I don't think it contains much more complexity than the other MODULES.

**Exercise 10.8.** A complete session consists of several statements followed by an end of file. Would the logic of the Calc2 MODULE body have been simplified if there were a PROCEDURE called session to take care of calling statement? What would be left for the Calc2 MODULE body? Do you think this would be a cleaner design?
☐

**Exercise 10.9.** Would this program be better if the routines in CalcStatement had been left in the Calc2 MODULE? What is the purpose of placing these functions in a separate MODULE?
☐

**Exercise 10.10.** When Calc2 encounters the end of file, it gratuitously prints the result 0. Modify the program so that it doesn't produce extraneous output at the end of each session.
☐

# Part III

# Advanced Data Types

The memory of a typical modern computer is a uniform sequence of cells, each capable of storing a single value. This makes good sense from a hardware designer's point of view, but it is a *featureless* environment in which to write programs. The data TYPES in Chapter 2 provide one major level of abstraction; they allow the memory to be interpreted as numbers, characters, or truth values. A second major abstraction is presented in Chapter 5 — ARRAYS superimpose a tabular structure upon the barren memory landscape.

Modula-2 has a particularly rich group of data structures. The basic data TYPES from Part I are adequate for most programs, but they are often not ideal. The advanced data structures presented in the next five chapters present interesting and useful alternatives. They enable the programmer to create more powerful abstractions. In each chapter we will try to explain why and when these alternatives should be used in addition to explaining how they are used.

# Chapter 11

# Enumerations

An *enumeration* is simply a list. Let me enumerate some advantages of Modula-2. Modula-2 is a coherent, powerful, elegant, modular, structured programming language.

(* Example 11.1 *)

```
TYPE
    Advantages = ( coherent, powerful,
                elegant, modular, structured );
```

The TYPE definition given above creates a new species called Advantages. Advantages has five distinct values: coherent, powerful, elegant, modular, and structured. We can declare variables or constants of this new TYPE, and we can write PROCEDURES that implement operations on this new TYPE. Here is a declaration that creates three variables that have the TYPE Advantages.

(* Example 11.2 *)

```
VAR
    primary, secondary, tertiary : Advantages;
```

You can use the variable primary with other variables that have the Advantages TYPE or with any of the constants that represent the values of the Advantages TYPE.

(* Example 11.3 *)

```
primary := structured;
secondary := primary;
```

The Modula–2 TYPE checking prohibits using a variable that is an Advantages TYPE with some other TYPE. Thus the following is *illegal* in Modula–2

(* Example 11.4 *)

```
primary := 30;
```

because primary is an Advantages TYPE and 30 is a CARDINAL.

You should use enumeration TYPES when variables are used to represent a few nameable alternatives. Enumeration TYPES are inappropriate for representing an employee's *salary*, but they might be ideal for representing an employee's *job category.*

(* Example 11.5 *)

```
TYPE
    Engineer = ( SupportTech, JrEngr, CustEngr, Engr,
    SrEngr, ProjSuper, ChiefEngr );
```

Modula–2's TYPE checking applies to enumeration TYPES. It is not possible to mix one enumeration TYPE with another without deliberately using Modula–2's TYPE relaxation facilities.

Enumerations are declared by placing parentheses around a list of identifiers.

**enumeration**

— Diagram 11.1 —

When an enumeration TYPE is exported from a MODULE that enumeration's *identifiers* (the constant values) are automatically exported.

Enumeration TYPES, like all objects stored in a digital computer, are actually assigned binary codes. The first item in the enumeration list is assigned the value 0, the next item is assigned the value 1, and so on. The function ORD can be used to determine the value associated with an enumeration constant or variable.

```
                                              (* Example 11.6 *)
MODULE EnumValues;
FROM InOut IMPORT WriteCard, WriteString, WriteLn;

TYPE
   Tastes = ( Sweet, Sour, Bitter, Salt );

BEGIN
   WriteString('Sweet = ');
   WriteCard(ORD(Sweet),2); WriteLn;
   WriteString('Sour   = ');
   WriteCard(ORD(Sour),2); WriteLn;
   WriteString('Bitter = ');
   WriteCard(ORD(Bitter),2); WriteLn;
   WriteString('Salt   = ');
   WriteCard(ORD(Salt),2); WriteLn;
END EnumValues.
```

The program printed the following:

```
Sweet  =  0
Sour   =  1
Bitter =  2
Salt   =  3
```

Notice that the program listed above works without *explicitly* declaring any variables or constants. An enumeration TYPE declaration automatically makes the identifiers in the enumeration list into constant identifiers. It is in the role of a constant identifier that they are passed to the ORD function.

Modula–2 only allows *assignment* and *comparison* operations on enumeration TYPES. Any other operations must be written by the programmer, usually as a PROCEDURE. The standard INC and DEC PROCEDURES work with enumeration variables. INC sets a variable to the next enumeration value in the list.

Let's modify the TypeValues MODULE to include some enumeration variables and some assignment and comparison operations using those variables.

```
                                              (* Example 11.7 *)
MODULE EnumValues2;
FROM InOut IMPORT WriteCard, WriteString, WriteLn;

TYPE
    Tastes = ( Sweet, Sour, Bitter, Salt );

VAR
    Candy, Lemon, PotatoChip, Caviar : Tastes;

BEGIN
    Candy := Sweet;
    Lemon := Sour;
    PotatoChip := Salt;
    Caviar := PotatoChip;
    WriteString('Candy = ');
    WriteCard(ORD(Candy),2); WriteLn;
    WriteString('Lemon = ');
    WriteCard(ORD(Lemon),2); WriteLn;
    WriteString('PotatoChip = ');
    WriteCard(ORD(PotatoChip),2); WriteLn;
    WriteString('Caviar = ');
    WriteCard(ORD(Caviar),2); WriteLn;
    WriteString('Caviar is Less Than Candy: ');
    IF Caviar < Candy THEN
        WriteString('True')
    ELSE
        WriteString('False')
    END;
    WriteLn;
END EnumValues2.
```

The EnumValues2 program printed the following:

```
Candy = 0
Lemon = 1
PotatoChip = 3
Caviar = 3
Caviar is Less Than Candy: False
```

TypeValues2 demonstrates the creation of a new, *named* TYPE and then the creation of variables with that TYPE. (The advantages of using named TYPES are detailed in Section 5.1.) It is also possible to create *anonymous* enumerations by placing an enumeration list in place of a TYPE name in a variable declaration.

```
                                          (* Example 11.8 *)
    VAR
        walls, ceilings, exterior:
            ( Beige, White, OffWhite, Pink, Undecided );
```

This declaration creates three enumeration variables. They may attain any of the following five values: Beige, White, OffWhite, Pink, or Undecided.

Enumerations and subranges work well together. Given the enumeration TYPE

```
                                          (* Example 11.9 *)
    TYPE
        Days = ( Sunday, Monday, Tuesday, Wednesday,
                 Thursday, Friday, Saturday );
```

we can declare a subrange named WeekDays with

```
                                          (* Example 11.10 *)
    TYPE
        WeekDays = [ Monday .. Friday ];
```

Operations involving the WeekDays TYPE may be subject to stricter bounds checking during execution or compilation, and they clearly express the programmer's intent to avoid weekend values.

**Exercise 11.1.** Complete the following enumeration TYPE declarations:

```
    TYPE
        MaritalStatus = _____;
        PrimaryColors = _____;
        Days = _____;
        SevenSisters = _____;
        Religions = _____;
        FreshWaterFish = _____;
        AutoMakers = _____;
        DeadLanguages = _____;
        DeadProgLang = _____;
```

□

**Exercise 11.2.** Write a PROCEDURE to output text representations of one enumeration TYPE from the previous exercise. Hint: see the WriteBool PROCEDURE from Example 4.1.

□

**Exercise 11.3.** Rewrite the `OneBuffer` MODULE (Example 8.2) using enumerations to identify the error conditions.
□

# 11.1. VAL

The VAL PROCEDURE is often used with enumeration TYPES to create an object with a specified TYPE and value. The first argument to VAL is the name of a Modula–2 data TYPE, the second argument is a CARDINAL value. For example one could set the variable Lemon (from Example 11.7) to the value Sour by using a standard assignment

(* Example 11.11 *)

```
Lemon := Sour;
```

or by using the VAL PROCEDURE

(* Example 11.12 *)

```
Lemon := VAL(Tastes,1);
```

(Remember that 1 is the ORD of Sour)

VAL is often used to relax Modula–2's strict TYPE checking as illustrated in the following nonsense program.

(* Example 11.13 *)

```
MODULE Nonsense;

TYPE
   Fable = (Esop, Wives, Fairy);
   Dream = (Scary, Boring, Sad, Exhilarating);

VAR
   story : Fable;
   memory : Dream;

BEGIN
   memory := VAL(Dream,ORD(Esop));
   story := VAL(Fable,ORD(Sad));
   memory := VAL(Dream,ORD(story)-1)
END Nonsense.
```

VAL makes it very easy to generate illegal enumeration values. Illegal enumeration values will often be caught during a programs execution. For example, if the enumeration constant Sad in the second statement of the nonsense MODULE body were replaced with the constant Exhilarating an illegal enumeration value would be produced.

One final note concerns the relationship between BOOLEANS and enumeration TYPES. You can think of BOOLEANS as if they were an enumeration defined by the following TYPE declaration:

(* Example 11.14 *)
```
TYPE BOOLEAN = (FALSE, TRUE);
```

BOOLEANS are built into Modula-2, you won't ever find a MODULE containing this declaration, but everything works as if BOOLEANS were declared as enumeration TYPES.

**Exercise 11.4.** Write a PROCEDURE to input BOOLEAN values. Consider carefully what input should be allowed to indicate a TRUE value and what input should be allowed for FALSE. Note that a PROCEDURE that required a user to type FALSE to indicate a FALSE value would be unpleasant. Allow (but don't require) abbreviations, alternate forms, upper/lower case, etc.
□

**Exercise 11.5.** Write a PROCEDURE to input the Tastes TYPE. This PROCEDURE should output a *menu* indicating that the user should enter 0 for Sweet, 1 for Sour, etc. Read in the number, check to make sure that it's a legal value, and then return a Tastes value using the VAL PROCEDURE.
□

## 11.1.1. Example — the Months Global MODULE

The following global MODULE exports an enumeration TYPE that names the months of the year, and a PROCEDURE called MonthLen that returns the number of days in a given month. Here is the DEFINITION MODULE.

(* Example 11.15 *)
```
DEFINITION MODULE Months;

TYPE
   MONTH = ( Jan, Feb, Mar, Apr, May, Jun,
             Jul, Aug, Sep, Oct, Nov, Dec );

PROCEDURE MonthLen(m : MONTH) : CARDINAL;

END Months.
```
The basic strategy for implementing the MonthLen PROCEDURE is

to look up the answer in a table. The indices of the table are the
MONTH TYPE, and the values in each slot indicate the number of
days in that month. The body of the MODULE is used to initialize
the table automatically.

Here is the Months IMPLEMENTATION MODULE.

```
                                          (* Example 11.16 *)
IMPLEMENTATION MODULE Months;

VAR
    Len : ARRAY MONTH OF CARDINAL;

PROCEDURE MonthLen (m : MONTH) : CARDINAL;
BEGIN
    RETURN Len[m]
FND MonthLen;

BEGIN
    Len[Jan] := 31; Len[Feb] := 28;
    Len[Mar] := 31; Len[Apr] := 30;
    Len[May] := 31; Len[Jun] := 30;
    Len[Jul] := 31; Len[Aug] := 31;
    Len[Sep] := 30; Len[Oct] := 31;
    Len[Nov] := 30; Len[Dec] := 31;
END Months.
```

**Exercise 11.6.** How could you check the parameter to MonthLen
to make sure it represented a valid MONTH? Would such checking
be justified? What checking is the compiler doing? How does using an enumeration parameter make the MonthLen PROCEDURE
more robust?
□

**Exercise 11.7.** Rewrite the MonthLen PROCEDURE so that it
works correctly for either a leap year or an ordinary year.
□

**Exercise 11.8.** Rewrite the MonthLen PROCEDURE so that it uses
a CASE statement rather than a table lookup. Which method do
you prefer and why?
□

**Exercise 11.9.** Write a PROCEDURE to calculate the cumulative
day of the year given a month and a day of the month and add it
to the Months MODULE. For example February 10 is the 41st day
of the year.

□

**Exercise 11.10.** Write a PROCEDURE to determine the month and the day of the month given the cumulative day of the year.
□

## 11.2. Example — Running a Maze

The most famous maze in history was built by Daedalus for Minos, king of Crete. The bloodthirsty Minotaur who inhabited the maze was fed seven young men and seven young women every year. Theseus eventually "solved" the maze and killed the Minotaur.

Today many people enjoy solving maze puzzles. The goal is to enter the maze at a given point, move through the labyrinth, and eventually find the route to the exit. People solve mazes through a combination of intelligence and trial–and–error. Intelligence is hard to program, but trial–and–error is easy for a computer.

We are going to use maze solving as an example twice in this book, once in this section and once in Section 13.4. The approach in this chapter is to use a two dimensional ARRAY of enumerations to represent the maze. This version uses *recursion* to implement the trial–and–error search. In Section 13.4 we are going to use a two dimensional ARRAY OF RECORDS to represent the maze. The increased information handling ability of the RECORDS will allow us to avoid recursion in Section 13.4's solution.

The solution in this chapter is called a *depth first* approach because each path is followed to its end before an alternative path is attempted. Our strategy is simple. From a given square in the maze we will first try going right, then try going straight, and then try left. Recursion easily enables us to go to the end of a path. If a path runs into a dead end before reaching the exit we back up to the last point where there was an alternative and try that path.

One complication of our strategy is that the meaning of "right" (or "left" or "straight") changes depending on how we get to a given point. It's easiest if we use the points of the compass to label the directions. If you enter a square from the North, going right means traveling West. Straight means traveling South. (See Figure 11.2.) The enumeration data TYPE listing the directions of travel is

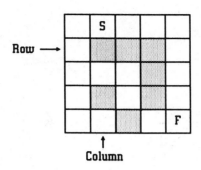

Figure 11.1. This two dimensional maze consists of White passages and Black walls. Paths are only allowed between White cells that share a left, right, top, or bottom wall. Diagonal connections do not constitute a path between White cells. The starting cell is labeled with S and the finish cell is labeled with F.

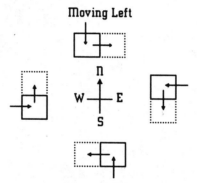

Figure 11.2. If you enter a maze cell from the North, "moving left" means moving to the East. All four possibilities are shown in this figure.

(* Example 11.17 *)

```
TYPE
    direction = (North, South, East, West);
```

We are going to represent the maze as a two dimensional ARRAY. Our maze is like a checkerboard. The walls are black and the paths are white. Each element in the ARRAY starts out as either black or white. When a square is visited we mark it as such to avoid running around in loops. When a path leads to the maze exit we mark all the squares on the trail back to the maze entrance as "path". We are using an *enumeration* data TYPE for the ARRAY elements because it is ideal for this situation.

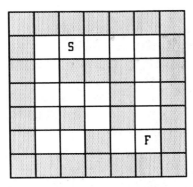

Figure 11.3. Placing an impermeable border around the active part of the maze simplifies the solution by eliminating edge tests. Placing sentinel values into data structures is a common technique.

(* Example 11.18 *)

```
TYPE
    color = (White, Black, Path, Visited);

VAR
    maze : ARRAY [0..6],[0..6] OF color;
```

Another complication of this approach is the *boundary* of the maze. At first glance it seems that we have to check the ARRAY subscripts constantly to avoid paths that lead outside the maze. We can avoid this complication by using a trick — making the actual maze ARRAY just larger than the desired maze. We can make the outer border of the maze all black, thereby avoiding any special case border tests. Thus the declaration above has an active area of five by five with a one row (column) safety zone surrounding the active area. (Figure 11.2.)

Two simple utility routines are necessary for this project: one to print a maze and one to initialize a maze. The initialization PROCEDURE could assign the values for one particular maze to the maze ARRAY. However it is much more flexible to have the initialization routine read in a maze definition from the console or a file. In either case the maze initialization routine must make sure that the border of the maze is set to all black so that we don't accidently trace a path off the active surface. These two PROCEDURES are left as exercises for the reader.

Our strategy for solving a maze is simple. From a given cell we try to run the maze by moving left, straight, or right. In pseudo code this is

If this square is anything but White Then
    go back to previous square
If this square is the destination Then success!
Otherwise mark this square as Visited
If left, straight, or right path succeeds Then
    Mark this square as Path and go back to previous
Otherwise go back to previous square

As we noted above moving left, straight or right is somewhat complicated. Therefore we have isolated these actions in separate PROCEDURES. By themselves these PROCEDURES are trivial. Alternatively the logic of these PROCEDURES could be incorporated directly into the maze running PROCEDURE at the expense of cluttering its body. Putting the logic of the direction PROCEDURES into the body of the maze running PROCEDURE would make it slightly more efficient by avoiding several subroutine calls, and it would reduce the stack space requirements of this recursive task. However neither of these arguments is persuasive here. (These two arguments might be more persuasive in a program designed to solve much larger mazes.)

Here is a table that shows moving *left* after entering a cell from a given direction.

| Entering from the | Left Neighbor | Entrance Direction |
|---|---|---|
| North | row, col + 1 | West |
| South | row, col − 1 | East |
| East | row + 1, col | North |
| West | row − 1, col | South |

Like many programs, the program to find a path through a maze consists of buckets of sweat surrounding just a bit of inspiration. The following program has omitted some of the details to focus on the major ideas of the program. Note that the *bodies* of the following four PROCEDURES are completely omitted: PrintMaze, InitMaze, Straight, and Right. The variable declarations are present as is the crucial RunMaze PROCEDURE along with the Left PROCEDURE. The body of the Maze MODULE is also present.

```
                                              (* Example 11.19 *)
(* Recursive program to solve a two dim. maze *)
MODULE Maze;
FROM InOut IMPORT Done, Write, WriteString,
    ReadString, WriteCard, WriteLn,
    OpenInput, CloseInput;

TYPE
    direction = (North, South, East, West);
    color = (White, Black, Path, Visited);

VAR
    maze : ARRAY [0..6],[0..6] OF color;
    destrow, destcol : INTEGER; (* the exit place *)

PROCEDURE InitMaze;
BEGIN (* student project *)
END InitMaze;

PROCEDURE PrintMaze;
BEGIN (* Student project *)
END PrintMaze;

PROCEDURE RunMaze
 (row,col : INTEGER; fromdir : direction) : BOOLEAN;
BEGIN
    IF maze[row,col] <> White THEN RETURN FALSE END;
    IF (row = destrow) AND (col = destcol) THEN
        maze[row,col] := Path;
        RETURN TRUE
    END;
    maze[row,col] := Visited;
    (* try the three directions *)
    IF Left(row,col,fromdir) THEN
        maze[row,col] := Path;
        RETURN TRUE
    END;
    IF Straight(row,col,fromdir) THEN
        maze[row,col] := Path;
        RETURN TRUE
    END;
    IF Right(row,col,fromdir) THEN
        maze[row,col] := Path;
```

```
        RETURN TRUE
    END;
    RETURN FALSE
END RunMaze;

PROCEDURE Left
    (row,col : INTEGER; from : direction) : BOOLEAN;
BEGIN
    CASE from OF
        North : RETURN RunMaze(row,col+1,West) |
        South : RETURN RunMaze(row,col-1,East) |
        East : RETURN RunMaze(row+1,col,North) |
        West : RETURN RunMaze(row-1,col,South)
    END
END Left;

PROCEDURE Straight
    (row,col : INTEGER; from : direction) : BOOLEAN;
BEGIN (* Student project *)
END Straight;

PROCEDURE Right
    (row,col : INTEGER; from : direction) : BOOLEAN;
BEGIN (* Student project *)
END Right;

BEGIN
    InitMaze;
    WriteString("Input Maze: "); WriteLn;
    PrintMaze;
    IF RunMaze(1,1,North) THEN
        WriteString("Maze Solution: "); WriteLn;
        PrintMaze
    ELSE
        WriteString("Solution not found."); WriteLn
    END
END Maze.
```

**Exercise 11.11.** Fill in the body of the InitMaze PROCEDURE.
□

**Exercise 11.12.** Fill in the body of the PrintMaze PROCEDURE.
□

**Exercise 11.13.** Fill in the body of the Right PROCEDURE.
□

**Exercise 11.14.** Rewrite RunMaze so that the logic of Straight, Left, and Right is incorporated directly. (Avoid the PROCEDURE calls.)

□

**Exercise 11.15.** Rewrite the Left PROCEDURE so that it uses table lookup instead of a CASE statement to perform its chore.

□

# Chapter 12

# SETS

A mathematical SET is a collection of objects. For example consider the primary colors Red, Green, and Blue. We can form eight distinct SETS from these three objects, ranging from the *null* SET (zero members) to the full SET with three members. The following program introduces the Primaries enumeration TYPE and eight constant SETS based on Primaries.

(* Example 12.1 *)

```
MODULE Sets;

TYPE
    Colors = ( Red, Green, Blue );
    Primaries = SET OF Colors;

CONST
    s0 = Primaries {};
    s1 = Primaries { Red };
    s2 = Primaries { Green };
    s3 = Primaries { Blue };
    s4 = Primaries { Red, Green };
    s5 = Primaries { Red, Blue };
    s6 = Primaries { Green .. Blue };
```

```
        s7 = Primaries { Red .. Blue };

BEGIN
END Sets.
```

In Modula–2 a SET is indicated by mentioning the name of the SET followed by a list of the members of the SET. The list of members is surrounded by *curly braces*. SET s0 is the *null* SET; s1, s2, and s3 each contain one member; s4, s5, and s6 contain two members; and s7 contains three members. Primaries is the base TYPE of all eight constant SETS.

SETS may be formed by listing their members as in s0 through s5. Whenever there are several consecutive members it is acceptable to either list the members or to indicate the range of members by using Modula–2's notation for subranges. Notice that SETS s6 and s7 use the subrange notation.

Modula–2 allows SET variables and SET TYPES in addition to the SET constants shown above.

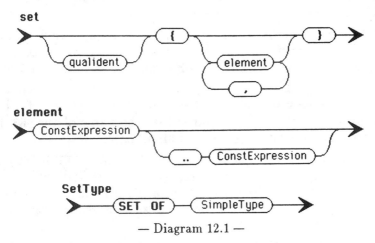

— Diagram 12.1 —

The diagram of a *SetType* pertains to declaring SET variables, or explicitly named SET TYPES.

Modula–2 SETS are more restricted than Pascal SETS. One restriction is the requirement that Modula–2 SETS are always based on an enumeration or a subrange. The number of elements that are allowed in a SET varies. Sometimes the number is small, often sixteen on sixteen bit computers or thirty–two on thirty–two bit computers. Some Modula–2 implementations allow SETS that are larger. The number of elements in the base TYPE of a SET may not exceed the number of elements that are allowed in a SET.

Another restriction of Modula–2 is that the base TYPE of a SET must be written in front of the list of SET members. This improves program clarity and eliminates ambiguities, especially when a program contains several subrange SETS.

## 12.1. BITSETS

Modula–2's only predefined SET TYPE is the BITSET. You might like to think of a BITSET as a SET whose base TYPE is the SET of bits in the native word of the computer. On a sixteen bit computer a BITSET acts as if it were declared as

(* Example 12.2 *)

```
TYPE
    BITSET = SET OF [ 0 .. 15 ];
```

The numbering of the bits in a machine word is a system dependent feature of Modula–2. However on many systems the first element of a BITSET, { 0 }, corresponds to the least significant bit of a machine word, the next element is the next bit, etc.

BITSETS are important in systems programming because they are often used to access special device registers in order to program a computer's peripheral devices. Examples are shown in Chapter 19.

It isn't necessary to mention the word BITSET in front of a list of elements of a BITSET. Remember that the name of the SET TYPE must always be written in front of all other SETS.

**Exercise 12.1.** One purpose of the standard TYPE BITSET is to provide a data abstraction for bits so that "bit fiddling" is easier. Do you think that the elaboration of BITSETS into a general SET notion applicable to enumerations and subranges is worthwhile?
□

**Exercise 12.2.** When have you used SETS in Pascal? Would SETS of sixteen or thirty–two members have been adequate for your Pascal SET applications? Several Pascal implementations allow SETS with 256 (or more) members. Can you think of an application for SETS that requires more than sixteen or thirty–two members?
□

## 12.2. SET Operations

One important SET operation is the membership test denoted by the IN operator. The IN operator tests whether a value (represented by an expression) is a member of a SET. The result is TRUE if the value is in the SET and FALSE otherwise. For example, the expression

```
5 IN { 2 .. 7 }
```

evaluates to TRUE because 5 is a member of the given BITSET. The IN operator requires an expression of a certain TYPE on the left hand side and a SET expression with that base TYPE on the right hand side. (An aside: IN is the *only* Modula–2 operator that allows or requires two different TYPES of operands.)

Modula–2 has four *operations* to form new SETS from existing SETS. These are SET union, intersection, difference, and symmetric difference.

- The *union* of two SETS is a SET that contains all the members in either of the two constituent SETS.
- The *intersection* of two SETS is a SET containing only those members that are in *both* of the constituent SETS.
- The *difference* of two SETS contains all of those members that are in the first SET but not in the second.
- The *symmetric difference* of two SETS contains only those members that are in only one of the constituent SETS.

The following table lists the operators for these four SET operations.

| SET Operations | |
|---|---|
| Operator | Operation |
| + | Union |
| − | Difference |
| * | Intersection |
| / | Symmetric Difference |

The meanings of these operations can be summarized in Modula–2 notation:

```
I IN (s1+s2)    means    (I IN s1) OR (I IN s2)
I IN (s1-s2)    means    (I IN s1) AND (NOT(I IN s2))
I IN (s1*s2)    means    (I IN s1) AND (I IN s2)
I IN (s1/s2)    means    (I IN s1) <> (I IN s2)
```

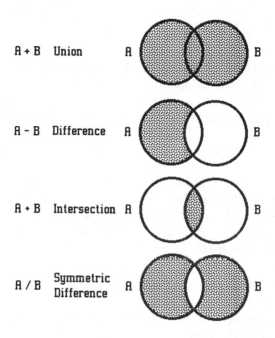

Figure 12.1. Modula–2's four set construction operators.

Here we assume that s1 and s2 are SETS of the same TYPE and that the variable I is a member of the base TYPE of s1. Some people use the term *exclusive or* for what we are calling symmetric difference.

| Relational Operators for SETS | |
| --- | --- |
| Operator | Operation |
| = | Equality |
| < > | Inequality |
| # | Inequality |
| <= | Inclusion |
| >= | Inclusion |

There are three conditional operators that can be used to *compare* SETS. The conditional operators produce a BOOLEAN result.

- The = operator and the < > (or #) operator can be used with SETS to test for *equality* or *inequality*.
- The >= operator or the <= operator can be used with SETS to test for SET *inclusion*. One SET is said to be included in another when all members of the first SET are also members

of the other.

The two SET inclusion operators are the opposite of each other. s1 <= s2 means that s1 is included in s2 while s1 >= s2 means that s2 is included in s1. Note that the operators > and < cannot be applied to sets.

**Exercise 12.3.** Here is a short program that contains several SET operations.

(* Example 12.3 *)

```
MODULE SetOps;

TYPE
    Color = ( Red, Green, Blue );
    Primaries = SET OF Color;

VAR
    ColorSetA, ColorSetB, ColorSetC : Primaries;

BEGIN
    ColorSetA := Primaries {Red};
    ColorSetB := ColorSetA + Primaries {Blue};
    IF ColorSetB <= Primaries {Green..Blue} THEN
      ColorSetC := Primaries {Green} - ColorSetB
    ELSE
      ColorSetC := ColorSetA / Primaries{Red..Blue}
    END
END SetOps.
```

What are the final values of the three SET variables?
□

**Exercise 12.4.** Modify the program in the previous exercise so that it symbolically prints the final values of the SET variables.
□

**Exercise 12.5.** The inversion of a SET has as members those elements that are not members of the original SET. How would you invert a set using Modula-2's set operators?
□

**Exercise 12.6.** Write a TYPE definition for a TYPE called Super-Set that is an ARRAY (as large as you want) OF BITSETS. Write PROCEDURES to perform union and difference operations on SuperSets. The skeleton for these two PROCEDURES is shown below.

```
                                            (* Example 12.4 *)
PROCEDURE SuperUnion
        (s1, s2 : SuperSet; VAR result : SuperSet);
BEGIN
END SuperUnion;

PROCEDURE SuperDiff
        (s1, s2 : SuperSet; VAR result : SuperSet);
BEGIN
END SuperDiff;
```

□

**Exercise 12.7.** Proceed as in the previous exercise to implement
the comparison operations equality, inequality, and inclusion for
SuperSets.
□

**Exercise 12.8.** Place your routines for SuperSets into a global
MODULE.
□

## 12.3. INCL and EXCL

The unique aspect of sets is our ability to establish their membership. Probably the simplest method is to state the membership
using set notation and assign that membership to a set.

```
                                            (* Example 12.5 *)
MODULE Members;

TYPE
        Color = ( Red, Green, Blue );
        Primaries = SET OF Color;

VAR
        walls, floor : Color;
        ColorSet : Primaries;

BEGIN
        walls := Red;
        floor := Blue;
           (* Constant members *)
        ColorSet := Primaries { Red, Blue };
           (* Variable members *)
```

```
    ColorSet := Primaries { walls, floor };
       (* Mixed members *)
    ColorSet := Primaries { walls, Blue }
END Members.
```

Individual members can be added to a SET using Modula–2's union set operator (+). Similarly the SET difference operator (-) can be used to remove a member from a set.

(* Example 12.6 *)

```
MODULE InclOps;

TYPE
    Color = ( Red, Green, Blue );
    Primaries = SET OF Color;

VAR
    floor : Color;
    ColorSet : Primaries;

BEGIN
    floor := Blue;
    ColorSet := Primaries {};
      (* Constant *)
    ColorSet := ColorSet + Primaries { Red };
      (* Variable *)
    ColorSet := ColorSet + Primaries { floor };
END InclOps.
```

Notice that we first initialized the SET to null before using the set union operator.

Modula–2's set operators are flexible and powerful, but they often aren't ideal for clearly expressing your ideas. Just as the standard INC PROCEDURE is often more expressive than an equivalent assignment statement, Modula–2's standard INCL and EXCL SET membership PROCEDURES are often more expressive than the equivalent operations using SET operators.

The INCL PROCEDURE makes the value of an *expression* into a member of the given SET. The first argument of INCL is a SET and the second is an expression. Naturally the TYPE of the expression must be the base TYPE of the SET. EXCL is the same as INCL except that the value of the given expression is excluded from membership in the given SET. Let's rewrite Example 12.6 using INCL to determine the membership of ColorSet.

(* Example 12.7 *)

```
MODULE Incl;

TYPE
    Color = ( Red, Green, Blue );
    Primaries = SET OF Color;

VAR
    floor : Color;
    ColorSet : Primaries;

BEGIN
    floor := Blue;
    ColorSet := Primaries {};
    INCL(ColorSet,Red);
    INCL(ColorSet,floor);
END Incl.
```

**Exercise 12.9.** Write a PROCEDURE to output a list of the members of a Primaries variable.
□

**Exercise 12.10.** Write InclSuper and ExclSuper for the SuperSets of Exercise 12.6.
□

# 12.4. Example — Packed BOOLEANS and the Sieve Revisited

The BOOLEAN representation that is built into Modula–2 is optimized for computations. However the common representation isn't ideal when many BOOLEANS are needed because each BOOLEAN occupies more than one bit of memory. On a sixteen bit computer, sixteen BOOLEANS could be packed into a single word to save space at the expense of execution speed. The standard Modula–2 BITSET data TYPE is ideal for representing densely packed BOOLEANS because it allows us to use every bit in a word of storage.

We will use the term *packed* BOOLEANS to describe TRUE/FALSE values optimized to occupy minimum space. Packed BOOLEANS are ideal for a program such as the Sieve of Eratosthenes (Example 6.11). In the sieve, the number of primes that can be found depends on how large an ARRAY OF BOOLEANS can be handled. Using packed BOOLEANS makes it possible to work with much larger ARRAYS.

The interface to our packed BOOLEAN data structure consists of two PROCEDURES. The PROCEDURE named readPB is passed an index as a parameter and then returns the current value of that packed BOOLEAN. Similarly the writePB PROCEDURE writes a BOOLEAN value into the indicated packed BOOLEAN. The packed BOOLEANS are used by client MODULES as if they were an ordinary ARRAY OF BOOLEANS, except that PROCEDURES are used for assignment and evaluation rather than simple ARRAY indexing.

```
                                        (* Example 12.8 *)
DEFINITION MODULE PackedBools;

(*
 * A packed Bool is a sequence of t/f
 * values organized for maximum
 * storage density, hence relatively slow access.
 * A single array 0..65535 of PBs is available.
 *)

PROCEDURE readPB (index : CARDINAL) : BOOLEAN;
PROCEDURE writePB (index : CARDINAL; val : BOOLEAN);

END PackedBools.
```

The following IMPLEMENTATION MODULE creates a single ARRAY of t/f values, using the individual bits in a memory cell for storage. Naturally we use an ARRAY OF BITSETS to store the packed BOOLEANS.

Our goal is a system that will provide as many true/false values as there are CARDINALS. On a sixteen bit computer, MAX(CARDINAL) is 65535 (64K) and it takes 4K words (64K DIV 16) for the BITSET ARRAY.

```
                                         (* Example 12.9 *)
    IMPLEMENTATION MODULE PackedBools;

    CONST
       (* The following consts are machine specific *)
       NCards = MAX(CARDINAL); (* s.b. 65535 *)
       NBits = 16; (* Bits per BITSET *)
       ArrayLen = NCards DIV NBits + 1;

    VAR
       pb : ARRAY [ 0 .. ArrayLen ] OF BITSET;

    PROCEDURE readPB(index : CARDINAL): BOOLEAN;
    BEGIN
       RETURN (index MOD NBits) IN pb[index DIV NBits]
    END readPB;

    PROCEDURE writePB(index : CARDINAL; val : BOOLEAN);
    BEGIN
       IF val THEN
         INCL(pb[index DIV NBits], index MOD NBits)
       ELSE
         EXCL(pb[index DIV NBits], index MOD NBits)
       END
    END writePB;


    END PackedBools.
```

To test the PackedBools MODULE we include a new version of the
Sieve of Eratosthenes (Example 6.11) that uses packed BOOLEANS
rather than ordinary BOOLEANS. This allows us to search much
farther for primes. We will also use the Long arithmetic package
generated in Section 5.7 to avoid the overflow problems that would
develop if we tried to use CARDINALS. With a version of Modula-2
that supports LONGCARDS we could avoid using the Long arithmetic package.

This program will print a list of primes less than 100,000. Therefore we need 50,000 (of the 65536) buckets from the Packed-
Boolean data structure and we need arithmetic that works
correctly up to 100,000.

```
                                           (* Example 12.10 *)
MODULE SieveL;
FROM InOut IMPORT WriteCard, WriteLn;
FROM PackedBools IMPORT readPB, writePB;
FROM Long IMPORT LONG, AddLong, WriteLong, CmpLong,
      IncLong, StringToLong, LongToCard;


CONST
    PageLength = 66;


MODULE WriteMod;
IMPORT LONG, WriteLong, WriteLn, PageLength;
EXPORT WRITELONG;


VAR
   line, col: CARDINAL; (* static *)

PROCEDURE WRITELONG (x : LONG);
BEGIN
   WriteLong(x,7);
   INC(col);
   IF col = 10 THEN col := 0; WRITELN END;
END WRITELONG;


PROCEDURE WRITELN;
VAR
   i : CARDINAL; (* dynamic *)
BEGIN
   INC(line); WriteLn;
   IF line = (PageLength - 4) THEN
       FOR i := 1 TO 7 DO WRITELN END;
   ELSIF line = PageLength THEN
       line := 0;
   END; (* IF *)
END WRITELN;


BEGIN (* WriteLnMod *)
   col := 0; line := 0; WRITELN; WRITELN; WRITELN
END WriteMod;


VAR
   last, three, suspect, convicted, prime : LONG;
```

```
BEGIN    (* Sieve of Eratosthenes *)
   StringToLong("50000",last);
   StringToLong("03",three);
   StringToLong("00",suspect);
   (* Init Packed Bools *)
   WHILE CmpLong(suspect, last) <= 0 DO
      writePB(LongToCard(suspect), TRUE);
      IncLong(suspect);
   END; (* WHILE *)
   (* Suspect - a possible prime
    * If suspect is TRUE
    * then calculate prime and rule out multiples *)
   StringToLong("00", suspect);
   WHILE CmpLong(suspect, last) <= 0 DO (* search *)
      IF readPB(LongToCard(suspect)) THEN
             (* found one *)
         AddLong(suspect, suspect, prime);
         AddLong(prime, three, prime);
         WRITELONG(prime);
         AddLong(prime,suspect,convicted);
         WHILE CmpLong(convicted, last) <= 0 DO
            (* rule out multiples of known prime *)
            writePB(LongToCard(convicted), FALSE);
            AddLong(convicted, prime, convicted);
         END (* WHILE *)
      END; (* IF *)
      IncLong(suspect)
   END (* WHILE *)
END SieveL.
```

This version of the sieve prints a much longer list of prime numbers, but it is much less readable and understandable than the original. For example the code

```
IF flags[suspect] THEN ...
```

is inherently much clearer than

```
IF readPB(LongToCard(suspect)) THEN ...
```

Both the LONG arithmetic package and the PackedBoolean package obscure the meaning of the program. If necessity forces you to obscure an algorithm as we are doing here, you should first write it and prove it in a clean form before the obscuring extensions are added.

**Exercise 12.11.** The PackedBoolean package is *much* slower than Modula-2's built in BOOLEAN TYPE. Similarly the LONG arithmetic package developed in Section 5.7 is much slower than CARDINAL arithmetic. What impact do these factors have on the execution speed of the Sieve program. Note that output to a computer terminal or printer is also slow. Do you suspect that the SieveL program is now so slow that it can't keep the terminal busy, or is the speed of the terminal still the bottleneck?
☐

**Exercise 12.12.** Expand the PackedBoolean package to allow up to 500,000 t/f values. Use a LONGCARD ARRAY index instead of a CARDINAL.
☐

**Exercise 12.13.** Rewrite this version of the Sieve using LONGCARDS instead of the LONG arithmetic package.
☐

# Chapter 13

# RECORDS

Situations often arise in programming where it helps to take two points of view towards a set of variables. For example the variables describing the characteristics of a sailboat might include the BoatManufacturer, the LengthOverAll, the LengthAtWater-Line, the SailArea, and the MaximumCrewSize. On the one hand we like to think about the *individual* variables and their values, for example we might like to assign the value 8 to the variable MaximumCrewSize. On the other hand it is often convenient to think of these variables as a *single entity*. We might want to pass this entire description of a sailboat to a PROCEDURE, or we might want to assign the values of one sailboat variable to another.

The Modula–2 RECORD data TYPE allows you to collect related data elements into a single variable. RECORDS allow you to adopt whichever point of view is convenient, a collection of variables or a single entity. Sailboats might be described using the following RECORD:

(* Example 13.1 *)

```
TYPE
   SailBoat =
      RECORD
        BoatManufacturer : ARRAY [0..15] OF CHAR;
        LengthOverAll, LengthAtWaterLine : CARDINAL;
        SailArea : CARDINAL;
        MaximumCrewSize : [4..16]
      END; (* RECORD *)
```

If the program that works with this SailBoat RECORD only deals with a single instance of the RECORD, the only advantage is the explicit grouping of the information. However if the program manipulates numerous SailBoats then the RECORD structure is an advantage. If there are ARRAYS OF SailBoats, or dynamically created SailBoats (See following chapter) then the RECORD structure is even more important.

Components of a RECORD can be any Modula–2 data TYPE including other RECORDS (see above) or ARRAYS.

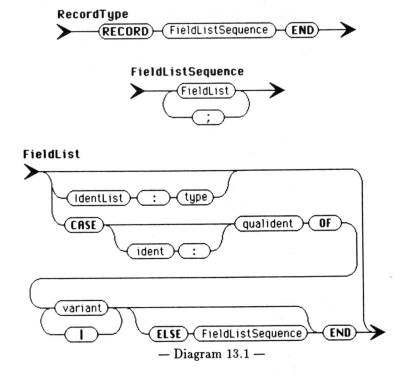

— Diagram 13.1 —

```
VAR Y :
    RECORD
        a : ARRAY BOOLEAN OF INTEGER;
        b : REAL;
        c, d : CARDINAL;
    END;
```

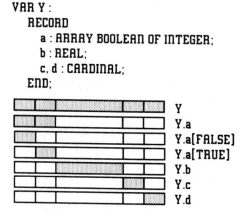

Figure 13.1. A RECORD contains named elements. In the figure, the named elements are shaded.

(The explanation of variant RECORDS is deferred until Section 13.3.)

The primary advantage of RECORDS is the ability to deal with the information as a group as well as individually. The following program MODULE illustrates both manipulations.

(* Example 13.2 *)

```
MODULE ShowSail;

TYPE
    SailBoat =
        RECORD
            BoatManufacturer : ARRAY [0..15] OF CHAR;
            LengthOverAll, LengthAtWaterLine : CARDINAL;
            SailArea : CARDINAL;
            MaximumCrewSize : [4..16]
        END; (* RECORD *)

VAR
    Irwin38, Irwin41 : SailBoat;

BEGIN
    Irwin38.BoatManufacturer := 'Irwin';
    Irwin38.LengthOverAll := 40;
    Irwin38.LengthAtWaterLine := 32;
    Irwin38.SailArea := 776;
    Irwin38.MaximumCrewSize := 6;
```

```
    Irwin41 := Irwin38;

    Irwin41.LengthOverAll :=  41;
    Irwin41.LengthAtWaterLine := 35;
    Irwin41.SailArea := 960;
  END ShowSail.
```

As you can see from this example, an *individual element* of a RECORD is designated by mentioning the name of the RECORD followed by a period followed by the name of the element. The *entire* RECORD is indicated by simply mentioning the name of the RECORD variable.

**Exercise 13.1.** Design RECORDS to describe

- a. Students.
- b. Major automobile companies.
- c. Archaeological artifacts for several
     prehistoric ancestors of Homo sapiens.
- d. Marketing information describing computer purchasers.
- e. Checking accounts.
- f. Video Cassette recorders.
- g. Congressmen.

□

**Exercise 13.2.** Write an interactive PROCEDURE in Modula–2 to input Sailboat TYPE variables. Prompt the user for each field, read in the response, and do some primitive error checking. Use any of the I/O routines from the MODULE InOut. The skeleton for this PROCEDURE is

```
PROCEDURE ReadSailBoat( VAR s : SailBoat );
(* body of proc *)
END ReadSailBoat;
```

□

## 13.1. The WITH Statement

When you are accessing several elements of a single RECORD it is bothersome to mention the name of the RECORD repeatedly. Modula-2 allows you to use the WITH statement to select a particular RECORD. Within the statement sequence defined by the WITH statement it is possible to refer to the elements of the RECORD without using the RECORD name as a prefix. This is an important simplification in many circumstances.

**WithStatement**

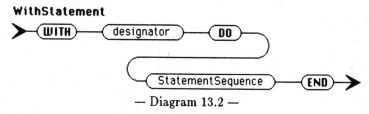

— Diagram 13.2 —

(In this context a designator is something that selects a particular variable, such as an element of a RECORD, an entire RECORD, an element of an ARRAY, a simple variable, etc.)

Let's rewrite the first example using the WITH statement to simplify the program.

```
                                            (* Example 13.3 *)
MODULE ShowSaill;

TYPE
   SailBoat =
      RECORD
         BoatManufacturer : ARRAY [0..15] OF CHAR;
         LengthOverAll, LengthAtWaterLine : CARDINAL;
         SailArea : CARDINAL;
         MaximumCrewSize : [4..16]
      END;

VAR
   Irwin38, Irwin41 : SailBoat;

BEGIN
   WITH Irwin38 DO
      BoatManufacturer := 'Irwin';
      LengthOverAll := 40;
      LengthAtWaterLine := 32;
      SailArea := 776;
```

```
      MaximumCrewSize := 6
   END;

   Irwin41 := Irwin38;

   WITH Irwin41 DO
      LengthOverAll :=  41;
      LengthAtWaterLine := 35;
      SailArea := 960
   END
END ShowSail1.
```

Using a WITH statement leads to several advantages. It collects a group of related operations thereby making the program more *readable*. The WITH statement often makes it possible to access the elements of a RECORD more *efficiently*. The gain in efficiency is especially important when you are working with ARRAYS OF RECORDS or dynamic RECORDS (See Chapter 14).

There is one important restriction that pertains to WITH statements — the statement sequence must never contain an assignment to the WITH statement's control variable. This restriction must be carefully observed by the programmer because the compiler is unable (or unwilling) to detect all possible violations of this rule. One example of an *erroneous* WITH statement is

```
                                      (* Example 13.4 *)
(* FOR loop incorrectly nested inside WITH *)
WITH sailboats[i] DO
     FOR i := 0 TO 10 DO
          (*
           * loop body
           *)
     END (* FOR *)
END (* WITH *)
```

The correct program structure for looping in conjunction with a WITH statement is to nest the WITH statement inside the loop instead of nesting the loop inside the WITH.

```
                                    (* Example 13.5 *)
  (* WITH correctly nested inside FOR loop *)
  FOR i := 0 TO 10 DO
      WITH sailboats[i] DO
           (*
            * loop body
            *)
      END (* WITH *)
  END (* FOR *)
```

**Exercise 13.3.** Rewrite the OneBuffer MODULE (Example 8.2) using RECORDS.

□


## 13.2. Example — Linked Lists

In Section 8.3 we presented a MODULE called OneBuffer that implemented a circular buffer. The buffer was accessed by calling deposit to place a character in the buffer or by calling withdraw to retrieve a character.

There is always a small time penalty that is imposed when you use a buffer. Naturally one goal of designing a good buffering scheme is to make it efficient. Nobody wants to waste time shuffling data into and out of holding bins.

Another consideration is *space* efficiency. Our need to conserve space often conflicts with our natural desire to make buffers large so that they can handle longer bursts of data. One drawback of circular buffers is that they have a fixed size. In a more space efficient buffering system space is allocated on–the–fly as necessary.

Let's see why space efficiency is often important. Consider a time–sharing computer system that is managing several hundred terminals. Usually most of the terminals are inactive, or sending and receiving data infrequently. However the system should be able to handle a long burst of data at high speed. Given 200 channels, it would be impractical to even allocate a small fixed size buffer for each channel. In this situation it's imperative for each terminal to have a buffer whose size reflects its current requirements.

One method is to use a *linked list* data structure. A linked list is similar to an ARRAY in that it consists of identical elements. However a linked list differs from an ARRAY because the number of

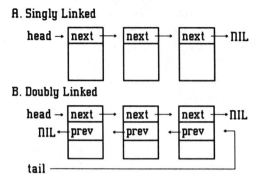

Figure 13.2. In a singly linked list, each element in the chain leads to the following element in the chain. Usually a special sentinel value, called NIL is used to mark the end of the chain. A doubly linked list has the additional property that each element in the list knows the previous element, allowing the list to be traversed in either direction.

elements varies and because each element contains a link to the next element. (Figure 13.2)

In this example we are going to write versions of deposit and withdraw that work with a pool of linked lists. Each element in the pool will be large enough to hold a few characters, the pool as a whole will be large enough to hold many characters. As before we will publish a DEFINITION MODULE that hides the actual buffers.

```
                                        (* Example 13.6 *)
(* Buffers using linked lists *)
DEFINITION MODULE LLBuf;

TYPE
   LINK;(* Opaque type. A link indicates a buffer *)

PROCEDURE deposit(ch : CHAR; chan : LINK);

PROCEDURE withdraw(VAR chan : LINK) : CHAR;

PROCEDURE cnt(chan : LINK) : CARDINAL;

PROCEDURE openbuf(VAR chan : LINK);

END LLBuf.
```

A client MODULE "opens" a buffering channel by calling openbuf
and passing it a LINK data TYPE. These link variables are tokens
that the buffering PROCEDURES (deposit, withdraw, and cnt)
use to locate the actual buffer. In this particular buffering system
each buffer is a RECORD, and there is an ARRAY OF RECORDS serv-
ing as a buffer pool. The LINK actually is an index into the ARRAY
of buffers, but this implementation detail is hidden from the
client.

All the linked lists are originally linked into a special list known as
the *free list*. The openbuf PROCEDURE pulls the first buffer off the
free list and returns its index to the client MODULE. Sometimes
deposit encounters a full buffer. When this happens deposit
must take another buffer RECORD from the free list and add it to
the clients list. Similarly when withdraw drains the last data from
a buffer RECORD that buffer is returned to the free list.

Notice that in the LLBuffers DEFINITION MODULE the LINK
parameter for the withdraw PROCEDURE is a *variable*. This is because the LINK is the index of the *first* buffer RECORD in the chain
of buffers allocated to a particular task. The value of the LINK
must be updated when withdraw drains a buffer and puts it back
on the free list.

Each task that has been allocated a buffer has at least one buffer
RECORD. There may be several buffers allocated to a task depending on how much data it has stored in the buffer. The first buffer
in one task's chain of buffers is special because it contains the
book keeping information for the entire chain. (Since this header
information isn't used in subsequent RECORDS in the chain, this
information could be placed into a separate RECORD. I placed all
the information into a single RECORD because the code seemed
simpler with only one RECORD TYPE.)

The data RECORD for the Buffers contains five book keeping
items plus the actual data storage space.

### A Chain of Buffers

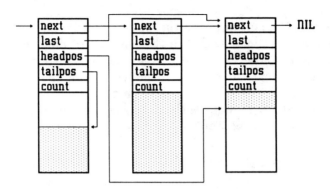

Figure 13.3. Each buffer contains a header plus a storage area. The next element of each buffer indicates the next buffer in the chain. In the first buffer in the chain, last is used to indicate the final buffer in the chain, headpos indicates the position of the head of the active data region, tailpos indicates the location of the tail of the active data, and count keeps track of the size of the buffer.

```
                                       (* Example 13.7 *)
(* completion of the LINK declaration
 *   in the definition module *)
TYPE
    LINK = [0..Nbuffers];

(*
 * Cbufs are the actual storage elements in the pool
 *)
TYPE
    Cbuf =
        RECORD
            (* The head and tail of the list *)
            next : LINK;
            last : LINK;
            (* indices into the first and last bufs *)
            tailpos : CARDINAL;
            headpos : CARDINAL;
            (* the number of chars in the buffer *)
            count : CARDINAL;
            (* The actual storage space *)
            data : ARRAY [0..CbufEnd] OF CHAR;
        END;
```

The next element indexes the next buffer in the chain, or it has the special value NULL to indicate the end of a chain of buffers. Last indexes the last buffer in the chain (the far end). The far end is also called the head and it is the end where data is deposited. The first buffer (the near end of the chain) is also known as the tail and it is where the data is withdrawn. The tailpos element indexes the next available datum from the tail of the chain, and the headpos element indexes the next available slot in the head of the chain. The role of count is left to your speculation. (Figure 13.3)

The only complication of depositing information into a buffer chain is allocating a new buffer when an existing buffer is full. Here is the pseudo code for depositing a character into a buffer

Place the character into the last buffer in the chain
    into the slot indexed by headpos
Increment headpos and count
If the last buffer is now full Then
    Link another buffer to the end of the buffer chain
    Point last at the new last buffer
    Set headpos to zero

Remember that headpos, count, and last are stored in the first RECORD in the chain.

Withdrawing is a bit harder because some withdrawals empty the first buffer in the chain. Thus the first buffer must be returned to the free list, and the second buffer becomes the first. Since the first buffer in a chain contains the book keeping variables, these must be transferred to the second before the first is discarded. Here is the pseudo code for withdrawing a character from a buffer:

Make sure there is a character in the buffer
Fetch the character indexed by tailpos in
    the first buffer of the chain
If the first buffer is now empty Then
    Copy the book keeping variables to the second buffer
    Change the client's link to indicate the second buffer
    Place the first buffer on the free list

The LLBuffers MODULE contains two additional public PRO-CEDURES: cnt and openbuf. Neither of these is complicated and I am not going to show you their pseudo code. Likewise the two private PROCEDURES in LLbuffers, GetBuf and DiscardBuf, are simple. Here is the complete code for the LLBuffers IMPLEMEN-TATION MODULE.

(* Example 13.8 *)

```
IMPLEMENTATION MODULE LLBuffers;
FROM InOut IMPORT WriteString, WriteLn;

CONST
    CbufEnd = 31;
    Nbuffers = 32;
    NULL = 0; (* no further links *)

(* completion of the LINK declaration *)
TYPE
    LINK = [0..Nbuffers];

(*
 * Cbufs are the actual storage elements
 * in the pool.
 * Each can hold CbufEnd+1 datums (characters).
 * Note: last, tailpos, headpos, and count
 * are valid only in the first buffer in the chain
 *)
TYPE
    Cbuf =
        RECORD
            next : LINK;
            last : LINK;
            tailpos : CARDINAL;
            headpos : CARDINAL;
            count : CARDINAL;
            data : ARRAY [0..CbufEnd] OF CHAR;
        END;

VAR
    Buffer : ARRAY [ 0..Nbuffers ] OF Cbuf;
    Free : LINK; (* Link to head of FreeList *)
    i : CARDINAL;

(* private - place a Buffer on freelist *)
PROCEDURE DiscardBuf(B : LINK);
BEGIN
    Buffer[B].next := Free;
    Free := B
END DiscardBuf;
```

```
(* private - get a Buffer from freelist *)
PROCEDURE GetBuf(VAR B : LINK);
BEGIN
  IF Free <> NULL THEN
     B := Free;
     Free := Buffer[Free].next
  ELSE
     WriteString("Ran out of buffers."); WriteLn;
     B := 0;
  END
END GetBuf;

PROCEDURE deposit(ch : CHAR; chan : LINK);
BEGIN
  WITH Buffer[chan] DO
    Buffer[last].data[headpos] := ch;
    INC(headpos);
    INC(count);
    IF headpos > CbufEnd THEN
       (* get a buffer from free list *)
       GetBuf(Buffer[last].next);
       last := Buffer[last].next;
       Buffer[last].next := NULL;
       headpos := 0;
    END; (* IF *)
  END (* WITH *)
END deposit;

PROCEDURE withdraw(VAR chan : LINK) : CHAR;
VAR
   ch : CHAR;
   temp : LINK;
BEGIN
  ch := 0C;
  WITH Buffer[chan] DO (* perform the withdraw *)
    IF count = 0 THEN
       WriteString("Can't withdraw from ");
       WriteString("an empty buffer"); WriteLn
    ELSE
       ch := data[tailpos];
       DEC(count);
       INC(tailpos);
    END (* IF *)
  END; (* WITH *)
```

```
     IF Buffer[chan].tailpos > CbufEnd THEN
       (* put buf back on free *)
       WITH Buffer[chan] DO
         Buffer[next].count := count;
         Buffer[next].last := last;
         Buffer[next].tailpos := 0;
         Buffer[next].headpos := headpos;
       END;
       temp := chan;
       chan := Buffer[chan].next;
       DiscardBuf(temp);
     END; (* IF *)
     RETURN ch
   END withdraw;

   PROCEDURE cnt(chan : LINK) : CARDINAL;
   BEGIN
       RETURN Buffer[chan].count
   END cnt;

   PROCEDURE openbuf(VAR chan : LINK);
   BEGIN
       GetBuf(chan);
       WITH Buffer[chan] DO
         headpos := 0;
         tailpos := 0;
         next := NULL;
         last := chan;
         count := 0;
       END (* WITH *)
   END openbuf;

   BEGIN
       (* initialize free list and links *)
       Free := 1;
       FOR i := 1 TO Nbuffers-1 DO
          Buffer[i].next := i+1
       END;
       Buffer[Nbuffers].next := NULL;
   END LLBuffers.
```

**Exercise 13.4.** Write a PROCEDURE to indicate whether free space is available? What is the simplest criteria?

□

**Exercise 13.5.** What is the special function of `Buffer[0]`? When is it used?

☐

**Exercise 13.6.** This version of `LLBuffers` fails badly when the free list is exhausted. Analyze the problem and implement a solution.

☐

**Exercise 13.7.** How could you check the integrity of the buffering system? For example is it feasible to make sure that none of the buffers have become stranded (not on any list)? What would you have to change to perform this check? (Remember that there may be several client MODULES, each with its own chain of buffers.)

☐

**Exercise 13.8.** Rewrite the `deposit` PROCEDURE without using WITH statements. Be careful, this is harder than it first seems. Do you think the WITH statement as used in the `deposit` PROCEDURE is good style? Is it hiding too much of the complexity in this instance? Is your version of `deposit` more readable, or less readable?

☐

## 13.3. Variant RECORDS

*Variant* RECORD allow a programmer to use RECORDS when a given RECORD has several similar, but distinct forms. Consider the following situation. A computer consulting firm keeps a RECORD of the skills of their employees. Each employee is primarily skilled in one particular operating system. The secondary skills of the employees are the particular languages and facilities of that operating system that they have mastered. Let's first define an enumeration TYPE listing a few common computer operating systems.

(* Example 13.9 *)

```
TYPE
    OpSYS = ( Unix, Idris, Xenix, RT11, MSdos, CPM );
```

We can now create a variant RECORD that defines the abilities of the consultants.

(* Example 13.10 *)

```
TYPE
   Consultant =
      RECORD
         name : ARRAY [0..20] OF CHAR;
         idnum : CARDINAL;
         DateOfHire : Date;
         Position : (Programmer, ProgAnalyst,
                     Analyst, SeniorAnalyst);
         CASE System : OpSYS OF
            Unix .. Xenix :
               UnixC, UnixF77, UnixM2,
               Yacc, Lex, S, MRS : BOOLEAN |
            RT11 :
               Macro, RtF77,
               RtPascal, RtM2 : BOOLEAN |
            MSdos, CPM :
               CpmPascal, DBii, CpmC : BOOLEAN
         END (* case *)
      END; (* record *)
```

In this RECORD the variant part deals with the particular skills of
a consultant for a particular operating system. The System field
in this RECORD is special. It is called the *tag field* because it's
value determines which of the variants is currently applicable. In
this case the tag field is an enumeration TYPE. The tag field
named System has six enumeration values: Unix, Idris, Xenix,
RT11, MSdos, and CPM.

For example the Consultant RECORD for an employee specializ-
ing in the RT11 operating system would have the System field of
the RECORD assigned the value RT11. An RT11 specialist might be
familiar with the Macro assembler, or the programming languages
RtF77, RtPascal, or RtM2. We wouldn't expect an Rt11 specialist
to work with C, Yacc, Lex, MRS, S, or DBii because they aren't
commonly available with RT11.

Let's suppose a programmer named Ada Lovelace is a Unix specialist. Naturally it is meaningless to inquire of her RT11 Macro
abilities. However it is unlikely that a compiler could check such
errors of logic. Therefore it is the *programmer's* responsibility to
ensure that programs only manipulate the parts of a variant
RECORD that are associated with the current value of the tag field.
It is acceptable to change the value of the tag field at any time,
but it is unwise to make any assumptions about the values in the

variant parts after changing the tag field.

As a general rule, one *makes assignments* to the tag field *before* making assignments to the variant fields. This rule is demonstrated in the previous example. As a second rule, one should *test* the value of the tag field *before* using the values in the variant fields.

Remember from the syntax diagram for RECORDS that a FieldList was either a declaration of variables of a given TYPE or a variant.

**variant**

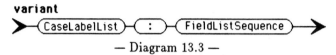

— Diagram 13.3 —

The syntax diagrams for CaseLabelLists and CaseLabels were given in Section 3.2. Notice the similarity of the syntax of the variant RECORD declaration and the CASE statement. CASE statements are often used in programs that deal with variant RECORDS. The following PROCEDURE is an example.

```
                                              (* Example 13.11 *)
PROCEDURE WriteConsult (c : Consultant);

PROCEDURE Twrite(t: BOLEAN; s : ARRAY OF CHAR);
BEGIN
   IF t THEN WriteString(s) END
END Twrite;

BEGIN
   WITH c DO
      WriteString(name); WriteString(' - ');
      CASE Position OF
         Programmer :
           WriteString('Programmer') |
         ProgAnalyst :
           WriteString('Programmer/Analyst') |
         Analyst :
           WriteString('Analyst') |
         SeniorAnalyst :
           WriteString('Senior Analyst')
      END;
      WriteLn;
      CASE System OF
         Unix .. Xenix :
                 CASE System OF
                 Unix :
```

```
                            WriteString('UNIX specialist') |
                    Idris :
                      WriteString('Idris specialist') |
                    Xenix :
                      WriteString('XENIX specialist')
                  END;
                  WriteLn;
                  WriteString('Skills: ');
                  Twrite(UnixC,'C ');
                  Twrite(UnixF77,'Fortran77 ');
                  Twrite(UnixM2,'Modula-2 ');
                  Twrite(Yacc,'Yacc ');
                  Twrite(Lex,'Lex ');
                  Twrite(S,'S ');
                  Twrite(MRS,'MRS');
                  WriteLn |
          RT11 :
                  WriteString('RT11 specialist');
                  WriteLn;
                  WriteString('Skills: ');
                  Twrite(Macro,'Macro ');
                  Twrite(RtF77,'Fortran77 ');
                  Twrite(RtPascal,'Pascal ');
                  Twrite(RtM2,'Modula-2');
                  WriteLn |
          MSdos, CPM :
                  IF System = MSdos THEN
                    WriteString('MSdos')
                  ELSE
                    WriteString('CP/M')
                  END;
                  WriteString(' Specialist'); WriteLn;
                  WriteString('Skills: ');
                  Twrite(CpmPascal,'Pascal ');
                  Twrite(DBii,'Dbase-II ');
                  Twrite(CpmC,'C');
                  WriteLn
          END (* case *)
        END (* with *)
      END WriteConsult;
```

Short circuit evaluation of BOOLEAN expressions applies to
RECORD variants. Notice that we were careful in WriteConsult to
check the value of tag fields before using the values of the variant

fields. It is acceptable to write

```
IF (System = MSdos) AND CpmPascal THEN ...
```

but it is *very* poor practice to write

```
IF CpmPascal AND (System = MSDOS)
```

Variant RECORDS save space because the compiler does not have to set aside separate storage for the variant parts. The compiler only needs to set aside enough space for the *largest* variant part. This is a trivial factor in a program with only a few copies of the RECORD, but it is a major consideration in a program with thousands of copies of a RECORD.

You should not assume anything about how the compiler implements the variant parts of a RECORD. In some languages it is possible to use variant RECORDS as a primitive TYPE transfer function. Don't do this in Modula–2 — instead use the built in TYPE transfer functions. The Modula–2 language specification has nothing to say about how a compiler implements data storage and programs that rely on the quirks of particular compilers are bad practice.

The FieldList syntax diagram (Diagram 13.1) shows the tag identifier as an optional part. Normally tag fields are explicitly named, but occasionally a tag field is nameless. This is called a *free variant*. Free variants were often used in Pascal as a machine dependent TYPE transfer system, but better methods of TYPE transfer are available in Modula–2.

## 13.4. Example — Breadth First Maze Search

In Section 11.2 we first presented the problem of writing a program to solve maze puzzles. The solution in that chapter was recursive. It implemented a *depth first* search strategy. Each path was followed to its conclusion. If the path didn't lead to the maze exit another path was attempted.

In a *breadth first* approach all paths are followed simultaneously, one step at a time. This avoids recursion, but it imposes an additional bookkeeping burden on the programmer. RECORDS are the ideal data structure for this additional burden. In the previous version the maze was represented as a two dimensional ARRAY of *enumerations*. Here we represent the maze as a two dimensional ARRAY OF RECORDS.

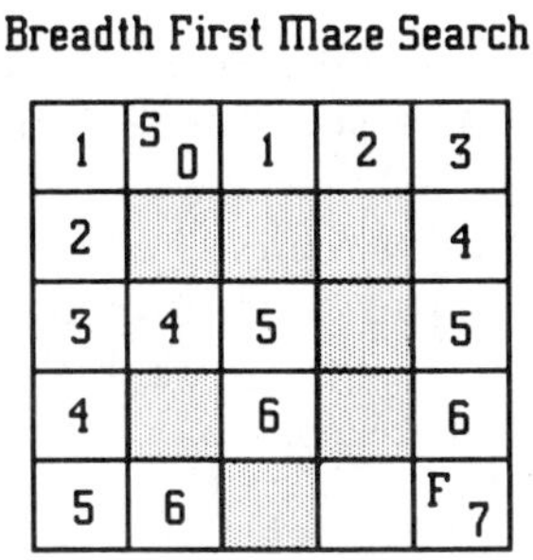

**Breadth First Maze Search**

Figure 13.4. Each cycle in a breadth first search pushes the path one step forward everywhere. In this diagram the numbers in each cell indicate the cycle during which they are first encountered.

The strategy for our breadth first search is to look at the neighbors of the entrance cell. All accessible neighbors (White) are treated as a group. If any of the members of this group are the exit cell then the maze is solved. Otherwise the accessible neighbors of the original group are made the new group, and the process is repeated. Eventually the maze is solved, or the new group is empty because there is no solution.

The MazeElement RECORD is the major record-keeping datum in this version of the maze solver.

```
                                         (* Example 13.12 *)
    TYPE
        Color = (White, Black, Visited, Path);

    TYPE
        Loc =
            RECORD
                row, col : INTEGER
            END;

    TYPE
        MazeElement =
            RECORD
                parent : Loc;
                data : Color;
                this, next : BOOLEAN
            END;

    VAR
        maze : ARRAY [0..6],[0..6] OF MazeElement;
```

We need to keep track of how we arrived at each cell using the
parent RECORD element so that we can show the path at the end
of a successful search. Then when we find the exit we can retrace
the path by using the parent links. The following element of the
RECORD is the data; it the same interpretation as the previous
maze program. White is a route through the maze, Black is a wall,
Visited is no longer of interest, and Path indicates a part of the
route to the exit.

The MazeElement RECORD keeps track of the members of the
current group and the next group (the accessible neighbors of the
current group) in the BOOLEAN variables this and next. Each
search of the neighbors of the members of the this group finds
accessible cells which are added to the next group.

The pseudo code for the breadth first maze search program is

> Set this to true for the entrance cell
> Set data to Visited for the entrance cell
> While the current group has some members
>   Search the maze for accessible neighbors
>      of the current group
>   Move next group into this group
>   Check each new member to see if it is the exit

The implementation of this algorithm is straightforward. The only
complication concerns deciding whether the current group has any
members. Rather than search through the entire maze once more,
we set a flag variable named more to TRUE while searching for
neighbors each time one is found.

Searching for accessible neighbors has been isolated into a PRO-
CEDURE named neighbors. Neighbors merely tries the four surrounding cells of the given cell. In the previous version of this program we used a maze grid that was larger than the working grid so
that we didn't need to worry about border problems. The same
trick is used in this program so that the neighbor PROCEDURE
isn't cluttered by edge sensing details.

The heart of the neighbors PROCEDURE is a nested PROCEDURE
called try that sees if a particular cell is White. If it is, the cell is
marked as visited, its parent is recorded, and it is logged into
the next group. The neighbors and try PROCEDURES don't war-
rant pseudo code descriptions.

The successful path is rediscovered by retracing, starting at the
exit and following the chain of parents. This is performed by a
PROCEDURE named retrace. Retrace is an infinite loop that

marks the current cell as path, and then moves to the parent cell. The loop ends when a cell is reached whose parents are noted as (0,0), which is the initialization value. This should be the entrance!

What follows is the breadth first solution of a five by five maze. In the interest of brevity printmaze and initmaze are omitted. Both of these would be similar to the versions in the previous version of this program. (Initmaze must set the parents row and column to zero for all cells so that retrace works correctly.)

(* Example 13.13 *)

```
MODULE MazeBreadth;
FROM InOut IMPORT WriteString, WriteCard, WriteLn;

TYPE
    Color = (White, Black, Visited, Path);

    Loc =
        RECORD
            row, col : INTEGER
        END;

    MazeElement =
        RECORD
            parent : Loc;
            data : Color;
            this, next : BOOLEAN
        END;

VAR
    maze : ARRAY [0..6],[0..6] OF MazeElement;
    dest : Loc; (* the exit place *)

PROCEDURE InitMaze;
BEGIN (* For the Reader *)
END InitMaze;

PROCEDURE PrintMaze;
BEGIN (* For the Reader *)
END PrintMaze;

PROCEDURE retrace;
VAR
    row, col : INTEGER;
```

```
      temp : Loc;
   BEGIN
      row := dest.row; col := dest.col;
      LOOP
         WITH maze[row,col] DO
            data:=Path;
            IF (parent.row=0) AND (parent.col=0) THEN
               RETURN
            END;
            temp:=parent
         END;
         row:=temp.row;
         col:=temp.col
      END
   END retrace;


   PROCEDURE neighbors
                  (r, c : INTEGER; VAR more : BOOLEAN);

   PROCEDURE try(row, col : INTEGER); (* nested *)
   BEGIN
      WITH maze[row,col] DO
         IF data = White THEN
            data := Visited;
            next := TRUE;
            parent.row := r;
            parent.col := c;
            more := TRUE
         END (* IF *)
      END (* WITH *)
   END try; (* PROCEDURE *)

   BEGIN (* neighbors *)
      try(r-1,c);
      try(r+1,c);
      try(r,c-1);
      try(r,c+1);
   END neighbors;

   PROCEDURE RunMaze(r,c : INTEGER) : BOOLEAN;
   VAR
      more : BOOLEAN;
      row, col : INTEGER;
   BEGIN
```

```
         maze[r,c].this := TRUE;
         maze[r,c].data := Visited;
         more := TRUE;
         WHILE more DO
            more := FALSE;
            (* search through maze for next level *)
            FOR row := 1 TO 5 DO
               FOR col := 1 TO 5 DO
                  IF maze[row,col].this THEN
                     neighbors(row,col,more);
                  END (* IF *)
               END (* FOR *)
            END; (* FOR *)
            (* move next into this and check for done *)
            FOR row := 1 TO 5 DO
               FOR col := 1 TO 5 DO
                  WITH maze[row,col] DO
                     this := next;
                     IF next AND (row = dest.row) AND
                           (col = dest.col) THEN
                        RETURN TRUE
                     END; (* IF *)
                     next := FALSE
                  END (* WITH *)
               END (* FOR *)
            END (* FOR *)
         END; (* WHILE *)
         RETURN FALSE
      END RunMaze;

BEGIN
   InitMaze;
   WriteString("Input Maze: "); WriteLn;
   PrintMaze;
   IF RunMaze(1,1) THEN
      retrace;
      WriteString("Maze Solution:"); WriteLn;
      PrintMaze
   ELSE
      WriteString("Solution not found."); WriteLn
   END
END MazeBreadth.
```

**Exercise 13.9.** Write `InitMaze` for this breadth first maze search.

□

**Exercise 13.10.** Write `PrintMaze` for this version of the maze search.

□

**Exercise 13.11.** What is the advantage of nesting the `try` PRO-CEDURE inside the `neighbors` PROCEDURE?

□

**Exercise 13.12.** Rewrite the `neighbors` PROCEDURE so that it doesn't call a PROCEDURE to examine each of the neighboring cells.

□

**Exercise 13.13.** It isn't necessary to keep track of parent and group information for *every* cell in the maze. Note that the black cells never have parents. Also there is a limit to the number of cells in a group, but in our scheme we have enough storage to mark every cell in the maze as being in a group. Would the solution be simplified if the group and parent information were separated from the maze ARRAY? How much storage would be saved? Is this a good idea for a small maze like the one we solved? Would it be a good optimization for a large maze?

□

**Exercise 13.14.** Explain the advantage, if any, of making a coordinate (`row`, `column`) into a RECORD in this program.

□

**Exercise 13.15.** Would the breadth first version of the maze program work if the entrance cell is in the interior of the maze (i.e. not on the border)? Would the depth first maze solver work if the entrance cell is in the interior?

□

# Chapter 14

# Dynamic Data

In many programs it is possible to decide, as the program is being designed, how many variables of each TYPE are needed. In these programs each variable is given a name at the outset and it can be referred to as needed using its name. Named variables are the rule in Modula–2 and many programmers never need Modula–2's dynamic (anonymous) data facilities.

However it is often impossible or impractical to decide at the outset exactly what data structures are needed. The solution is to use *dynamic data allocation*. Dynamic data allocation creats a datum (a *dynamic data structure*) during the course of execution of a program. Dynamic data structures are managed in Modula–2 using POINTERS. The PROCEDURE named ALLOCATE is used to create dynamic data, the DEALLOCATE PROCEDURE is used to discard dynamic data structures. Both of these PROCEDURES must be imported from a global MODULE named Storage and they are discussed in Section 14.2.

Dynamic data allocation is necessary partly because sometimes it is impossible to tell *how many* of each variable are required. For example it may be impossible to decide how many elements are needed in an ARRAY. However the major use of dynamic data allocation is to create *arbitrary data structures*, such as circular lists, trees, and graphs. It would be clumsy to include all these data structures in Modula-2.

Modula-2 has only three built-in *structured* data TYPES: ARRAYS, SETS, and RECORDS. Other data structures can be created using Modula-2's facilities for dynamic data. The major new tool for using dynamic data is the POINTER. A POINTER is a variable that points to a dynamically allocated variable. (Sometimes in systems programming POINTERS are used more flexibly.) A POINTER can be used to access the variable to which it points.

The value of a POINTER variable is established whenever dynamic data is created (using the ALLOCATE PROCEDURE). It is possible to assign one POINTER to another or to compare POINTERS but arithmetic operations on POINTERS are prohibited. The special value NIL is compatible with all POINTER TYPES and may be assigned to a POINTER to indicate that the POINTER doesn't point to anything.

Some people understand POINTERS by thinking about how POINTERS are *implemented*. A POINTER variable actually contains the main storage (memory) address of whatever it points to. In low level or assembly language programming the concept of the *address* of a variable is common. However it is usually easier to refer to variables by name, so high level languages such as Modula-2 try to disguise the addresses of items. When a variable is created dynamically it doesn't have a name — our only reference is its address. Thus POINTERS are necessary for dynamic data.

## 14.1. POINTERS

A simple POINTER declaration is

```
                                        (* Example 14.1 *)
    VAR
        chptr : POINTER TO CHAR;
```

This declaration establishes two things: (1) the variable named chptr is a POINTER TYPE, and (2) it points to a CHAR variable. When the program containing chptr starts to execute, chptr is uninitialized. An uninitialized POINTER is a loaded gun — it may be pointing randomly at your most sensitive data. It is the programmer's responsibility to initialize chptr, typically by allocating a CHAR variable, before it is used. Using an uninitialized POINTER is a baffling and common novice programming error.

In Modula-2 POINTER TYPES are usually used for creating *dynamic* data structures. The previous declaration creates a mundane data structure — there is either a CHAR to which chptr points or there isn't. Dynamic data structures are usually based around RECORDS. A more practical (likely) POINTER declaration is

(* Example 14.2 *)

```
VAR
    ListHead : POINTER TO ListElement;
```

For a linked list of INTEGERS, the ListElement TYPE might be defined as

(* Example 14.3 *)

```
TYPE
    ListPtr = POINTER TO ListElement;

    ListElement =
        RECORD
            Next : ListPtr;
            Value : INTEGER
        END; (* RECORD *)
```

The Next element of the RECORD points to the next element in the list and the Value element of the RECORD contains the numeric information. A linear list as exemplified by this declaration is the simplest useful data structure that can be constructed with POINTERS.

As we saw in Example 14.1, POINTER TYPES are declared by mentioning the TYPE to which a POINTER points.

**PointerType**

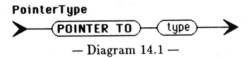

— Diagram 14.1 —

Modula–2 declarations must usually be ordered so that something referenced in one declaration is itself defined in an *earlier* declaration. This rule is relaxed for POINTERS — the TYPE to which a POINTER points may be defined in a declaration that comes after the POINTER declaration. Thus it is acceptable for the ListPtr declaration to preceed the ListElement declaration.

*Opaque* export is limited to subranges and POINTERS. Because of the limitations of subranges, most opaque export is of POINTERS. Opaque export is often used when a MODULE wants to hide the details of a RECORD. This is accomplished by opaquely exporting a POINTER to the given RECORD, and then exporting PROCEDURES to mediate between the clients POINTERS and the locally managed

RECORDS.

In Modula–2 every ordinary variable has a certain TYPE. The TYPE of a variable denotes what operations are allowed and what other variables are compatible. In Modula–2 every POINTER variable is associated with the TYPE of the variable to which it points. Just as a CHAR is fundamentally incompatible with an INTEGER, a POINTER TO CHAR is fundamentally incompatible with a POINTER TO INTEGER. In various other languages POINTERS aren't associated with specific variable TYPES and represent a major relaxation of usage checking.

Even though Modula–2's strict TYPE checking applies to POINTERS, they do embody difficult and error–prone programming. This is not to say that POINTERS represent bad style or that they should be avoided. Rather it is a frank admission that logical programming errors involving POINTERS are more insidious than most other forms of logical errors. POINTERS are to data what goto's are to code. The difference is that control structures remove the need to use goto's, whereas POINTERS remain a necessary tool.

Dynamic data structures are implemented in Modula–2 using POINTERS. Thus programs that use dynamic data structures must use POINTERS. Obviously POINTERS should not be (and in practice in Modula–2 never are) used in more mundane circumstances. The danger of POINTERS is reduced because most programmers sophisticated enough to use dynamic data structures are capable enough to handle POINTERS.

Some languages allow POINTERS to point towards any data item. This is not encouraged in Modula–2. In Modula–2, as in Pascal, ordinary POINTERS only point to dynamically allocated data items. POINTERS are not intended as a general facility — they are for dynamic data structures. In Modula–2 it is possible to use several built–in systems programming facilities to circumvent the ordinary rules (See Chapter 16). These mechanisms are not (and should not be) widely used.

Modula–2 allows only three POINTER operations: *assignment, equality comparison*, and *dereferencing*. Note that arithmetic and general comparisons are not allowed because they aren't needed for managing dynamic data structures. In languages that use POINTERS more generally there is a richer set of POINTER operations. Modula–2's spartan collection of POINTER operations reflects their circumscribed usage in Modula–2.

## 14.1.1. POINTER Assignment

A POINTER either points to something, or it doesn't. In Modula–2 a special value named NIL is reserved to mean that a POINTER doesn't actually point at anything. For example the assignment

(* Example 14.4 *)

```
ListHead := NIL
```

indicates that ListHead doesn't point to anything. By implication this means there aren't any elements in the list.

In general POINTERS are only compatible with other POINTERS of the same TYPE. However the value NIL is compatible with all POINTER TYPES. The value NIL usually is used to mark the terminus of a dynamic data structure although other techniques are available. For example in the linear list described above (Example 14.3) the Next element of the final ListElement RECORD would be set to NIL.

In most Modula–2 assignment statements the right hand side can be a complicated expression involving arithmetic and BOOLEAN operations. However a POINTER assignment can only transfer the value in one POINTER to another. Expressions (arithmetic or logical operations) are not allowed on the right hand side. (See Section 16.3 for a relaxation of this rule that applies to systems programming.)

If nextrec and finalrec are both POINTERS to the same TYPE of object

(* Example 14.5 *)

```
VAR
    nextrec, finalrec : POINTER TO SomeListElem;
```

one can make the assignment

(* Example 14.6 *)

```
nextrec := finalrec
```

This assignment means that the POINTER variable nextrec is made to point towards the same object as finalrec. The variable that they point to is not affected in any way by this assignment.

Once the general idea of POINTERS begins to become clear, the next hurdle is understanding the meaning of the assignment given directly above. It helps to remember that the "value" of a pointer determines what it points to, the "pointed to" item has its own value.

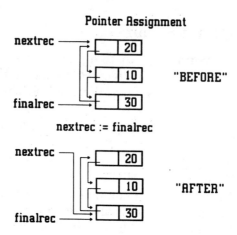

Figure 14.1. Assigning one pointer to another makes them point at the same object. The "pointed to" objects are not altered.

## 14.1.2. Dereferencing

*Dereferencing* means accessing the thing to which a pointer is pointing. Dereferencing a POINTER is a two step process: first the value of the POINTER itself is used to locate the "pointed to" item, and then the "pointed to" item is accessed.

The Modula–2 dereferencing operator is the caret (^). Let's first look at a simple example of using the dereferencing operator. Suppose that nextrec and finalrec are both POINTERS to the same TYPE of variable. We saw above how we could make them point to the same variable. However let's suppose in this example that they are pointing to different variables. We can assign the value of the variable pointed to by nextrec to the variable pointed to by finalrec using the following assignment.

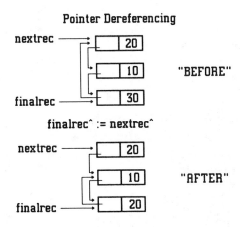

Figure 14.2. Pointer dereferencing means accessing whatever the pointer points at. In this diagram, the object that finalrec points at is assigned the value of the object that nextrec points at.

(* Example 14.7 *)

```
finalrec^ := nextrec^
```

After this assignment finalrec and nextrec continue to point to different variables. However as a result of the assignment statement those two variables have the same value.

We noted before that POINTERS often point to RECORDS. Let's suppose that finalrec and nextrec are POINTERS to ListElement RECORDS (from Example 14.3). The notation

(* Example 14.8 *)

```
finalrec^
```

denotes the entire RECORD that finalrec points to. Individual elements of a RECORD can also be selected.

(* Example 14.9 *)

```
finalrec^.Next := NIL;
finalrec^.Value := 330
```

The WITH statement is also applicable to POINTER dereferencing. The two assignments from immediately above can be expressed as

```
                                    (* Example 14.10 *)
WITH finalrec^ DO
    Next := NIL;
    Value := 330
END
```

Remember that when you use the WITH statement with ARRAYS OF RECORDS you must be careful not to change the ARRAY index in the body of the WITH statement. Similarly it would be disastrous to point finalrec to a different variable inside the body of the WITH statement.

## 14.1.3. POINTER Comparison

There are only two legal POINTER comparisons in Modula–2: *equality* and *inequality*. POINTERS are equal if they point to the same thing. POINTERS that are inequal are pointing to different places. It is acceptable to compare a POINTER with the POINTER constant NIL to see if it is actually pointing to something. As in all comparisons, the result is a BOOLEAN.

Short circuit evaluation of BOOLEAN expressions is important with POINTERS. For example the statement

```
                                     (* Example 14.11 *)
    IF (ListHead <> NIL) AND (ListHead^.Value = 0) THEN ...
```

works perfectly even if ListHead has the special value NIL. It is a disaster to write

```
                                     (* Example 14.12 *)
    IF (ListHead^.Value = 0) AND (ListHead <> NIL) THEN ...
```

because if ListHead is NIL then it isn't actually pointing to something. The expression ListHead^.Value has no meaning if ListHead isn't pointing to something.

## 14.2. ALLOCATE and DEALLOCATE

In most systems it is possible to set aside a region of memory that is allocated as necessary during a program's execution. In Modula–2 this region is typically managed by the routines in a global MODULE named Storage. Storage must interact with the operating environment of the program to determine the size and location of the free memory area, and it must interact with the routines in the program that need to use portions of the free memory. Storage contains three routines that are visible externally: ALLOCATE, DEALLOCATE, and Available.

(* Example 14.13 *)

```
DEFINITION MODULE Storage;

FROM SYSTEM IMPORT ADDRESS;

PROCEDURE ALLOCATE
            (VAR a : ADDRESS; size : CARDINAL);

PROCEDURE DEALLOCATE
            (VAR a : ADDRESS; size : CARDINAL);

PROCEDURE Available (size : CARDINAL) : BOOLEAN;

END Storage.
```

Let's suppose that we have a linked list of ListElement RECORDS. There is a POINTER to the first RECORD in the list. The Next field of the first RECORD points to the following RECORD, and so on. The Next element of the last RECORD is NIL. In addition to the POINTER indicating the head of the list, let's suppose that a POINTER named finalrec is pointing to the last ListElement RECORD in the list. The following program fragment will add a new ListElement RECORD to the end of the list, update the finalrec POINTER, and set the next field of the new (final) RECORD to NIL.

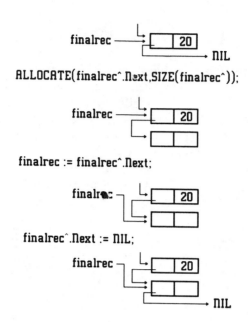

Figure 14.3. It takes three steps to place an object onto the end of a list. The steps must occur in the given order.

```
                                            (* Example 14.14 *)
ALLOCATE(finalrec^.Next, SIZE(finalrec^));
finalrec := finalrec^.Next;
finalrec^.Next := NIL
```

The DEALLOCATE PROCEDURE releases the storage occupied by a dynamically allocated variable. Naturally great havoc will ensue if the POINTER passed to DEALLOCATE doesn't point to a dynamically allocated variable of the expected TYPE. DEALLOCATE takes the same parameters as ALLOCATE. If the given POINTER actually points at a dynamic variable of the given TYPE, DEALLOCATE is safe. You should be extremely cautious if you are using any of Modula–2's TYPE relaxation or system programming facilities in conjunction with POINTERS.

The Available routine from Storage returns the value TRUE if a region of the requested size is available. It should be called before ALLOCATE if you want your program to handle the problem of running out of memory.

In older implementations of Modula–2 there are built in PROCEDURES called NEW and DISPOSE that provide access to the facilities of the Storage MODULE. If you use NEW and DISPOSE you must manually import ALLOCATE and DEALLOCATE. The purpose of NEW and DISPOSE is to intercept your storage management requests and translate them into calls to ALLOCATE and DEALLOCATE, thus they must be visible.

As you might expect, the task of storage management is system dependent and the ALLOCATE and DEALLOCATE PROCEDURES are provided with each system to handle the low level quirks in managing free memory. Modula-2 attempts to segregate system dependent operations into external MODULES. Removing environmental features from the compiler makes Modula-2 easier to implement and easier to adapt to various systems.

**Exercise 14.1.** Write a program that reads in a series of numbers and stores them in a linear list of ListElement RECORDS (from Example 14.3).
□

**Exercise 14.2.** Modify the program produced in Exercise 1 to sort and print the complete list of numbers. Use the insertion sort algorithm from Exercise 5.7 of Section 5.3. Is it easier to exchange the ListElements, exchange only the values, or rearrange the POINTERS (relink the list) to swap the two elements? When would it be easier to relink the list than exchange the values?
□

**Exercise 14.3.** Modify the LLBuffers global MODULE (Example 13.8) so that the Cbuf buffers are allocated dynamically. DiscardBuf should continue to place free buffers back on the free list. GetBuf should get a buffer from the free list if possible and dynamically allocate a buffer when necessary. Naturally the buffer indices used throughout LLBuffers will have to be changed to POINTERS. Discuss the advantages and disadvantages of dynamically allocating the Cbuf buffers.
□

**Exercise 14.4.** Modify LLBuf (Example 13.8) so that it is more flexible. Instead of using an ARRAY of Cbuf RECORDS you should maintain linked lists of dynamically allocated Cbuf RECORDS. The LINK that indicates one particular buffer element should be changed from a subrange TYPE to a POINTER TYPE. Note that the opaque export of LINK from the DEFINITION MODULE doesn't need to be changed. The IMPLEMENTATION MODULE will require simple changes throughout to replace ARRAY indexing with POINTER indirection. The major change will be in the private routines GetBuf and DiscardBuf.

The major design decision is whether to continue to manage a free list. One alternative is to continue to use a free list. ALLOCATE will only be called when a buffer is needed and the free list is empty. DEALLOCATE will never be called, all emptied buffers will be placed on the free list. The second strategy is to return all emptied buffers to the Storage MODULE. This avoids the task of managing the free list in the LLBuf MODULE. If calls to ALLOCATE and DEALLOCATE are time consuming, the first approach is probably better. The second approach is simpler and should probably be used if accessing Storage has a low overhead.
□

**Exercise 14.5.** Use a linked list data structure to represent packed BOOLEANS. Write a global MODULE to implement this service. The client should be able to request a packed BOOLEAN ARRAY of arbitrary length, and then the client should be able to read or write any BOOLEAN in the ARRAY. Opaque TYPE export is probably best since the actual linked list of BOOLEANS should be hidden from the client.
□

# 14.3. Example — Binary Trees

One useful data structure is the *tree*. Each node in a tree has POINTERS to nodes that are lower in the tree. Each node in a *binary tree* has exactly *two* POINTERS to other nodes. Often these two POINTERS are called the left POINTER and the right POINTER.

One common use of a binary tree is storage of *ordered* information. For any given node in an *ordered* binary tree, all nodes to the left have "smaller" values and all nodes to the right contain "larger" values. For any given body of information, suitable meanings must be created for "smaller" and "larger." Numeric data can be ordered by its value, text can be ordered alphabetically, complex data sets can be ordered by complex criteria.

There are two advantages to an ordered binary tree.
- It is easy to search because it is ordered. From each node it is possible to decide whether the target lies in the left or the right subtree. Thus an optimal search is easy.
- It is easy to insert new nodes because it is a tree. Inserting new nodes requires updating of just three links.

Binary trees are only easy to sort if they are balanced, meaning that the left and right subtrees of the upper nodes have roughly the same number of elements. The principal disadvantage of a binary tree is the difficulty of converting an unbalanced tree into a balanced one.

The example in this section tackles the problem of reading in a list of words, and then printing the sorted list of words with a count of their occurrences. Let's first think about possible solutions that don't use dynamic data structures.

We could store the words in an ARRAY as we read them in, then sort the ARRAY and print the results. One problem is duplicates. Each time we read in a word we have to search through the entire list to see if it is a duplicate. As you know searching a large ARRAY is time consuming. If we don't search each time we are going to waste enormous amounts of storage because in a typical document there are many repetitions and relatively few unique words. Another problem with using an ARRAY is that we don't know in advance how large an ARRAY will be required.

Using an ordered binary tree solves this dilemma. Because the tree is always sorted it is easy to search for duplicates each time a word is read in. Keeping the tree sorted means that printing the results is easy — no final sort is necessary. Finally since the tree is allo-cated dynamically we don't need to determine its size in advance.

Let's first examine the data structure used to implement this binary tree.

( * Example 14.15 * )

```
TYPE
   Word = ARRAY [0..9] OF CHAR;

   NodePtr = POINTER TO node;

   node =
      RECORD
         left, right : NodePtr;
         wrd : Word;
         cnt : CARDINAL
      END;
```

Each node of the tree is a RECORD that contains storage for a Word (an ARRAY of ten characters), POINTERS to the left and right sub nodes, and a count of the number of times the word has been en-countered. One of these nodes is allocated each time a unique word is encountered.

First let's examine the FillTree PROCEDURE. This one is easy. All we need to do is read a word from the input. If we don't en-

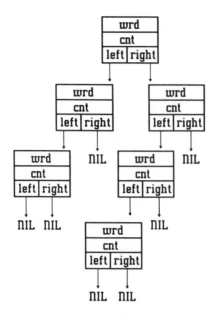

Figure 14.4. A binary tree.

counter end of file we call the Insert PROCEDURE to put the word
into the tree. When end of file occurs we are done.

The logic for inserting a word into the tree is a little harder.
FillTree directs the Insert PROCEDURE to start its search at the
root node. If the root node doesn't contain the word, Insert calls
itself (recursion) to examine either the left half of the tree or the
right half. Whenever Insert reaches the end of a branch without
encountering the search word, a new node must be allocated for
the word. The recursion terminates when the word is encountered
or when the end of a branch is encountered. Here is the pseudo
code for the recursive Insert PROCEDURE:

> If the node POINTER is NIL
>> Allocate a new node
>> Install the word in the node and set the reference count to one
> Otherwise if the word is stored in the current node Then
>> Add one to the reference count
> Otherwise search the appropriate (left or right) subtree

Insert uses the StrCmp PROCEDURE (from Strings, Example
8.1) to compare two character strings. StrCmp returns an INTEGER
value indicating whether the strings are equal, the first string is
less than the second, or the first is greater than the second.

Printing the tree is similar to searching the tree. The basic strategy is this; for any given node first print the left subtree, then print the data in the node itself, and then print the right subtree. Starting at the root node and following this strategy prints the entire tree. Using recursion leads to a surprisingly simple routine. A pseudo code version isn't necessary to understand the PrintTree PROCEDURE.

The SortCountWords program imports StrCmp from Strings and ALLOCATE from the STORAGE MODULE along with several familiar PROCEDURES from InOut.

```
                                        (* Example 14.16 *)
MODULE SortCountWords;
(*
 * Read in a text file, store it in a sorted binary
 *    tree, then write out the sorted list of words
 *    with a count of the number of times each word
 *    occurred in the text.
 *)
FROM Strings IMPORT StrCmp;
FROM InOut IMPORT WriteLn, WriteCard,
     ReadString, WriteString;
FROM Storage IMPORT ALLOCATE;

TYPE
    Word = ARRAY [0..9] OF CHAR;

    NodePtr = POINTER TO node;

    node =
       RECORD
          left, right : NodePtr;
          wrd : Word;
          cnt : CARDINAL
       END;

VAR
    root : NodePtr;

PROCEDURE FillTree;
VAR
    wrd : Word;
BEGIN
    root := NIL;
```

```
    LOOP
       ReadString(wrd);
       IF wrd[0] = 0C THEN EXIT END;
       Insert(wrd,root);
    END (* LOOP *)
END FillTree;

PROCEDURE Insert
       ( value : Word; VAR node : NodePtr );
BEGIN
   IF node = NIL THEN
       (* end of branch, create node *)
       NEW(node);
       WITH node^ DO
             left := NIL; right := NIL;
             cnt := 1; wrd := value
       END (* WITH *)
   ELSE WITH node^ DO (* search further *)
       CASE StrCmp(value,wrd) OF
             +1 : Insert(value,right) |
             -1 : Insert(value,left) |
              0 : INC(cnt)
       END (* CASE *) END (* WITH *)
   END (* IF *)
END Insert;

PROCEDURE PrintTree(node : NodePtr);
BEGIN
   IF node # NIL THEN
      WITH node^ DO
        PrintTree(left);
        WriteCard(cnt,4); WriteString("  ");
        WriteString(wrd); WriteLn;
        PrintTree(right)
      END (* WITH *)
   END (* IF *)
END PrintTree;

BEGIN (* program *)
   FillTree;
   PrintTree(root)
END SortCountWords.
```

**Exercise 14.6.** Rewrite the Insert routine from SortCount-

Words so that it is not recursive. Which implementation is more efficient?

□

**Exercise 14.7.** Rewrite the PrintTree routine from SortCountWords so that it avoids recursion. Hint: the major problem is that you have to backtrack to print the tree. Backtracking is handled automatically in a recursive version whereas you have to backtrack explicitly in a non–recursive version. The solution to this problem will be easier if you modify the ListElement RECORD so that each node contains a POINTER back to its parent node as well as POINTERS to its subtrees.

□

**Exercise 14.8.** Each activation of Insert consumes a certain amount of memory as space is set aside for Insert's parameters and local variables. By reducing the number of parameters, Insert can be made more space efficient and its maximum depth of recursion can be increased. Which of Insert's two parameters could be a global variable? Rewrite Insert accordingly.

□

**Exercise 14.9.** Write a PROCEDURE that counts the number of nodes in a left subtree and the number in a right subtree. A binary tree is balanced if there are the same number of nodes in the root's left subtree as in its right subtree.

□

**Exercise 14.10.** What are the advantages of keeping a binary tree approximately balanced? Hint: think about the depth of recursion for subroutines such as Insert? What is the worst case input for a program such as SortCountWords?

□

**Exercise 14.11.** Write a PROCEDURE to find the node that is in the "middle" of the tree, i.e. the node whose word is in the middle of the sorted list.

□

# Chapter 15

# Procedure Variables

In the previous chapter we introduced the idea of a POINTER variable that could be used to access some other variable. In this chapter we introduce a similar idea — the concept of a procedure variable that can be used to *invoke* a PROCEDURE.

Normally we invoke a PROCEDURE by using its name. For example searching an ARRAY for a value is a common operation. If the ARRAY is ordered (sorted) we should use the efficient *binary* search algorithm.

```
                                        (* Example 15.1 *)
  index := bsearch(x,t)
```

The variable named x is assumed to be an ARRAY, t is assumed to be compatible with the elements of x, and bsearch is a PROCEDURE that performs a binary search. The ARRAY indice of t is returned and placed in the CARDINAL variable named index. However suppose that the ARRAY is not ordered. Now we are forced to use the slower *linear* search.

```
                                        (* Example 15.2 *)
  index := lsearch(x,t)
```

The variables x and t have the same meaning as before, and lsearch obviously performs a linear search. In both of these examples we are invoking a PROCEDURE by using its name.

It is also possible to invoke one of the search PROCEDURES using a procedure variable. The procedure variable can indicate either a linear search or a binary search PROCEDURE. The declaration

(* Example 15.3 *)

```
VAR
    srch : PROCEDURE(ARRAY OF Item, Item) : CARDINAL;
```

introduces a procedure variable named srch. It can attain as its *value* any PROCEDURE with the following characteristics: its first parameter is an ARRAY OF Item, its second parameter is an Item, and it returns a CARDINAL value. Notice that the procedure *variable* declaration indicates only the TYPES of the parameters unlike a PROCEDURE declaration, which also supplies the names for the parameters.

We can make the srch procedure variable indicate the bsearch PROCEDURE with the following assignment statement.

(* Example 15.4 *)

```
srch := bsearch
```

Notice that bsearch followed by a parameter list (Example 15.1) indicates a call of bsearch whereas bsearch without the parameter list (Example 15.4) is used in the assignment of bsearch to the srch procedure variable.

Similarly srch can indicate the lsearch PROCEDURE with the assignment

(* Example 15.5 *)

```
srch := lsearch
```

In either case, once one or the other has been established a search can be performed using the variable srch to invoke the appropriate PROCEDURE.

(* Example 15.6 *)

```
index := srch(x,t)
```

It is important to distinguish between a procedure variable, such as srch, and an actual PROCEDURE such as lsearch. Lsearch was created by writing a series of statements and operations; it embodies a particular algorithm, may have bugs, may be inefficient, and so on. Srch is simply a variable that can be used to activate *any* PROCEDURE that has compatible parameters (and result). Srch doesn't embody any algorithm, it isn't "written," it is neither buggy nor correct; in short it is as blameless as any other variable.

The syntax diagram for a ProcedureType is

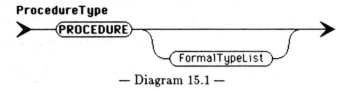

— Diagram 15.1 —

A FormalTypeList is a list of the TYPES of the parameters of a
ProcedureType.

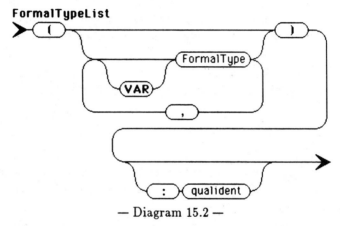

— Diagram 15.2 —

Modula–2 includes a predefined ProcedureType called PROC. A
PROC is a PROCEDURE without parameters or result. It works as if
it were defined by the following declaration.

(* Example 15.7 *)

```
TYPE PROC = PROCEDURE
```

Several restrictions apply to procedure variables:
- You can't assign a *standard* PROCEDURES, e.g. TRUNC or
  ODD, to a procedure variable. This restriction allows the
  compiler to implement the standard PROCEDURES flexibly.
  PROCEDURES supplied in external MODULES, such as the WriteLn PROCEDURE from the InOut MODULE can be assigned to
  procedure variables.
- You can't assign a *local* (nested) PROCEDURE to a procedure
  variable.
- You must never activate a procedure variable without first
  assigning it an actual PROCEDURE.

- PROCEDURE variables can only be assigned a value or activated. They cannot be compared and there are no arithmetic or other operations that apply to them.

There are several similar sounding terms that have very different meanings. Let's pause for a moment to make sure that all of the following are clearly understood.

- A PROCEDURE is a collection of data and statements.
- A PROCEDURE *declaration* is the part of a Modula–2 program where a PROCEDURE is detailed.
- *Activating* a PROCEDURE means making it start to execute.
- A procedure *variable* can be used to activate any PROCEDURE with compatible parameters and result. Procedure variables are to PROCEDURES as POINTERS are to dynamic data.

Procedure variables are commonly used in two situations — as *elements* of RECORDS and as *parameters* for PROCEDURES. Storing procedure variables in RECORDS makes it possible for a data structure to associate operations (PROCEDURES) with particular items. Using procedure variables as PROCEDURE parameters makes it possible to create PROCEDURES that perform standard operations on a variety of data TYPES because the interface to a data TYPE is passed in the procedure variables. This second common use of procedure variables is illustrated in the following section.

## 15.1. Example — The Quicksort

The quicksort is an efficient method for sorting. Its major advantage is that it is much faster than the exchange (insertion) sort that was outlined in Exercise 5.7 of Section 5.3. The problem with all sorting is that the difficulty more than doubles whenever the number of items to be sorted doubles. It is more than twice as hard (meaning it takes more than twice as long) to sort 200 items than it is to sort 100 items.

The key idea of the quicksort is that it quickly partitions the problem into two smaller problems, then into four even smaller problems, and so on until the sort is complete. The advantages of the quicksort recommend it whenever there are more than a few tens of items to be sorted.

The quicksort operates by placing an element into its final position. For any given item, its final position is such that all the items below it are less than it and all the items above it are greater. The quicksort moves an element into its final position, thus partitioning the data into two pieces, a lower piece and an upper piece. Then quicksort calls itself to sort these two pieces. Here is the first cut pseudo code for quicksort. Note that x is the list to be sorted.

> Place x[0] into its final position
> (This partitions the list into two pieces)
> Sort the bottom part of the list
> Sort the top part of the list

Obviously the hard part of this process is placing an element into its final position in the list. First we need to agree on a few terms. The *homing* element is the list element that is going to be placed into its final home in the list. In the pseudo code given above, x[0] is the homing element. The list is divided into three pieces: the top of the list contains elements greater than the homing element, the bottom of the list contains elements less than or equal to the homing element, and the middle of the list, which has not yet been examined. (Note, the terms top and bottom don't make graphic sense, if you imagine the list drawn from top to bottom of a sheet of paper. However the terms do make sense when you look at the code, and see the comparisons "bottom less than top", etc. Just as in the battle for space in a corporate skyscraper, the bottom is the home of the small fry.) Here is a more detailed pseudo code explanation of the quicksort process:

> Make the homing element the bottom element of the list
> Set top to indicate the top of the list
> Set bottom to zero (the bottom of the list)
> While the middle of the list exists
>     (Note, at this point X[bottom] is the homing element)
>     While X[top] is bigger than X[bottom]
>         Set top to top minus one
>     Swap x[top] with x[bottom]
>     (Note, at this point X[top] is the homing element)
>     While x[bottom] is smaller than x[top]
>         Set bottom to bottom plus one
>     Swap x[bottom] with x[top]
> Sort the bottom part of the list
> Sort the top part of the list

The idea here is that the top and bottom indexes move inexorably towards the middle of the list. Each time top is decreased (or bottom is increased) the new element in the top (bottom) of the list is compared with the homing element. It the new element is too small (too big) it is placed into the other list by swapping. Even–

| The Quicksort on a five element ARRAY | | | | | |
|---|---|---|---|---|---|
| 7 | −3 | 9 | 300 | 0 | Initial |
| 0 | −3 | 9 | 300 | 7 | After first inner WHILE |
| 0 | −3 | 7 | 300 | 9 | After second inner WHILE |
| 0 | −3 | 7 | 300 | 9 | After first inner WHILE |
| 0 | −3 | 7 | 300 | 9 | After second inner WHILE |
| 0 | −3 | 7 | 300 | 9 | Initial, first recursion |
| −3 | 0 | 7 | 300 | 9 | After first inner WHILE |
| −3 | 0 | 7 | 300 | 9 | After second inner WHILE (First recursion terminates) |
| −3 | 0 | 7 | 300 | 9 | Initial, second recursion |
| −3 | 0 | 7 | 9 | 300 | After first inner WHILE |
| −3 | 0 | 7 | 9 | 300 | After second inner WHILE (Second recursion terminates) (Sort terminates) |

Figure 15.1. This figure shows the operation of the Quicksort method on a five element array. The "homing" element in underlined, and the first and last elements are indicated by the carets.

tually the top list meets the bottom list, thereby placing the homing element into its final position.

First let's examine the quicksort algorithm for an ARRAY OF REALS. Once the basic algorithm is working we will turn to procedure variables to *generalize* the solution. We have embedded the PROCEDURE in a short program MODULE to provide a minimal environment for go/nogo testing of the sort.

```
                                            (* Example 15.8 *)
MODULE TestSort;
FROM InOut IMPORT WriteLn;
FROM RealInOut IMPORT WriteReal;

PROCEDURE qsort(VAR x : ARRAY OF REAL;
                        first, last : INTEGER);
VAR
   bot, top : INTEGER;
   temp : REAL;
BEGIN
   bot := first;
   top := last;
   WHILE bot < top DO;
        WHILE (x[bot] <= x[top]) AND (bot<top) DO
           DEC(top)
        END;
        temp := x[top] (* swap *);
        x[top] := x[bot];
        x[bot] := temp;
        WHILE (x[bot] <= x[top]) AND (bot<top) DO
           INC(bot)
        END;
        temp := x[top]; (* swap *)
        x[top] := x[bot];
        x[bot] := temp
   END; (* outer WHILE *)
   IF first<(bot-1) THEN qsort(x,first,bot-1) END;
   IF (bot+1)<last THEN qsort(x,bot+1,last) END;
END qsort;

VAR
   data : ARRAY [0..4] OF REAL;
   i : INTEGER;
BEGIN (* Test qsort *)
   data[0] := -7.; data[1] := -3.; data[2] := 9.;
   data[3] := 300.; data[4] := 0.;
   qsort(data,0,4);
   FOR i := 0 TO 4 DO;
      WriteReal(data[i],4);
   END;
   WriteLn;
END TestSort.
```

We are going to modify this version of the quicksort using procedure variables to make it work with any TYPE of ARRAY, not
just an ARRAY OF REALS. First we must analyze exactly how the
REALS are embedded in this version of the algorithm, and then we
must devise a way to make the algorithm work with other data
TYPES. Examining the code, we find that REALS are mentioned or
manipulated in the following places in the qsort PROCEDURE:

- The qsort PROCEDURE has an ARRAY OF REALS parameter.
- The variable named temp is a REAL.
- The inner WHILE loops both compare two REAL elements of
  the ARRAY.
- The code to swap (exchange) two elements of the ARRAY uses
  REALS in assignment statements.

In order for qsort to work with any TYPE of ARRAY we need a
way to compare two ARRAY elements and we need a way to swap
two ARRAY elements. If both of these facilities are provided via
procedure variables, we can interact with the ARRAY through its
*indices* without ever dealing directly with the *elements* and their
unknown data TYPE. First we need a PROCEDURE to compare two
ARRAY elements. The routine should accept two indices and return a BOOLEAN indicating whether the first element is less than or
equal to the second. The second PROCEDURE must swap two AR-
RAY elements. The routine should accept two indices and then
swap those two elements. Both of these routines are made available to qsort via procedure variables. Since qsort is a useful
PROCEDURE, we will place it into a global MODULE. First here is
the DEFINITION MODULE for qsort.

```
                                        (* Example 15.9 *)
DEFINITION MODULE Qsort;

(*
 * procedure types to compare and swap
 *     array elements
 *)
TYPE
   CompProc = PROCEDURE( INTEGER, INTEGER) : BOOLEAN;
   SwapProc = PROCEDURE( INTEGER, INTEGER);

(*
 * Sort an array using the Quick Sort method.
 * You must supply the array bounds and procedures
 *     to swap and compare array elements.
 * Any array may be sorted, notice the array is not
```

```
*     a parameter.
 *)
PROCEDURE qsort(first, last : INTEGER;
                comp : CompProc; swap : SwapProc);

END Qsort.
```

Now here is the IMPLEMENTATION MODULE for the qsort PROCEDURE.

(* Example 15.10 *)

```
IMPLEMENTATION MODULE Qsort;

PROCEDURE qsort(first, last : INTEGER;
                comp : CompProc; swap : SwapProc);
VAR
   bot,top : INTEGER;

BEGIN
   bot := first;
   top := last;
   WHILE bot < top DO;
        WHILE comp(bot,top) AND (bot<top) DO
           DEC(top)
        END;
        swap(bot,top);
        WHILE comp(bot,top) AND (bot<top) DO
           INC(bot)
        END;
        swap(bot,top);
   END; (* outer WHILE *)
   IF first < (bot-1) THEN
      qsort(first,bot-1,comp,swap)
   END;
   IF (bot+1) < last THEN
      qsort(bot+1,last,comp,swap)
   END;
END qsort;

END Qsort.
```

One interesting result is that qsort becomes easier to read and understand because the busywork is performed in outside PROCEDURES.

Here are PROCEDURE that will compare and swap elements for an
ARRAY OF INTEGERS.  These PROCEDURES would be programmed
in the MODULE that imported the Qsort MODULE and they would
be supplied as parameters to the qsort PROCEDURE.

(* Example 15.11 *)

```
VAR
    x : ARRAY[0..99] OF INTEGER;

PROCEDURE compint(i, j : INTEGER) : BOOLEAN;
BEGIN
    RETURN x[i] <= x[j]
END compint;

PROCEDURE swapint(i, j : INTEGER);
VAR
    t : INTEGER;
BEGIN
    t := x[i]; x[i] := x[j]; x[j] := t
END swapint;
```

Here is a program MODULE that uses the qsort PROCEDURE to sort
an ARRAY OF RECORDS.  The following program first initializes the
RECORDS in the reverse order and then sorts them using qsort.
Notice that we don't have to import the CompProc and SwapProc
TYPES from Qsort.  These would only be needed if qsort were
called using procedure variables as parameters rather than actual
PROCEDURES as parameters.

(* Example 15.12 *)

```
MODULE TestQsortAgain;
FROM InOut IMPORT WriteCard, WriteLn;
FROM Qsort IMPORT qsort;

TYPE Ritem =
        RECORD
            index : CARDINAL;
            cnt : CARDINAL;
            txt : ARRAY [0..20] OF CHAR;
        END;

VAR
    r : ARRAY [0..999] OF Ritem;
    i : CARDINAL;
```

```
PROCEDURE compRitem (u,v : INTEGER) : BOOLEAN;
BEGIN
   (* comparison only depends upon index field *)
   RETURN(r[u].index <= r[v].index)
END compRitem;

PROCEDURE swapRitem (a,b : INTEGER);
VAR
   x : Ritem;
BEGIN
   x := r[a]; r[a] := r[b]; r[b] := x
END swapRitem;

BEGIN (* TestQsortAgain *)
   FOR i := 0 TO 999 DO
      WITH r[i] DO
         index := 999-i;
         cnt := 0;
         txt := ''
      END
   END; (* FOR *)

   qsort(0,999,compRitem,swapRitem);

   FOR i := 0 TO 999 DO
      WriteCard(r[i].index,5);
      IF (i MOD 15) = 14 THEN WriteLn END
   END; (* FOR *)
   WriteLn
END TestQsortAgain.
```

**Exercise 15.1.** Write a version of bsearch (From Section 5.2) that uses procedure variables to make it work with any TYPE of ARRAY.
□

**Exercise 15.2.** Write the compare and swap PROCEDURES for BITSETS, CHARS, and some fixed length ARRAY OF CHARS.
□

**Exercise 15.3.** Rewrite the insertion sort routine (from Example 5.7 of Section 5.3) to use procedure variables.
□

**Exercise 15.4.** How might you use procedure variables in con-junction with the desk calculator program? (Example 4.14 from

Section 4.9)

☐

**Exercise 15.5.** The first version of qsort, Example 15.8, will work with *any* ARRAY OF REALS. It is not bound to any *particular* ARRAY. The second version of qsort, Example 15.10 relies on procedure variable parameters. The two sets of PROCEDURES that are supplied, Example 15.11 are each bound to a *specific* ARRAY. How would you modify this system of PROCEDURES for performing the quicksort so that the compare and swap would be bound to a given ARRAY TYPE rather than bound to a specific ARRAY variable of that TYPE? (Hint: Accessing an individual element binds the compare and swap routines to a specific variable. Could you use another procedure variable to solve the problem?) Write a version of qsort, based on Ex 15.10, that can sort any of several ARRAYS of some TYPE as well as several different TYPES.

☐

# Part IV

# Systems Programming

Most programming is concerned with using a computer to accomplish a given result. For example a program that prints a list of prime numbers is mostly concerned with the algorithm for discovering primes. *Result* oriented programs are often called *applications* programs. In order for applications programs to operate they must be supported by *systems* programs. Systems programs are concerned with the computer itself. Systems programs send commands to the computer's peripheral devices, they manage the file system, and they allocate space and time so that applications programs can execute.

Systems programming is different from applications programming. An applications program creates its own environment and then proceeds from start to finish to accomplish a given result. A systems program exists in the midst of a melee. There are usually several different operations in progress simultaneously and the systems program must manage them concurrently. In addition systems programs must control the computer peripherals. Whereas an applications program is analogous to an airline pilot who is responsible for flying a plane from one city to another, a systems program is more like an air traffic controller who must simultaneously manage several planes converging on a single airport.

Systems programming is only possible with programming languages that support hardware management and concurrency management. Hardware management includes accessing specific addresses on a computer, relaxing TYPE checking so that storage can be allocated and data can be transferred to peripheral devices, handling interrupts, and performing input/output tasks. Concurrency management involves dealing with several simultaneous processes, such as managing interrupts and managing subordinate (user) processes. All these facilities are available in Modula–2.

# Chapter 16

# TYPE Relaxation

There are two purposes for having a given TYPE for every variable. First the TYPE of a variable indicates what operations apply to that variable. This makes variables more expressive. In addition the TYPE of a variable imposes certain restrictions on that variable. Variables can only be used with compatible variables. This makes programs more robust and it eliminates numerous common errors.

Systems programs often need flexible TYPE relaxation rules. For example how do we use streams to send REALS (or RECORDS, or SETS, or POINTERS) to files when streams (as defined in the Streams global MODULE) are always CHAR or WORD oriented?

Modula–2 offers several different forms of TYPE relaxation. To convert items from one TYPE to another Modula–2 allows TYPE names to be used as TYPE transfer functions. Also Modula–2 includes two primitive TYPES, WORD and ADDRESS. These two TYPES enable many otherwise impossible operations. WORD and ADDRESS must be imported from the SYSTEM MODULE, which is the first topic in this chapter.

# 16.1. The SYSTEM MODULE

The SYSTEM MODULE is different from the common global
MODULES that were discussed in Chapter 9. It isn't an ordinary
MODULE that was written by a programmer, rather it is a set of
data TYPES and operations that are treated specially by the compiler.

Even though the SYSTEM MODULE is *not* an ordinary MODULE, you
can imagine that its basic properties are defined by a DEFINITION
MODULE similar to the following.

(* Example 16.1 *)

```
DEFINITION MODULE SYSTEM;

TYPE
   WORD; ADDRESS;

(* Return the Address of any datum *)
PROCEDURE ADR(x : AnyType): ADDRESS;

(* Return the size of a Variable *)
PROCEDURE SIZE(x : AnyType): CARDINAL;

(* Return the size of a TYPE *)
PROCEDURE TSIZE(AnyType): CARDINAL;

END SYSTEM.
```

This is a *minimal* SYSTEM MODULE — most versions of Modula-2
have SYSTEM MODULES that contain additional facilities. By its
nature and design the SYSTEM MODULE is system dependent. You
will have to examine the documentation for your version of
Modula-2 to learn about the capabilities present in your SYSTEM
MODULE.

Here are some facilities that are often present in SYSTEM
MODULES:
  • Many versions of Modula-2 have facilities to support corou-
    tines in their SYSTEM MODULE. Typically the NEWPROCESS
    PROCEDURE is used to create a coroutine and the TRANSFER
    PROCEDURE is used to shift from one coroutine to another.
    Here are typical definitions for NEWPROCESS and TRANSFER.

(* Example 16.2 *)

```
PROCEDURE NEWPROCESS
    (P: PROC; A: ADDRESS; N: CARDINAL; VAR Q: ADDRESS);
```

```
PROCEDURE TRANSFER(VAR P, Q: ADDRESS);
```

The parameters for NEWPROCESS are the following: P identifies the PROCEDURE that is the body of the coroutine, A is the ADDRESS of its workspace, N is the size of its workspace, and Q is the coroutine descriptor that is initialized by the call to NEWPROCESS. The parameters for TRANSFER are the following: P is the coroutine descriptor of the current coroutine and Q is the coroutine descriptor of the coroutine that is activated.

- Many versions of Modula–2 have an additional PROCEDURE (often called IOTRANSFER) to support co–routines that are used to manage *interrupt driven* I/O devices. Here is a typical definition of IOTRANSFER.

(* Example 16.3 *)

```
PROCEDURE IOTRANSFER(P, Q : ADDRESS; vec : CARDINAL);
```

The variable named P stores the state of the interrupt handler, Q identifies the coroutine that is activated by the call to IOTRANSFER, and vec identifies a particular hardware interrupt. When the interrupt occurs, the coroutine that suspended itself by calling IOTRANSFER will be reactivated. See Chapter 18.

- Many versions of Modula–2 have an additional PROCEDURE (often named LISTEN) that can be called within a critical region to enable hardware interrupts temporarily.

(* Example 16.4 *)

```
PROCEDURE LISTEN;
```

- Many versions of Modula–2 have additional PROCEDURES to access Input and Output instructions. For example the Logitech Modula–2 compiler for the IBM PC contains the following PROCEDURES for accessing the machine's I/O address space.

```
                                             (* Example 16.5 *)
PROCEDURE INBYTE(Port : CARDINAL; VAR W : WORD);
PROCEDURE INWORD(Port : CARDINAL; VAR W : WORD);
PROCEDURE OUTBYTE(Port : CARDINAL; W : WORD);
PROCEDURE OUTWORD(Port : CARDINAL; W : WORD);
```

- Many versions of Modula–2 have additional PROCEDURES to
  access operating system services. For example the Logitech
  Modula–2 contains a PROCEDURE called DOSCALL that is used
  to invoke MS–DOS operations. In addition there is a PRO-
  CEDURE that causes a software interrupt so that the routines
  that manage the interrupts can be invoked.

```
                                             (* Example 16.6 *)
PROCEDURE DOSCALL(fn : CARDINAL);
PROCEDURE SWI(intnumber : CARDINAL);
```

These routines are specific to Logitech's version of Modula–2
on the IBM PC. You may need these facilities to write programs specifically for the PC, you should avoid these facilities if you want to move your program from one environment
to another.

The purpose of the SYSTEM MODULE is to force programmers to
acknowledge those parts of a program that use these risky or
machine dependent facilities. PROCEDURES and data TYPES from
the SYSTEM MODULE can only be used by importing them. This
differs from the handling of the more innoccuous *standard* PRO-
CEDURES, which are automatically imported into all MODULES.

The ADR and SIZE PROCEDURES must be handled specially because
they accept any data TYPE as a parameter. The TSIZE PROCEDURE
must be handled specially because it accepts a TYPE name rather
than a variable name. The only other Modula–2 PROCEDURES
that use TYPE name as parameters are VAL, MIN, and MAX.

## 16.2. WORD

The WORD data TYPE corresponds to a unit of storage in the computer's main memory. A WORD occupies as much *space* as a CARDINAL or INTEGER, but it is not interpreted numerically. A WORD is merely a unit of storage, it has no numeric (or other) interpretation. WORDS are usually used when information is being *moved*, unlike the data TYPES from Chapter 2 and Part III, which are usually used when information is being *manipulated* or *interpreted*. The only operation that can be performed with a WORD is assignment — arithmetic, logical, and comparison operations are not allowed.

WORDS are often used as formal parameters for PROCEDURES. When used in this way WORDS are compatible with most actual parameters that occupy the same amount of storage as a WORD. The exact list of data TYPES that are compatible with WORDS is implementation dependent. In all other situations WORDS are *incompatible* with all other data TYPES.

WORDS make it is possible to write PROCEDURES that accept any actual parameters that occupies a single WORD of storage. The ReadWord and WriteWord PROCEDURES from the Streams MODULE use WORD parameters so that they can be used to manage streams of INTEGERS, CARDINALS, BOOLEANS, enumerations, BITSETS, etc.

An even more remarkable capability exists when the formal parameter of a PROCEDURE is declared to be an ARRAY OF WORD. An ARRAY OF WORD formal parameter is compatible with everything (in most implementations of Modula–2). The following PROCEDURE will write any data TYPE to output stream named S.

```
                              (* Example 16.7 *)
    PROCEDURE WriteWords(S : STREAM; x : ARRAY OF WORD);
    VAR
        i : CARDINAL;
    BEGIN
        FOR i := 0 TO HIGH(x) DO WriteWord(S,x[i]) END
    END WriteWords;
```

The WriteWords PROCEDURE can be passed a RECORD, an ARRAY, a REAL, etc. and it will write the correct number of WORDS of information to the output stream S. Note that WriteWords relies upon the WriteWord PROCEDURE from the Streams MODULE.

**Exercise 16.1.** Write the ReadWords PROCEDURE.
□


## 16.3. ADDRESS

Just as a special data TYPE (WORD) is required for generic memory access, a special ADDRESS data TYPE is required for generic POINTER operations. In all versions of Modula–2 the ADDRESS TYPE is compatible with all POINTER TYPES. In addition in many versions of Modula–2 the ADDRESS TYPE is compatible with CARDINALS, LONGCARDS, or LONGINTS.

The ADDRESS TYPE usually behaves as if it were declared

                                                          ( * Example 16.8 * )
```
TYPE ADDRESS = POINTER TO WORD;
```

Because of their special properties, ADDRESSES aren't limited to accessing WORDS.

Our first encounter with memory addresses was in Chapter 14. The address of an item is used when you need to communicate an item's *location* rather than its *value*. In Chapter 14 memory addresses were used in conjunction with dynamic memory allocation. If an executing program needs to use a small region of memory, it is concerned with the *location* of the region.

Modula–2 only allows three operations on ordinary POINTER TYPES: *assignment*, *comparison* (for equality or inequality), and *dereferencing* (accessing whatever it points towards). POINTER operations are usually TYPE checked carefully and it is usually illegal to create expressions with mixed POINTER TYPES. In some implementations of Modula–2 these restrictions are relaxed for the ADDRESS TYPE and limited arithmetic operations are available between ADDRESSES and one of the three numeric TYPES mentioned above. Always remember that ADDRESS is an implementation dependent TYPE. It obeys different rules in different Modula–2 systems.

Dynamic memory allocation is one of the few situations where *programmers* are *required* to use POINTERS. Addresses of items are used throughout Modula–2, but the details are taken care of by the compiler. However, there are situations where POINTERS are convenient, especially for *efficiency* and *flexibility* in systems programming. Examples are given in Chapter 17.

## 16.3.1. SIZE, TSIZE, and ADR

Most operations in Modula-2 involve known TYPES and therefore the language itself is able to take care of the machine level details. Even operations involving ordinary POINTERS involve known TYPES because ordinary POINTERS always point at a particular TYPE of variable. Using ADDRESS POINTERS completely disguises the TYPE of the pointed at variable. This is the advantage of using ADDRESS POINTERS, but it is also the major problem because the burden for handling many machine dependent details shifts from the language itself to the programmer.

ADDRESS POINTERS should only be used when you don't care about the *interpretation* of the item pointed towards. However in using ADDRESS POINTERS you often do care about the *size* (in memory storage units) of the item.

The routines TSIZE and SIZE from the SYSTEM MODULE indicate how much storage is required to store a variable or a TYPE. SIZE is passed the name of a variable as its parameter, TSIZE is passed the name of a TYPE. Both return the storage requirements of their parameter. The actual number that is returned has system dependent interpretation.

TSIZE may be passed the name of a variant RECORD TYPE along with the variant tags and it will determine how much size is occupied by a dynamically allocated instance of that particular RECORD variant, or it can simply be passed the name of the variant RECORD TYPE and it will determine the maximum space occupied by that RECORD.

Don't assume that TSIZE(WORD) is equal to one. Two or four fundamental storage units are usually used to store WORDS. On some systems ADDRESS POINTERS can be incremented. Often you can make an ADDRESS POINTER point at the next word in memory by incrementing it by TSIZE(WORD). (Note that this is system dependent — on at least one Modula-2 system TSIZE returns the number of bits of storage.)

You can determine the memory location of something by using the ADR PROCEDURE. ADR requires the name of a variable (of any TYPE) and it returns an ADDRESS POINTER to that variable.

## 16.3.2. A Stack Storage System

The following MODULE implements a *stack* storage system. In a stack items are stored by placing them above any existing items, much as one dish can be stacked on top of others. When items are removed from a stack, the most recent additions are removed first. Thus the term Last In First Out (LIFO) is often used to describe this type of storage system.

The routine PUSH (or POP) is passed a WORD count and a POINTER to the WORDS to be pushed onto (or popped off of) the stack. Passing a POINTER to PUSH (or POP) is usually more efficient than passing the thing itself, and it is also a common way to circumvent Modula-2's TYPE checking. The stack is simply an ARRAY OF WORDS that is declared within the MODULE. First we'll show the DEFINITION MODULE.

(* Example 16.9 *)

```
DEFINITION MODULE Stack;
FROM SYSTEM IMPORT WORD, ADDRESS;

PROCEDURE POP(wc : CARDINAL; p : ADDRESS);
PROCEDURE PUSH(wc : CARDINAL; p : ADDRESS);

END Stack.
```

This program was originally developed using a Modula-2 compiler that allowed ADDRESS POINTERS to be incremented or decremented. On that system incrementing an ADDRESS POINTER by TSIZE(WORD) would make it point at the next WORD in memory. The IMPLEMENTATION MODULE for Stack is

(* Example 16.10 *)

```
IMPLEMENTATION MODULE Stack;
FROM SYSTEM IMPORT TSIZE, WORD, ADDRESS;
FROM InOut IMPORT WriteString, WriteLn, WriteCard;

CONST
   Top = 500;

VAR
   s : ARRAY[0..Top] OF WORD;
   sp : CARDINAL;

PROCEDURE CheckSp;
BEGIN
```

```
    IF sp = 0 THEN
        sp := 1;
        WriteString('Stack Underflow'); WriteLn
    END;
    IF sp > Top THEN
        sp := Top;
        WriteString('Stack Overflow'); WriteLn
    END;
END CheckSp;

PROCEDURE PUSH(count : CARDINAL; p : ADDRESS);
BEGIN
    WHILE count > 0 DO
        s[sp] := p^;
        INC(sp);
        CheckSp;
        DEC(count,TSIZE(WORD));
        INC(p,TSIZE(WORD));
    END (* WHILE *)
END PUSH;

PROCEDURE POP(count : CARDINAL; p : ADDRESS);
BEGIN
    p := p + count;
    WHILE count > 0 DO
        DEC(p,TSIZE(WORD));
        CheckSp;
        DEC(sp);
        p^ := s[sp];
        DEC(count,TSIZE(WORD));
    END (* WHILE *)
END POP;

BEGIN
    sp := 0;
END Stack.
```

The count parameter supplied to these routines is presumably created by the user of these routines using the SIZE or TSIZE PROCEDURES. It must be decremented by TSIZE(WORD) each time through the loop. The addresses passed to these two routines might be created using the ADR function or they might be ordinary POINTERS pointing at something created dynamically.

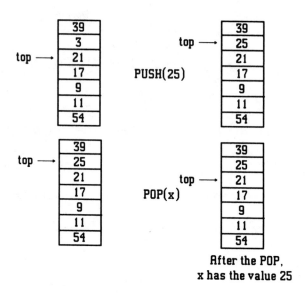

Figure 16.1. PUSH adds an element to the top of the stack; POP retrieves the top element from the stack.

The following program MODULE exercises some of the routines in the Stack MODULE.

```
                              (* Example 16.11 *)
MODULE TryStack;
FROM SYSTEM IMPORT TSIZE, SIZE, ADR;
FROM Stack IMPORT PUSH, POP;
FROM InOut IMPORT WriteString, WriteInt, WriteLn;
FROM RealInOut IMPORT WriteReal;

VAR
    b : ARRAY [0..99] OF CHAR;
    x : REAL;
    i : CARDINAL;
    powers : ARRAY [0..15] OF REAL;

BEGIN
    b := 'Powers of 2 using REALs';
    PUSH(SIZE(b), ADR(b));
    b := '';
    x := 1.;
    FOR i := 0 TO 15 DO
```

```
      PUSH(TSIZE(REAL), ADR(x));
      x := x * 2.
   END;
   POP(SIZE(powers), ADR(powers));
   POP(SIZE(b), ADR(b));
   WriteString(b); WriteLn;
   FOR i := 0 TO 15 DO
      WriteReal(powers[i],10);
      WriteLn
   END;
END TryStack.
```

This program illustrates the flexibility of the Stack routines — it definitely *doesn't* illustrate good programming practice. The program first pushes a string variable and sixteen REALS onto the stack, then it pops an ARRAY of sixteen REALS and then the string variable. Looking at the resulting values indicates correct operation of the stack for this test case, although this is certainly not an exhaustive test. Since this stack has no idea what TYPES of variables it contains, it can't possibly notice (or complain) that individual REALS have been deposited and then an ARRAY OF REALS has been withdrawn.

**Exercise 16.2.** What happens in PUSH and POP if the count parameter is not a multiple of TSIZE(WORD)? Suggest at least two remedies and rewrite the Stack MODULE using the best solution.
□

**Exercise 16.3.** Notice that the routine named CheckSp is called once each time through the loops inside PUSH and POP. This is extremely inefficient, since at the outset of either PROCEDURE it is possible to determine if the stack will overflow inside the body of the loop. Rewrite the Stack MODULE using a more efficient test for overflow and underflow.
□

**Exercise 16.4.** What is the advantage of passing POINTERS to the Stack MODULE rather than passing the items themselves using ARRAY OF WORD parameters?
□

**Exercise 16.5.** Write a variant of the Stack MODULE that keeps track of the size of each datum on the stack. One possibility is for PUSH to place the size of the data after the data itself. Another possibility is to use a separate stack to keep track of the sizes of the items on the main stack. In either case POP should check the size of the stacked datum with the size of the request.

☐

## 16.4. TYPE Names as TYPE Transfer Functions

In Section 2.3 we introduced the TYPE transfer functions named CARDINAL and INTEGER. If you are an astute reader you may have noticed that these functions aren't included in the list of standard functions in Appendix III. The reason is simple — *any* TYPE name can be used as a TYPE transfer function.

For example if b is a BITSET, it can be incremented by one using the following assignment.

(* Example 16.12 *)
```
b := BITSET(CARDINAL(b) + 1)
```

TYPE transfer functions truly act as if they were *functions*. They can be used wherever *functions* can be used, including expressions and value parameters. They cannot be used where variables (designators) are required such as variable parameters or the left hand side of an assignment statement. Thus both of the following plausible statements using TYPE transfer functions are *incorrect*. (b is a BITSET.)

(* Example 16.13 *)
```
CARDINAL(b) := CARDINAL(b) + 1;
INC(CARDINAL(b));
```

The first is wrong because a function isn't allowed on the left of an assignment operator, the second is wrong because a function isn't allowed as a variable parameter.

A particular bit of an INTEGER can be tested by using the TYPE name BITSET as a transfer function. The following PROCEDURE returns TRUE if its numeric parameter is odd by checking the low bit of its INTEGER parameter.

(* Example 16.14 *)
```
PROCEDURE Odd(x : INTEGER) : BOOLEAN;
BEGIN
   RETURN(0 IN BITSET(x))
END Odd;
```

Note there is no guarantee that the test 0 IN BITSET(x) will work on all systems — remember that the numbering of bits in a BITSET is implementation dependent.

TYPE names can be used as TYPE transfer functions even for
TYPES that aren't built into Modula–2. Here is an example.

(* Example 16.15 *)

```
MODULE xfer;
FROM SYSTEM IMPORT ADR;

TYPE
   Day = (Workday, Weekend, Holiday,
               Vacation, Sickday, Personal);
   XXX = [1..365];

VAR
   d : Day;
   x : XXX;
   i : INTEGER;
   b : BITSET;

BEGIN
   i := INTEGER(d) + INTEGER(x);
   d := Day(b);
   x := XXX(INTEGER(d) * INTEGER(b));
END xfer.
```

The ability to use a TYPE name as a TYPE transfer function even
applies to TYPES that occupy many storage locations. Normally
the ARRAYS A and B in the following MODULE would be incompatible because they are declared to be different TYPES. TYPE names
used as TYPE transfer functions allow them to be assigned to each
other.

(* Example 16.16 *)

```
MODULE T;
FROM InOut IMPORT WriteString, WriteLn;

(* Two incompatible array types *)
TYPE
   A = ARRAY [0..10] OF CHAR;
   B = ARRAY [0..10] OF CHAR;

(* Two incompatible array variables *)
VAR
   a : A;
   b : B;
```

```
BEGIN
  a := "MTA";
  b := B(a);
  WriteString(b); WriteLn
END T.
```

This capability works for RECORDS and SETS. The only restriction is this — the two variables must be the same size.

Modula-2's TYPE transfer functions can be used to implement variable length ARRAYS. This practice strays towards the unacceptable, but sometimes there aren't any alternatives. For example one might declare a POINTER variable as

(* Example 16.17 *)
```
VAR
    STR = POINTER TO ARRAY [0..999] OF CHAR;
```

Normally one would allocate the entire ARRAY OF 1000 CHARS.

(* Example 16.18 *)
```
ALLOCATE(STR, SIZE(STR^));
```

However its possible to allocate less than the full amount.

(* Example 16.19 *)
```
ALLOCATE(STR,200);
```

This would create an ARRAY OF two hundred CHARS. Allocating a partial ARRAY makes it the programmer's responsibility to keep track of the actual length of the ARRAY. This is very risky territory. For example it would be wrong to assign one foreshortened ARRAY to another, even if they were both the same length because the Modula–2 compiler (unaware of the foreshortening) would generate code to copy all 1000 supposed elements.

**Exercise 16.6.** Which statements in the following MODULE are *wrong*? Which are unnecessarily *complicated*, which are *correct*?

(* Example 16.20 *)

```
MODULE x;
FROM SYSTEM IMPORT ADR;

TYPE
   R =
      RECORD
         a, b : ARRAY[0..9] OF REAL
      END;
   S = [0..9];
   A = ARRAY S OF REAL;
   PTI = POINTER TO INTEGER;
   E = ( e, n, u, m );

VAR
   rec : R;
   ar : A;
   sub : S;
   int : INTEGER;
   p : POINTER TO REAL;
   enum : E;

BEGIN
   (* 1 *) INTEGER(sub) := 0;
   (* 2 *) sub := S(0);
   (* 3 *) enum := E(sub);
   (* 4 *) ar := A(rec.a);
   (* 5 *) rec := A(ar);
   (* 6 *) rec.a[CARDINAL(m)] := FLOAT(sub);
   (* 7 *) INC(CARDINAL(sub));
   (* 8 *) enum := E(int) - E(sub);
   (* 9 *) int := INTEGER(sub);
   (* 10 *) int := INTEGER(ar[sub]);
   (* 11 *) p := ADR(rec.a);
   (* 12 *) ar[int] := p^;
   (* 13 *) int := TRUNC(p^);
   (* 14 *) int := PTI(p)^;
   (* 15 *) sub := int;
   (* 16 *) sub := sub + int;
   (* 17 *) sub := S(e) + S(int);
END x.
```

□

## 16.5. Example — Generic Quicksort

In Section 15.1 I presented two versions of the quicksort algorithm. In Example 15.8 the fifteen line quicksort PROCEDURE was embedded in a thirty line program MODULE. That version of quicksort was tailor made to sort one TYPE of ARRAY — obviously a more general version is desirable.

The second version of quicksort in Section 15.1 is somewhat more general. In Example 15.10 the quicksort PROCEDURE is housed in a global MODULE. It interacts with the data structure that is being sorted via two PROCEDURES: one to compare two elements of the data structure and one to swap two elements. This is an improvement but it is still not a completely general solution.

The major remaining problem is that the routines to compare and swap data elements are bound to a particular ARRAY. The two routines take as parameters the ARRAY indices. The actual ARRAY is attached (in the code) to the compare and swap routines. Ideally one should be able to sort any one of a dozen different ARRAYS OF INTEGERS using a generic routine to compare a pair of INTEGERS. The solution to this problem is to use POINTERS and TYPE transfer functions.

The second problem with the approach in Example 15.10's quicksort is the swap PROCEDURE. It should be possible to engineer a generic swap using the tools in this chapter. This minimizes the amount of code that a client must supply.

Thus we can generalize the quicksort implementation by using systems programming techniques. This is a good idea for quicksort because it is a completely general algorithm. We should strive to implement it generically. An application specific algorithm would usually be programmed more in the style of Example 15.8.

The basic change to quicksort is its parameters. The earlier versions used array indices, this version will use ADDRESS POINTERS. This immediately brings us to the first problem. Given a POINTER to the first element in the data structure, how can we construct a POINTER to the next (or previous) element? Obviously we also need to know the size of each element, thus the size of each element must be a parameter. As before the PROCEDURE to compare elements must be passed.

The QSORT DEFINITION MODULE is

(* Example 16.21 *)

```
DEFINITION MODULE QSORT;
FROM SYSTEM IMPORT ADDRESS;

(*
 * PROCEDURE TYPE to compare ARRAY elements
 *    (not exported)
 *)
TYPE
  CompProc = PROCEDURE(ADDRESS, ADDRESS) : BOOLEAN;

(*
 * Sort  an ARRAY using the Quick Sort  method.
 * The client must supply:
 *     pointers to the first and last elements
 *     a procedure to compare two array elements
 *     the size of an element in bytes
 *)
PROCEDURE Qsort(first, last : ADDRESS;
               comp : CompProc; size : CARDINAL);

END QSORT.
```

Examine the parameters carefully. They are the key to under-standing this version of quicksort.

Any program that makes use of ADDRESS pointers, the WORD data TYPE, and other systems programming features is not going to be directly portable. The goal here is to write a version of quicksort that is completely general on a particular system, and one that can be modified without too much trouble for another system. This version of quicksort was developed using the DECWRL Modula–2 compiler. Some of the code (to be explained below) is specific to this compiler.

```
                                          (* Example 16.22 *)
IMPLEMENTATION MODULE QSORT;
(*
 * The quicksort for any data structure
 *     Note various dependencies on the
 *     DECWRL Modula-2 compiler
 *)
FROM SYSTEM IMPORT ADDRESS, WORD, TSIZE;

(*
 * Qsort() is the externally visible routine.
 * It simply calls dosort().
 *
 * Notice, dosort() and swap() are nested inside
 *    Qsort() so they can pick up the size and comp
 *    arguments with minimum fuss (from surrounding
 *    scope).
 *)
PROCEDURE Qsort(first, last : ADDRESS;
                  comp : CompProc; size : CARDINAL);

(*
 * dosort implements the quicksort algorithm on
 *    arbitrary data
 *)
PROCEDURE dosort(first, last : ADDRESS);
VAR
   bot,top : ADDRESS;
BEGIN
   bot := first;
   top := last;
   WHILE bot < top DO;
       WHILE comp(bot,top) AND (bot<top) DO
           top := top - size
       END;
       swap(bot,top);
       WHILE comp(bot,top) AND (bot<top) DO
           bot := bot + size
       END;
       swap(bot,top);
   END; (* outer WHILE *)
   IF first < (bot-size) THEN
     dosort(first,bot-size)
```

```
      END;
      IF (bot+size) < last THEN
         dosort(bot+size,last)
      END;
   END dosort;

   (*
    * Swap the things pointed at by a and b.
    *    Things are size bytes long.
    *    Note: DECWRL @c is important here!
    *    Note: DECWRL TSIZE returns size of something
    *    in bits.
    *    (Word alignment is assumed and required.)
    *)
   PROCEDURE swap(a,b : ADDRESS);
   VAR
      i : CARDINAL;
      t : WORD;
   TYPE
      wp = POINTER @c TO WORD;
   VAR
      x, y : wp;
   BEGIN
     x := a;
     y := b;
     FOR i := 1 TO size BY TSIZE(WORD) DIV ByteSize DO
        t := x^;
        x^ := y^;
        y^ := t;
        x := wp(ADDRESS(x) + TSIZE(WORD) DIV ByteSize);
        y := wp(ADDRESS(y) + TSIZE(WORD) DIV ByteSize);
     END (* FOR *)
   END swap;

CONST
    ByteSize = 8;

BEGIN (* the Qsort procedure *)
    size := size DIV ByteSize; (* convert to bytes *)
    dosort(first,last);
END Qsort;

END QSORT.
```

The first thing you might notice is the strange use of the TSIZE facility. The DECWRL compiler TSIZE returns the number of *bits* in a data type. For this software we are more interested in the number of bytes, thus all TSIZE values are immediately converted to bytes.

The second thing you might notice is the strange construct "@c" in the declaration of the wp TYPE. The "@c" is a DECWRL Modula–2 extension that means "Turn off all validity checks for these POINTERS." This is necessary because the use of POINTERS in the swap PROCEDURE wouldn't pass the stringent (and admirable) POINTER validity checks of DECWRL Modula–2.

The third strange coding practice in this version of quicksort is the use of the variables x and y in the swap PROCEDURE. Swap is passed a pair of ADDRESS POINTERS and it picks up the size of the data structures from its surrounding scope — the Qsort PROCEDURE. However as I mentioned above the DECWRL Modula–2 compiler performs very strict POINTER checking and there is no way to turn it off for the built in ADDRESS TYPE. Thus I am forced to invent a new TYPE called wp that has the usage checking disabled. However the wp TYPE doesn't allow POINTER arithmetic, only the built in ADDRESS TYPE supports POINTER arithmetic. Therefore I have to use the ADDRESS TYPE transfer function in the swap PROCEDURE.

These are the problems that occur when useful software must be forged in a particular programming environment. However once these implementation difficulties are overcome, the result is a powerful routine.

In the following program this new version of quicksort is called on to sort a multi–dimensional data structure. An Ritem contains a key element (an INTEGER) and a small ARRAY OF REALS. The ARRAY OF Ritems is sorted by its key, and each ARRAY OF REALS is also sorted.

```
                                       (* Example 16.23 *)
(*
 * Exercise the Qsort proc
 *    uses DECWRL specific features
 *)
MODULE TestQsortAgain;
FROM InOut IMPORT WriteCard, WriteLn;
FROM RealInOut IMPORT WriteReal;
FROM QSORT IMPORT Qsort;
FROM random IMPORT Random;
FROM SYSTEM IMPORT TSIZE, ADDRESS, ADR;

TYPE Ritem =
   RECORD
      index : CARDINAL;
      samples : ARRAY [0..10] OF REAL;
   END;

VAR
   r : ARRAY [0..999] OF Ritem;
   i, j : CARDINAL;

PROCEDURE compRitem(u,v : ADDRESS) : BOOLEAN;
VAR
   a, b : POINTER @c TO Ritem;
BEGIN
   a := u;
   b := v;
   (* comparison only depends upon index field *)
   RETURN a^.index <= b^.index
END compRitem;

PROCEDURE compREAL (u,v : ADDRESS) : BOOLEAN;
VAR
   a, b : POINTER @c TO REAL;
BEGIN
   a := u;
   b := v;
   RETURN a^ <= b^
END compREAL;

(* fill up r - random stuff in this version *)
PROCEDURE collect;
```

```
VAR
   i, j: INTEGER;
BEGIN
   FOR i := 0 TO 999 DO
     WITH r[i] DO
         index := Random() MOD 100;
         FOR j := 0 TO 10 DO
           samples[j] :=
                     FLOAT(Random() MOD 20 * index);
         END
     END
   END (* FOR *)
END collect;

BEGIN (* TestQsortAgain *)
   collect;
   FOR i := 0 TO 999 DO
     WITH r[i] DO (* sort the individual arrays *)
         Qsort(ADR(samples[0]),ADR(samples[10]),
                 compREAL,TSIZE(REAL));
     END
   END;

   (* sort the works *)
   Qsort(ADR(r[0]),ADR(r[999]),
               compRitem,TSIZE(Ritem));

   FOR i := 0 TO 999 DO
     WITH r[i] DO
         WriteCard(index,5);
         FOR j := 0 TO 10 DO
             WriteReal(samples[j],7)
         END;
         WriteLn
     END
   END (* FOR *)
END TestQsortAgain.
```

The collect PROCEDURE is straightforward — its purpose is simply to load the Ritems with random values. The PROCEDURES named compRitem and compREAL are passed POINTERS, and they RETURN BOOLEANS indicating the ordering of the items pointed at by their parameters. POINTER checking is turned off using the DECWRL "@c" Modula–2 extension, and each PROCEDURE contains internal POINTER variables of the appropriate TYPE to make it easy to access the items.

The body of TestSort first calls collect to initialize r, then it sorts each of the 1000 samples ARRAYS and then it sorts r itself. Finally r is printed.

**Exercise 16.7.** Name at least two advantages of having Qsort call dosort to perform the actual sorting.

□

**Exercise 16.8.** What is the advantage of having the dosort PROCEDURE pick up comp and size from its surrounding scope?

□

**Exercise 16.9.** Rewrite the QSORT MODULE without using nested PROCEDURES.

□

**Exercise 16.10.** Is there any way to use open ARRAY parameters to interchange two items (variable size) without the tedious WORD–by–WORD method used in the swap PROCEDURE?

□

**Exercise 16.11.** When you assign one ARRAY (or RECORD) to another the compiler is likely to generate machine code that uses special computer instructions to move data with minimum overhead. Unfortunately the swap PROCEDURE copies one datum to another one WORD at a time. Can you think of a more efficient algorithm for the swap PROCEDURE?

□

**Exercise 16.12.** Copying numerous bytes from one place to another could be speeded up without compiler assistance by writing a special routine in machine language. Investigate your Modula-2 system to find out if it is possible to link your Modula-2 programs to routines written in the host computers own assembly language. Can you think of other instances when it might be advantageous to code a part of a problem in assembly language?

□

**Exercise 16.13.** Modify the compRitem PROCEDURE so that Ritems are compared based on the following weighting formula:

```
index + samples[0]/2 + samples[1]/4 +
        samples[2]/8 + . . .
```

□

**Exercise 16.14.** How would you modify the QSORT global MODULE to export the swap PROCEDURE?

□

# Chapter 17

# Programming Hardware

One aspect of systems programming is writing programs that actually control the computer hardware. Every computer contains *peripheral devices* to transfer data between the computer and the outside world. For example most computers are connected to terminals so that people can interact with the computer. Most computers capable of running Modula–2 are also connected to disks so that information can be stored for long periods of time. Most computers are connected to printers, and most larger computers have clocks so that they can keep track of time. Even simple computers, such as a computer controlling a microwave oven, has a small collection of switches and sensors used for input and a few actuators used for output.

A computer's peripherals are attached to the computer using *interfaces*. The details naturally vary, but most computers assign addresses to the interfaces, much as if they were memory. On some computers a part of the main memory space is reserved for interfaces, on other computers there is a separate address space reserved solely for interfaces. A special location used for accessing an interface, in memory space or in some other addressable space, is usually called a *device register*.

Smaller computers are often dedicated to a single task and they are content to wait busily for something to happen on a particular interface. For example a computer controlling a microwave oven spends most of its time *polling* its switches and sensors waiting for a change.

More powerful computers are usually reluctant to wait for events. The preferred approach is to have the event *interrupt* the ongoing activities. Usually the overhead for dealing with peripheral devices is small. Once the peripheral device has been serviced the main task can be resumed where it left off. This is somewhat like cooking while chatting with your dinner guests.

One problem that occurs when several things are happening at once is that events become unsynchronized. The peripheral interfaces can often be thought of as either being *consumers* of data or *producers* of data. For example a keyboard interface is a producer, a printer interface is a consumer. Systems programmers strive to keep the producer's data from being ignored and the consumer's from being starved. The small sections of code that coordinate producers and consumers are called *critical regions* and it is necessary to make sure that production and consumption are temporarily suspended during a critical region.

This chapter discusses the basic aspects of programming hardware: accessing specific hardware locations and programming critical regions. Chapter 19 focuses on writing routines in Modula-2 that service interrupts.

These aspects of Modula-2 are not always available. When Modula-2 is used on a computer with a fully developed time-sharing operating system these facilities are probably not available (to ordinary users). When Modula-2 is used on a single-user computer with a fully developed operating system these facilities may or may not be included. On more rudimentary computers low-level facilities for accessing hardware are probably available.

## 17.1. Located Variables

One normal function of the compiler is to allocate space for the variables in a program. In some Modula–2 implementations it is possible for a programmer to override the compiler and specify the location of a variable. One common use of located variables is to provide a named variable to access a device register. Another common use is to allow a program to communicate with the operating system, or to communicate (using an agreed region of memory) with another program.

Many Modula–2 implementations allow you to specify a fixed location for a variable by following the variable name with a number enclosed in square brackets. This part of the Modula–2 syntax is not described in the syntax diagrams because this facility isn't provided in *all* installations.

For example on the Digital Equipment Corporation LSI–11 family of microcomputers the AAV11–C Analog Output interface consists of four data registers often located at address 170440B.

```
                                    (* Example 17.1 *)
VAR dac [ 170440B ] : ARRAY [0..3] OF INTEGER;
```

Suppose that two of the channels of the analog output device are wired to a video display or graphics plotter. By writing x and y values to the interface we can draw points on the display or plotter. The following local MODULE contains a PROCEDURE named point that draws a point at the given coordinate. The local MODULE also contains the declarations for the *located* variables. Since the memory locations that are accessed by located variables exist statically, it is preferable to declare located variables statically. Thus located variables are ordinarily declared in the declaration part of a global MODULE.

```
                                              (* Example 17.2 *)
    MODULE Dac;
    EXPORT Point;

    VAR
        dac [ 170440B ] : ARRAY [0..3] OF INTEGER;

    PROCEDURE Point(x,y : INTEGER);
    BEGIN
        dac[0] := x; dac[1] := y
    END Point;

    END Dac.
```

There is also a POINTER technique for accessing absolute memory
locations. Simply declare a POINTER to a given TYPE and then use
the TYPE relaxation methods outlined in the previous chapter to
coerce the POINTER to point towards a specific device register.
Here is the previous local MODULE rewritten using POINTER techniques.

```
                                              (* Example 17.3 *)
    MODULE DacPtr;
    EXPORT Point;

    TYPE
        P = POINTER TO INTEGER;

    VAR
        px, py : P;

    PROCEDURE Point(x, y : INTEGER);
    BEGIN
        px^ := x;
        py^ := y
    END Point;

    BEGIN
        px := P(170440B);
        py := P(170442B)
    END DacPtr.
```

This version is bulkier but it only uses the *standard* features of
Modula–2 whereas the earlier version uses located variables, an *optional* feature of Modula–2.

The MODULE body in the DacPtr MODULE is used to initialize the POINTERS to the AAV11–C's device registers. Thus this MODULE relies upon the fact that MODULE bodies are automatically activated when their surrounding context is created. TYPE transfer functions are used in the DacPtr MODULE body to initialize the POINTER variables.

Naturally any program that uses located variables is machine dependent. Even different models of essentially the same computer may use different locations for devices. You should confine such dependencies to a few MODULES to make your programs more maintainable.

## 17.2. MODULE Priorities

Every computer program that manages interrupts has potential problems with *critical regions*. Interrupts imply simultaneity — the hardware interface and interrupt handler software apparently operate at the same time as the main task of the computer. In many computers there are numerous interfaces capable of producing interrupts, so there are numerous activities appearing to happen simultaneously.

We will use the OneBuffer MODULE first presented in Chapter 8 to illustrate the problem. The OneBuffer MODULE implements a small circular buffer that can be used to coordinate the activities of a producer and a consumer. Typically a producer calls deposit to save a character in a buffer, a consumer calls withdraw to retrieve a character from a buffer, and either may examine the cnt variable to determine how many characters are stored in a buffer.

Whether these routines work acceptably depends on how they are used. If they are used in an ordinary applications program they work correctly. However the routines fail if either the producer or the consumer (or both) are *interrupt* handlers. Let's examine these routines more closely to see why.

Remember that an interrupt can occur at any time. Since each statement in Modula–2 can be translated into more than one machine instruction it is even possible for an interrupt to occur in mid–statement. Let's suppose that data is being deposited into a buffer by an interrupt handler and that it is being drained by an ordinary applications task. Buffers are often used to provide an interface between an interrupt task and an ordinary task.

| Ordinary Task | Interrupt Task |
|---|---|
| 1. withdraw is called. | |
| 2. DEC is called to decrement cnt.<br>  a. DEC fetches the value of cnt from main memory.<br>  b. DEC subtracts one from the value. | |
| | 3. An interrupt occurs. (The ongoing task, DEC is suspended.) |
| | 4. deposit is called.<br>  a. INC increments cnt.<br>  b. The data is put into the buffer.<br>  c. INC increments head. |
| | 5. The interrupt handler is finished. |
|   c. DEC resumes. It places the value of cnt back into memory. | |
| 6. INC increments tail. | |
| 7. A value is returned from withdraw. | |

Figure 17.1. Here is one scenario that demonstrates how an interrupting task can corrupt shared variables. Note — Step 2c places an incorrect value into the cnt variable. The change to cnt that occurred during the interrupt service routine is lost.

In our scenario deposit is called by the interrupt task and withdraw is called by the ordinary task. Deposit modifies the variables head and cnt while placing items into the buffer. Withdraw modifies the variables tail and cnt while with drawing items from the buffer. If withdraw is interrupted while modifying tail there is no problem because the tail variable is ignored by deposit. However if withdraw is interrupted while updating cnt there may be problems because deposit also modifies cnt. Since cnt is the only variable shared by deposit and withdraw, it should be protected so that it can't be corrupted during an interrupt.

Let's be more specific to show how cnt can be corrupted by an interrupt that occurs at the wrong time. We will assume that an interrupt occurs during withdraw just after we've fetched the cnt variable and subtracted one from it (in the last line of the with-draw PROCEDURE) but before the new value has been written back into cnt. According to our scenario, the interrupt service routine immediately calls deposit, deposit puts an element into the buffer, increments the head variable, and then increments the cnt variable. A simple, ordinary interrupt service routine.

The problem is that the withdraw PROCEDURE resumes exactly where it left off. Before the interrupt occurred it read and then decremented the value of cnt. Withdraw's copy of cnt was safe-ly preserved during the interrupt service routine, and after the in-terrupt withdraw places the *incorrect* value back into the cnt variable. The increment to cnt performed by the service routine is ignored causing the producer and consumer to be out of step.

This is an insidious problem because it doesn't occur every time, and it might not even occur often. The interrupt has to occur at exactly the right point to cause a problem. Usually everything will be ok. Since cnt is one too low, at some point or another data will be missing and in many situations a missing character won't be very noticeable. However if you envision this same synchroni-zation problem occurring during the output of data to a disk you can see why systems programmers strive for perfection.

A similar problem can arise if the interrupt handler interrupts it-self (deposit) rather than withdraw. If deposit is interrupted just at its onset the second interrupt will proceed to deposit its character into the buffer before the first interrupt gets a chance. Only after the second interrupt is completed will the first inter-rupt proceed. At best there will a reversal of the data in the buffer. It's also possible that the buffer indices cnt or head could be corrupted by nested producer interrupts, or that data will be lost.

The solution is to disable interrupts during the critical regions. We could make the *entire* OneBuffer MODULE into a critical re-gion. However it is usually preferable to delimit critical regions as finely as possible because interrupts are disabled during a critical region. If the period of time that interrupts are suspended is too long then you are likely to lose data because most interrupts must be serviced within a fixed period of time.

The syntax diagrams for local, program, and IMPLEMENTATION MODULES indicate that they can have a *priority*. (DEFINITION MODULES can't have a priority.)

**priority**

— Diagram 17.1 —

The exact interpretation of the priority is machine dependent, but the general effect is to gain control over when interrupts are allowed. A PROCEDURE inside a prioritized MODULE may call other PROCEDURES from that MODULE, PROCEDURES from other MODULES that have a higher priority, or PROCEDURES from a MODULE that doesn't have a priority. It is not permissible for a PROCEDURE in a prioritized MODULE to call a PROCEDURE from a MODULE with a lower priority.

Some computers have a range of interrupt priorities. For example in the LSI–11 there are four interrupt priorities: four, five, six, and seven. The analog output interface usually is configured to interrupt at priority four. This assignment is done by the engineers who configure the computer hardware and it is not controllable (at least on the LSI–11) in software. Corresponding to the hardware interrupt priorities on the LSI–11 are software controllable *processor priority levels*. For example when the processor is set to priority level five the interrupts from level five and four are prohibited. As I mentioned above, the processor must not remain at a high priority level for very long. Typically the priority level is only raised for a few tens of microseconds.

Here is a rewritten version of the OneBuffer MODULE. It uses a local MODULE to protect the manipulation of the cnt variable and the entire deposit PROCEDURE. This local MODULE is assigned the priority four so that we prohibit level four (or less) interrupts. This guarantees that our critical regions are protected. The DEFINITION MODULE for OneBuffer is unchanged, so we will only show the new IMPLEMENTATION MODULE.

```
                                        (* Example 17.4 *)
IMPLEMENTATION MODULE OnePBuffer;
(*
 * Circular buffering.
 *    Deposit places a character into a buffer.
 *    Withdraw removes a character from a buffer.
 *    Cnt contains the current count of chars
 *       in the buffer.
 *    It is used to determine if a buffer is
 *       full or empty.
 *    Cnt should be considered "read-only".
 *)
CONST
   BufEnd = BufSize-1;

VAR
   x : ARRAY [0..BufEnd] OF CHAR;
   head, tail : CARDINAL;

MODULE crit[4];
IMPORT cnt, x, head, BufSize, BufEnd;
EXPORT deposit, DecCnt;

PROCEDURE deposit(ch : CHAR);
BEGIN
   IF cnt < BufSize THEN INC(cnt) ELSE RETURN END;
   x[head] := ch;
   IF head = BufEnd THEN
      head := 0
   ELSE
      INC(head)
   END
END deposit;

PROCEDURE DecCnt;
BEGIN
   DEC(cnt)
END DecCnt;

END crit; (* module *)

PROCEDURE withdraw() : CHAR;
BEGIN
```

```
   IF cnt > 0 THEN DecCnt ELSE RETURN OC END;
   IF tail = BufEnd THEN
      tail := 0
   ELSE
      INC(tail)
   END;
   RETURN x[tail]
END withdraw;

BEGIN (* initialization for Buffer MODULE *)
   head := 0;
   tail := BufEnd;
   cnt := 0;
END OnePBuffer.
```

Handling errors in the presence of interrupt driven producers or consumers can be extremely difficult. The previous version of OneBuffer (Example 13.8) printed error messages to flag obvious problems. Error messages are usually inappropriate in interrupt handlers. Where should they be displayed? Will the time or space devoted to printing error messages lead to further errors?

The two obvious problems associated with these circular buffers are attempting to read data from an empty buffer and attempting to place data into a full buffer. An interrupting producer faced with a full buffer has few options other than to discard the data. Similarly an *interrupting* consumer faced with an empty buffer has a major problem. One solution is to make the buffers large enough to handle all conceivable cases and to attempt to balance interrupt rates with the throughputs in the rest of the system. Unfortunately it's often impossible to figure out how large a buffer will suffice for all conceivable cases. Another solution is to use a more flexible buffering system such as the linked list buffer presented in Section 13.2. Obviously neither solution is foolproof.

A problem known as *deadlock* occurs whenever two tasks are competing for a resource and each is preventing the other from making progress. We can easily imagine a different version of the OneBuffer MODULE where it would be acceptable to call withdraw even if the buffer were empty. (In the version of OneBuffer presented above it is an error to call withdraw if the buffer is empty.) Faced with an empty buffer, withdraw would simply wait for deposit to deposit something. (This would be a good strategy if withdraw were being called by an ordinary task, and it would usually be a bad strategy if withdraw were called by an interrupt driven task.) However withdraw must be modified if we want it to be able to wait for deposit to place something in the buffer. As written above, if withdraw enters the critical region before it realizes that it has to wait for input, it would disable interrupts indefinitely and keep the producer (deposit) from ever depositing data into the buffer. This is classic deadlock.

One solution to the deadlock problem in Modula–2 is a PROCEDURE called LISTEN. It enables interrupts (even within a critical region) by lowering the machine's current processor priority level. Just lowering the level isn't a guarantee that the desired interrupt will occur, thus LISTEN should be called within a loop that waits for some event. LISTEN must be imported from the SYSTEM MODULE, and it may not be present in all versions of Modula–2.

The following dec PROCEDURE calls LISTEN to wait for the producer to deposit data into the buffer. This PROCEDURE would have to be substituted for the original version of dec in Example 17.4, LISTEN would have to be imported into OneBuffer from the SYSTEM MODULE, and then LISTEN would have to be imported into the local MODULE crit.

(* Example 17.5 *)

```
(*
 * Wait for a non-empty buffer while allowing
 *   interrupts
 *)
PROCEDURE DecCnt;
BEGIN
    WHILE cnt = 0 DO LISTEN END;
    DEC(cnt)
END dec;
```

Another solution to the deadlock problem is to avoid entering the critical region if the resource isn't available. This solution can be attained by modifying the withdraw PROCEDURE from Example 17.4 while retaining the original version of the dec PROCEDURE. Since withdraw is *outside* of the crit MODULE, we don't have to lower the processor priority to wait for interrupts, we merely avoid entering the critical region (avoid calling dec) until there is something in the buffer.

(* Example 17.6 *)

```
PROCEDURE withdraw( ) : CHAR;
BEGIN
   (* wait for something in the buffer *)
   WHILE cnt = 0 DO END;
   DecCnt;
   IF tail = BufEnd THEN
      tail := 0
   ELSE
      INC(tail)
   END;
   RETURN x[tail]
END withdraw;
```

We've shown two methods that an ordinary consumer task can apply to wait for an interrupt driven producer. Similar approaches could be taken to allow an ordinary producer to wait when confronted by a full buffer, assuming the presence of an interrupt driven consumer. Neither approach was taken in Example 17.4, which ignores both types of errors.

Just as an interrupt is presumed to take only a small amount of time away from the main task, a critical region is presumed to disable interrupts for only a short period. Many interfaces require responses to their interrupts within a given period or they will lose data. Critical regions must be clearly defined and they must never involve time consuming operations.

# Chapter 18

# Coroutines

*Coroutines* are built into Modula–2 so that it may be used to write interrupt handlers, runtime systems, event driven programs, and even complete operating systems. Coroutines are a primitive concept. They allow programmers to manage situations where several things are (or appear to be, or are best thought of as) happening simultaneously.

Coroutines are used to organize programs so that control can be transferred from one task to another. For example in a time–sharing operating system a single computer is shared between numerous users. Each user program executes several times each second during its *time slice*. A time–sharing system written in Modula–2 could view the user programs as coroutines and could use coroutine transfers to switch from one to another.

Coroutines can also be used in simpler cases, such as a program used by a scientist who is collecting and analyzing experimental data. During most experiments there are several distinct tasks that must be managed simultaneously. For example in a neuro-physiological experiment the separate tasks might be providing a stimulus for a neuron, recording electrical activity in the neuron, and displaying the data. All these tasks must be managed as the experiment progresses. Using a coroutine for each task is the pre–

ferred solution.

Another area where coroutines are useful is in managing the hardware of the computer. Most computers can perform calculations and other internal operations much faster than they can send (or receive) data to peripheral devices. Because of the speed imbalance it is important to allow the computer to work on other tasks while the transfer is occurring. Most computers use interrupts that can suspend the active task whenever the peripheral device needs attention. Modula-2 allows programmers to assign coroutines to each peripheral device. These coroutines will be activated automatically when the interrupts occur.

The three coroutine uses mentioned above all deal with systems programming. Another use for coroutines is in applications programs whose problem domain can be viewed concurrently. For example software is often developed to simulate complex systems — plasmas, nuclear explosions, geo–politics, traffic patterns, biological systems, etc. One approach to these problems is to develop relatively simple routines that model the behavior of one element of the simulation. Then all of these routines are executed once each time the simulation clock ticks. Coroutines are ideal for simulations, because the structure of a coroutine solution is close to the structure of the problem.

## 18.1. Coroutines and Subroutines

Coroutines are similar to subroutines. Coroutines and subroutines are both bundles of statements and data. However the differences are probably more important than the similarities.

A subroutine is a *hierarchical* structure. Each time a subroutine is called it establishes a new, deeper context. Subroutines are nested, thus calling a subroutine is analogous to placing a document on top of all the other documents on your desk. It is even possible for a subroutine to call itself either directly or indirectly. When a subroutine is called its local datums are *created* automatically and it starts to execute from the *beginning*.

Coroutines aren't hierarchical. Calling a coroutine does not establish a new context, rather it reactivates (except for the first call) an *existing* context. Obviously it is useless for a coroutine to call itself. Calling a coroutine is like switching from one pile of documents on your desk to another. When a coroutine is called its local data already exists, and it starts to execute from wherever it left off. A coroutine is created using the NEWPROCESS call and a coroutine only starts executing from the beginning the first time it is called.

When a subroutine is called it always starts at the beginning, works towards a conclusion, and then finishes and returns. A subroutine may call other subroutines while it is executing, but the return from a subroutine implies that the task is complete.

Coroutines start from wherever they left off. They usually execute for a period of time and then transfer control to some other coroutine. Thus while subroutines embody a directed attack on a problem, coroutines embody an interleaved (or intermittent) approach to an activity.

Subroutines often use parameters that direct them towards a particular problem. Coroutines can't use parameters because they don't start from the beginning each time. It is possible to pass information to a coroutine using global variables.

## 18.2. PROCESS, NEWPROCESS, and TRANSFER

Coroutines are created and managed using the PROCESS data TYPE and the NEWPROCESS and TRANSFER calls. All three of these items must be imported from the SYSTEM MODULE in every MODULE that uses coroutines.

The PROCESS data TYPE is used to describe the execution *state* (status) of a coroutine. The state may contain different items on different machines, but it usually contains
- The address where a coroutine should be resumed.
- The location of the coroutine's stack.
- The location of the coroutine's local data.

When a coroutine transfer occurs the state of the calling coroutine is recorded in a PROCESS variable and the state of the called coroutine is restored from a PROCESS variable. Thus PROCESS variables are central to all interactions with coroutines.

Coroutines must be created before they can be used. Creating a coroutine initializes a coroutine descriptor variable to enable a successful first call of the coroutine. The NEWPROCESS PROCEDURE requires several parameters. Coroutines are written as PROCEDURES without parameters. Obviously NEWPROCESS needs to know what PROCEDURE contains the coroutine. In addition every coroutine needs an area of storage for its local stack and variables. Therefore NEWPROCESS is also passed the address and the size of the coroutine's workspace. Finally NEWPROCESS requires the co–

routine descriptor variable that will be initialized. Note that
NEWPROCESS doesn't actually activate a coroutine, it simply initializes a coroutine descriptor variable so that the coroutine may
subsequently be activated by calling TRANSFER.

The size of a coroutine workspace depends on how much storage is
used by the coroutine. Simple coroutines need only a few tens of
words. Complicated coroutines may need thousands of words of
storage. Beware of coroutines that call recursive PROCEDURES, coroutines that contain ARRAY local variables, or coroutines that call
PROCEDURES from global MODULES. The amount of storage required by coroutines varies from implementation to implementation and you should consult the literature for your system for
more guidance.

Coroutines are activated using the TRANSFER PROCEDURE.
TRANSFER requires two parameters, a coroutine decscriptor (an
ADDRESS TYPE) variable to store the state of the calling coroutine
and an initialized PROCESS variable that describes the state of the
called coroutine. The first call to TRANSFER in a program initializes the PROCESS variable for the caller, hence the caller *becomes* a
coroutine as a result of *calling* a coroutine.

The following is a simple example of coroutines. The program
MODULE creates a coroutine called buzz that simply writes the
letter "Z" to the terminal. The program alternates between the
buzz coroutine and the main coroutine (which writes the letter
"B" to the terminal).

(* Example 18.1 *)

```
MODULE Bee;
FROM SYSTEM IMPORT PROCESS, TRANSFER, NEWPROCESS,
     SIZE, ADR;
FROM InOut IMPORT Write;

VAR
   co, main: PROCESS;
   WorkSpace : ARRAY [1..200] OF CARDINAL;

PROCEDURE buzz; (* coroutine *)
BEGIN
  LOOP
    Write('Z');
    TRANSFER(co,main)
  END (* LOOP *)
END buzz;
```

```
BEGIN
  NEWPROCESS(buzz, ADR(WorkSpace), SIZE(WorkSpace), co);
  LOOP
    Write('B');
    TRANSFER(main,co)
  END (* LOOP *)
END Bee.
```

The Bee program was written for a version of Modula-2 that contains a special TYPE called PROCESS to identify coroutines. In newer versions of Modula-2 the role of PROCESS in the Bee program is carried out by the ADDRESS TYPE. Also many Modula-2 implementations place the coroutine facilities in a standard global MODULE named Coroutines rather than in the special SYSTEM MODULE.

Most coroutines are written as an infinite loop. Whenever execution reaches the end of *any* coroutine the whole program completes. The only way to deactivate a coroutine that is "finished" is to stop calling it.

The TRANSFER PROCEDURE is careful to read the PROCESS variable of the called coroutine before it updates the PROCESS variable of the calling coroutine. Thus the previous example could be rewritten using a single PROCESS variable to keep track of which coroutine will operate next. This rewrite also incorporates a small change to the buzz coroutine to show that a program exits whenever a coroutine exits.

(* Example 18.2 *)

```
MODULE NewBee;
FROM SYSTEM IMPORT PROCESS, TRANSFER, NEWPROCESS,
     SIZE, ADR;
FROM InOut IMPORT Write, WriteString, WriteLn;

VAR
   next : PROCESS;
   WorkSpace : ARRAY [1..200] OF CARDINAL;

PROCEDURE buzz; (* coroutine *)
VAR
   i : CARDINAL;
BEGIN
  FOR i := 1 TO 100 DO
    Write('Z');
    TRANSFER(next, next)
```

```
   END; (* FOR *)
   WriteLn; WriteString('Buzz Exiting'); WriteLn
END buzz;

BEGIN
   NEWPROCESS(buzz,ADR(WorkSpace),SIZE(WorkSpace),next);
   LOOP
     Write('B');
     TRANSFER(next, next)
   END; (* LOOP *)
   WriteLn; WriteString('Main exiting'); WriteLn
END NewBee.
```

This program writes the letter "Z" one hundred times interleaved
with the letter "B" one hundred and one times, and then writes
the message "Buzz Exiting." The message "Main exiting" never
appears.

## 18.3. Example — The Polling Term Program

*Networking* means connecting computers together so that they
can be used cooperatively. For example a small computer in a
research lab might be connected to a larger mainframe so that
data collected by the lab computer can be analyzed on the mainframe. Or perhaps a word processor used by a secretary might be
connected to another computer so that the two computers can
share a printer.

There are numerous ways to interconnect computers. One simple
method is to connect a serial data communications line between
the machines. A serial link is easy to install, most computers have
compatible serial protocols, and serial data can even be sent over
telephone lines for long distance communications.

Software is needed to manage computer systems that are connected by serial lines. The Term program is one of the building blocks
in a software communications system. Term allows one computer
to act as a terminal for another. Everything that is typed on the
console of the first is sent to the second, and everything that is
output by the second is displayed on the terminal of the first. The
role of the computer running Term is simply to pass along the
character data.

In this version of Term we are going to use a simple *polling* approach. Polling means testing the interface periodically waiting for
data (rather than writing an interrupt handler that is called au-

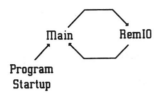

Figure 18.1. In this polling version of the Term program the coroutine handlers alternate.

tomatically when data is present). I wrote this program using two coroutines — one to manage the local keyboard/display and one to manage the communications with the remote computer. The major advantage of this approach is that it converts easily to the interrupt driven approach shown in the next chapter. A more efficient organization could be used if the only goal was to write a polled version of Term.

The approach that I am taking here is appropriate for a personal computer. On a multi-user computer a virtual terminal program would have to be constructed based on the capabilities of the host operating system. On a personal (by this I mean single-user) computer the operating system is often quite simple. Thus it doesn't get in your way when you try to send data to/from a serial port. Naturally there are personal computers where this approach wouldn't work.

This version of the term program was written for the IBM PC. It was compiled and tested using the Logitech Modula-2 system and it relies on several facilities from Logitech's SYSTEM MODULE. This program would be easy to modify for a different compiler on the PC, but it might be very hard to adapt to another computer.

The Term program uses operating system calls to send data to/from the keyboard/display of the IBM PC. The DOS calls are accessed using Logitech's DOSCALL PROCEDURE. The parameters to DOSCALL are relatively unimportant, at least from the conceptual point of view. Details can be found in the MS–DOS reference manual. The comments after each DOSCALL indicate the activity. Note that the keyboard is polled. If nothing has been typed the KbdCh variable is set to 0C following the call, otherwise it is assigned the value of the key that has been struck.

The RemIO coroutine is used to send data to/from the remote computer. RemIO reads the status register of the serial port interface. A character is transmitted if there is something to transmit and the transmit buffer is empty. A character is read from the in–

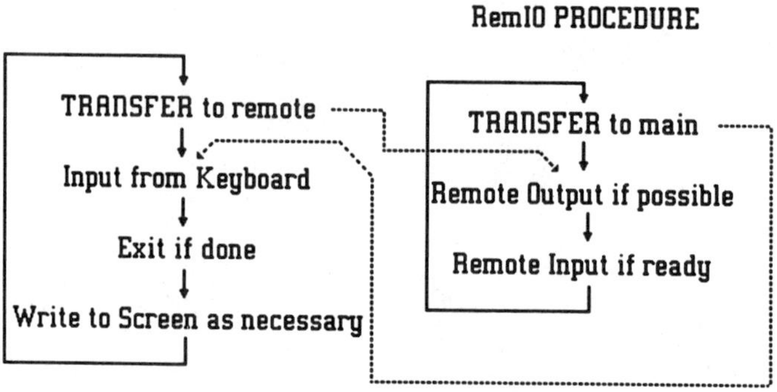

RemIO PROCEDURE

Figure 18.2. In this more detailed diagram of the Term program, ordinary flow of control is shown as a solid line and coroutine transfers are shown as a dashed line. The function of the main coroutine is to manage the local keyboard and screen. The function of the RemIO coroutine is to manage communications with the remote system.

terface if one is waiting.

The buffering in this program is very primitive. A variable named KbdCh contains any data that has been read from the keyboard. Once KbdCh has been transmitted it is set to 0C. Similarly RemCh contains any character that has been received from the interface. RemCh is set to zero as soon as it is displayed on the screen. Conceptually these single character buffers could be replaced with larger buffers to provide better decoupling between the producers and the consumers. This was done for this program, but the resulting code obscured the operation of the coroutines. Hence I decided on this simpler, but less realistic approach.

(* Example 18.3 *)

```
MODULE TermPoll;
(*
 * Virtual Terminal program for the IBM/PC
 *  running PCDOS. Uses Logitech Modula-2/86
 *  specific imports from SYSTEM
 *)

FROM SYSTEM IMPORT
    PROCESS, TRANSFER, NEWPROCESS, (* standards *)
    SIZE, ADR, WORD, (* standards *)
    DOSCALL, INBYTE, OUTBYTE; (* Dos specific *)
```

```
CONST
   Para = 16; (* sixteen bytes in a paragraph *)

VAR
   main, remote : PROCESS;
   WorkSpace : ARRAY [ 0 .. 127 ] OF CARDINAL;
   KbdCh, RemCh : CHAR;
   ready : BOOLEAN;

MODULE REMOTE;
IMPORT TRANSFER, INBYTE, OUTBYTE, WORD,
    KbdCh, RemCh, remote, main;
EXPORT RemIO;

PROCEDURE RemIO;
(* Polling handler for an 8250 Asnyc
    Serial I/O chip *)
CONST
   DataReg = 03F8H;
   StatReg = 03FDH;
   RcvRdy = 0;
   XmtRdy = 5;
VAR
   stat : WORD;
BEGIN
   LOOP
      TRANSFER(remote, main);
      INBYTE(StatReg,stat);
      IF (KbdCh # 0C) AND (XmtRdy IN BITSET(stat))
         THEN OUTBYTE(DataReg,KbdCh);
         KbdCh := 0C
      END;
      IF RcvRdy IN BITSET(stat) THEN
         INBYTE(DataReg,RemCh)
      END;
   END
END RemIO; (* procedure *)

END REMOTE; (* module *)

BEGIN
   KbdCh := 0C; RemCh := 0C;
   NEWPROCESS(RemIO, ADR(WorkSpace),
               SIZE(WorkSpace) DIV Para, remote);
```

```
    LOOP
        TRANSFER(main,remote);
        (* Poll kbd *)
        IF KbdCh = 0C THEN
            DOSCALL(6H, 0FFH, KbdCh, ready)
        END;
        (* exit on escape *)
        IF KbdCh = 33C THEN EXIT END;
        (* write screen as necessary *)
        IF RemCh # 0C THEN
            DOSCALL(6H, RemCh);
            RemCh := 0C
        END;
    END
END TermPoll.
```

This example is set up so that the coroutines execute consecutively — more elaborate strategies are certainly possible.

**Exercise 18.1.** Rewrite the `TermPoll` program using two device drivers: one to output characters to the serial port and one to input characters from the serial port.
□

**Exercise 18.2.** Rewrite the `TermPoll` program so that "keyboard" input can come from a disk file or so that output destined for the terminal display can alternatively be written to a disk file. This technique is called spooling or logging. You can activate the spooling function by entering a special control code from the terminal keyboard.
□

# Chapter 19

# Device Drivers

One important feature of Modula-2 is the ability to write coroutines that serve as device drivers (also called interrupt handlers) for *interrupting devices*. This ability considerably enhances Modula-2's suitability for systems programming, and it means that many systems can be written entirely in Modula-2 without resorting to lower level languages.

Working directly with hardware interrupts using Modula-2 is realistic only on machines dedicated to a single user or on machines where the entire system is written in Modula-2. This makes Modula-2 suitable for programming computers for laboratory or factory automation, stand alone workstations, or for writing entire operating systems for larger computers.

Writing an entire operating system is well beyond the scope of this book. Instead this chapter focuses on using Modula-2 to write device drivers that might be used in a dedicated computer, for example a computer collecting scientific data in a laboratory or a computer graphics workstation computer.

Device drivers in Modula-2 are coded as *coroutines*, which were discussed in Chapter 18. Inside a device driver you ordinarily need several facilities that have already been discussed. For example device drivers always access computer hardware, possibly using the techniques for *located* variables from Section 17.1. Also device drivers often involve *critical regions* and the possibility of *deadlock*, discussed in Section 17.2.

This chapter brings all these facilities together in several examples of interrupt handlers. But first we need to talk about the missing ingredient, the IOTRANSFER PROCEDURE that links a coroutine to a specific interrupt.

## 19.1. IOTRANSFER

Modula–2 interrupt handlers are written as coroutines. When an interrupt occurs the corresponding coroutine is automatically invoked, causing an unscheduled transfer to the coroutine from somewhere in the main program.

The IOTRANSFER PROCEDURE is included in many versions of the Modula–2 SYSTEM MODULE. Systems that lack IOTRANSFER (or equivalent) are valid Modula–2 systems but they usually aren't used for writing device drivers. You should consult your local Modula–2 guide for details about your version of IOTRANSFER.

IOTRANSFER binds an interrupt handler coroutine to a specific interrupt. Most computers identify individual interrupts with small whole numbers called *interrupt vector locations*. (Technically an interrupt vector location is an address in memory where the address of an interrupt service routine is stored. When the interrupt occurs the processor uses the address stored in the interrupt vector location to transfer to the appropriate routine. However this level of understanding of interrupt vectors isn't really necessary to write interrupt handlers in Modula–2.)

IOTRANSFER requires three parameters. The first parameter is a coroutine descriptor variable that is used to transfer control to the coroutine handler when the interrupt occurs. The second parameter is a coroutine descriptor variable to which control is immediately transferred. After the interrupt is serviced this second parameter may again be used to return control to whatever was interrupted. The third parameter identifies the interrupt vector location.

A coroutine establishes itself as an interrupt handler by calling IOTRANSFER. Thus there are three steps in the process of forming an interrupt coroutine:

1. The interrupt handler coroutine must be *created* using the NEWPROCESS PROCEDURE.
2. The interrupt handler coroutine must then be *invoked* normally using the TRANSFER PROCEDURE.
3. The interrupt handler must then perform any necessary *initialization* (of itself or of the managed device) and then call IOTRANSFER to suspend itself until an interrupt occurs.

Once an interrupt handler is created and working it is invoked automatically each time an interrupt occurs. Suppose a device driver coroutine executes the coroutine call

(* Example 19.1 *)
```
IOTRANSFER(driver, main, 40B)
```

to suspend itself while waiting for the interrupt identified by location 40B. Note that each call to IOTRANSFER can only catch one interrupt. When the interrupt finally occurs, the driver coroutine will be activated *as if* the interrupted program executed the coroutine call

(* Example 19.2 *)
```
TRANSFER(main, driver)
```

The TRANSFER call isn't embedded in the interrupted program because it isn't known in advance where the interrupted program will be executing when the interrupt occurs. Modula–2 creates the *illusion* that the device handler coroutine was called by an ordinary coroutine TRANSFER when actually it was called in response to an interrupt.

After servicing the interrupt, the coroutine suspends itself while waiting for another interrupt by calling IOTRANSFER. If another interrupt is not about to occur the suspended main coroutine can be reactivated using the ordinary TRANSFER call.

IOTRANSFER can *only* be used in MODULES with an assigned priority, because an interrupt handler should always be thought of as a critical region. Any PROCEDURES that are called from within an interrupt handler should also reside in a MODULE with assigned priority to ensure that they aren't interrupted.

## 19.2. Example — A Clock Driver

Our first example of a coroutine interrupt handler will control a programmable real–time clock. This will provide timing information within a program. The clock is programmed to interrupt once every ten milliseconds. Each time the clock interrupts a variable named Time is incremented, and the rest of the program uses this variable to keep track of time. The interrupt handler only allows Time to range from zero to 999, thus the time is reset once every ten seconds.

This clock interrupt handler is written as a local MODULE within the testbed program. This entire driver is specific to the LSI–11 computer and its programmable clock peripheral device, the KWV11.

```
                                          (* Example 19.3 *)
MODULE TIME;
FROM SYSTEM IMPORT SIZE, ADR, IOTRANSFER, TRANSFER,
        NEWPROCESS, PROCESS;
FROM InOut IMPORT WriteString, WriteLn;

VAR
    Time : CARDINAL; (* 0 to 999, local time ref. *)

MODULE clock [4];(* clock at priority 4 on PDP11 *)
IMPORT Time, ADR, SIZE, NEWPROCESS, PROCESS,
    TRANSFER, IOTRANSFER;

VAR
    comain, cotick : PROCESS;
    wsp : ARRAY [0..199] OF CARDINAL;

PROCEDURE tick; (* coroutine interrupt handler *)
VAR
    CSR [0170420B] : BITSET;
    CNT [0170422B] : CARDINAL;
CONST
    GO = {0};
    Model = {1};
    Rate1K = {5};
    IntEnb = {6};
    Mode = GO + Model + Rate1K + IntEnb;
BEGIN
    CNT := -10; (* twos compl. of desired count *)
```

```
      LOOP
         IF Time = 999 THEN
            Time := 0
         ELSE
            INC(Time)
         END;
         CSR := Mode;
         IOTRANSFER(cotick, comain, 0440B);
      END (* LOOP *)
   END tick;

   BEGIN (* clock module body *)
      Time := 999;
      NEWPROCESS(tick, ADR(wsp), SIZE(wsp), cotick);
      TRANSFER(comain, cotick);
   END clock;

   BEGIN (* program module body *)
      LOOP
         (* wait for Time to advance to zero *)
         WHILE Time <> 0 DO END;
         WriteString('tick'); WriteLn;
         (* wait for Time to advance past zero *)
         WHILE Time = 0 DO END;
      END (* LOOP *)
   END TIME.
```

This program is written for a version of Modula–2 that uses the special PROCESS TYPE to describe coroutines. The coroutine facilities of this version of Modula–2 are in the SYSTEM MODULE.

The tick coroutine interrupt handler is created and first called from the body of the clock MODULE. It then works by itself for the duration of the program. Notice that nothing is exported from the clock MODULE. Tick communicates with the rest of the program using the Time variable that is imported into the clock MODULE. This interrupt handler could easily be incorporated into a more useful program, such as a program that applies a time stamp to the information it processes.

One advantage of writing device handlers in a high level language such as Modula–2 is that they become much easier to test and debug. We can develop this driver for the programmable clock inside a simple program that verifies that its operation is essentially correct. In Modula–2 it is easy to develop coroutine interrupt handlers because it is easy to bind a coroutine interrupt handler

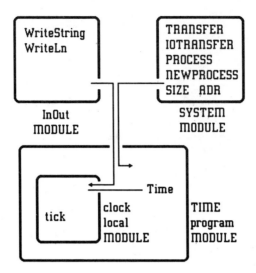

Figure 19.1. The TIME program uses a local MODULE to manage the KWV11 hardware. It imports from the InOut global MODULE and from the SYSTEM MODULE.

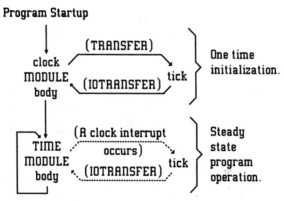

Figure 19.2. The initialization code for the clock MODULE is in its body. Once the initialization is complete, the tick coroutine is called each time the KWV11 hardware generates an interrupt.

into an ordinary program. Programming systems that require interrupt handlers written in low level languages often add to the difficulty by making it hard to bind the interrupt handler into an ordinary program. Thus there is a double penalty, the handler is hard to write and hard to understand because it is written in a low level language and it is hard to test because special operations are required to bind it to a program.

**Exercise 19.1.** The clock MODULE is a local MODULE. This is fine for testing, but it's probably best to separate the driver from the application. Rewrite the program so that it is in two pieces, the clock IMPLEMENTATION MODULE and the TIME application program. What should be exported from clock?
□

**Exercise 19.2.** Using the facilities shown here, write a program that displays a digital clock on the screen of your terminal.
□

## 19.3. Example — Timing a Spike Train

Here is a more involved use of a programmable clock. For a series of neurophysiology experiments it's necessary to time the inter-spike intervals for a series of nerve impulses. This timing information is then used to construct histograms, autocorrelograms, and cross–correlograms. Our interest here is the device driver that collects the spike data, not with the analysis software.

The device driver and the analysis software were originally written by Dan Ts'o. The device driver was written using a structured assembler and the applications software was written in the C programming language. The hardware consisted of an LSI–11/23 CPU, a programmable clock interface, a parallel input interface, a simple X–Y display, and a small amount of circuitry to condition the nerve spike signals.

The device driver is connected to the rest of the program using a circular buffer called the event buffer. The event buffer uses indices for the head and the tail of the data and of course there are slots for the data itself. Each slot in the event buffer is two words long: one word holds the timing information and the other has several bit flags that indicate which (of several) spike occurred.

This driver uses an interesting technique to avoid critical region problems. Critical regions occur when two separate processes share (for writing) a variable. In this system, there aren't any shared variables. The head index is written by the interrupt routine, the tail index is written by the application routines. The interrupt handler *compares* the head with the tail index to detect buffer overflow. The application routines perform the same comparison to find the end of the filled part of the buffer. Thus in this fairly simple case we avoid some of the difficulty of many device drivers.

Let's first take a look at the original assembly language device driver.

```
;KWV-11 Clock definitions
define   KWVCSR    170420   ;Status register
define   KWVBUF    KWVCSR+2;Buffer register
define   KWVVEC    440 ;Clock vector
define   KWVPSW    KWVVEC+2;New PSW
define   KWVPRI    300 ;Priority

define   ST2VEC    KWVVEC+4;St2 vector
define   ST2PSW    ST2VEC+2

define   KWVGO     1    ;GO bit
define   KWVMD0    0    ;Operating modes
define   KWVMD1    2
define   KWVMD2    4
define   KWVMD3    6
define   KWV10K    30   ;10kHZ rate
define   KWVOVIE   100  ;Overflow interrupt enable
define   KWVOVFL   200  ;Overflow bit
define   KWVORUN   10000    ;Overrun flag
define   KWVS2GO   20000    ;GO on ST2
define   KWVS2IE   40000    ;ST2 interrupt enable

define   KWVSET    KWV10K+KWVMD3+KWVS2IE+KWVOVIE+KWVGO

struct   kwvdev
    int kwv.csr
    int kwv.buf
end

; DRV11 parallel input port definitions
define   DRVCSR    172470
define   DRVOUT    DRVCSR+2
define   DRVINP    DRVCSR+4

struct   drvdev
    int drv.csr
    int drv.out
    int drv.inp
end

;Definitions of the event circular buffer
```

```
define   EBUFSIZ 512.

extern   ecb

struct   ebuf
    pointer  e.begin
    pointer  e.end
    block    e.buf EBUFSIZ words
end

proc start
    ; init vectors
    mov #kwvint,@#KWVVEC
    mov #KWVPRI,@#KWVPSW
    mov #kwvint,@#ST2VEC
    mov #KWVPRI,@#ST2PSW

    ;Set up clock
    mov #KWVSET,@#KWVCSR
end

proc kwvint
    ; save register 0, then put event buf addr into it
    push r0
    mov ecb+e.end,r0

    ;Put spike info into event buffer
    mov DRVINP,(r0)+

    ;Put clock overflow info into event buffer
    if < bit #KWVOVFL,KWVCSR> ne
        bis #KWVOVFL,-2(r0)
    end

    ;put time into event buffer
    mov KWVBUF,(r0)+

    ; circularize if necessary
    if <cmp r0,#ecb+ebuf> his
        mov #ecb+e.buf,r0
    end

    ;Check for event buffer overflow
    if <cmp r0,ecb+e.begin> eq
```

```
        bis #EVNTOVF,errflag
    else
        mov r0,ecb+e.end
    end

    ;Re-init clock
    mov #KWVSET,KWVCSR

    pop r0
    rti
end
```

Don't feel any obligation to understand the details of this assembly language driver. I have included it merely to show you what a device driver looks like in assembly language. Actually this assembly language device driver is more readable than most because of the explicit control structures.

The start PROCEDURE must be called initially to set up the interrupt vectors in specific regions of memory. Once the vectors are established the programmable clock is enabled and the application program starts to run. From this point forward the application program is one process and the handler is another.

A ST2 (Schmitt Trigger 2) interrupt occurs whenever a nerve impulse is detected. First the interrupt handler reads the DRV11 parallel input device to determine which spike caused the interrupt. This information is placed in the event buffer. Next the handler reads the clock to determine the time, and then places the time into the event buffer. The remainder of the handler consists of checks for clock overflow, event buffer overflow, etc.

Notice that this single handler is written to take care of two interrupts: a clock overflow or a spike arrival. This is a very difficult feature to imitate using Modula-2. Instead I have written two separate but similar handlers, one for each type of interrupt. This is the only organizational difference between the original assembly language version and my version in Modula-2.

The DEFINITION MODULE for the interval timer exports the event buffer data TYPE.

```
                                        (* Example 19.4 *)
DEFINITION MODULE CorInt;

TYPE
  EVENT = SET OF(Spike0, Spike1, Overflow);

CONST
  EbufSize = 256;

VAR
  EventBuf :
    RECORD
      begin, end : CARDINAL;
      buf : ARRAY [0 .. EbufSize-1] OF
          RECORD
             activity : EVENT;
             time : CARDINAL;
          END; (* buf record *)
    END; (* EventBuf record *)

END CorInt.
```

Here is the IMPLEMENTATION MODULE:

```
                                        (* Example 19.5 *)
IMPLEMENTATION MODULE CorInt;

FROM SYSTEM IMPORT ADR, SIZE, IOTRANSFER, TRANSFER,
  NEWPROCESS, PROCESS;

CONST
  Kwv10K = { 3,4 }; (* 10 khz clock rate *)
  KwvMd3 = { 1,2 }; (* Mode 3 operation *)
  KwvS2IE = { 14 }; (* Schmitt Trig 2 Int Enable *)
  KwvOvIE = { 6 }; (* Overflow Interrupt Enable *)
  KwvGo = { 0 }; (* The Go bit *)
  KwvSet = Kwv10K+KwvMd3+KwvS2IE+KwvOvIE+KwvGo;

VAR
  Kwv [ 0170420B ] :
    RECORD
      KwvCsr : BITSET;
      KwvBuf : CARDINAL;
    END;
```

```
      Drv [ 0172470B ] :
         RECORD
            DrvCsr : BITSET;
            DrvOut : BITSET;
            DrvInp : BITSET;
         END;
      WspSpike, WspOvf : ARRAY [ 0..199 ] OF CARDINAL;
      CoSpike, CoOvf, CoMain : PROCESS;

(* Device driver for spike (schmitt trigger)
      interrupts *)
PROCEDURE SpikeInt;
VAR
   newend : CARDINAL;
BEGIN
   LOOP
      IOTRANSFER(CoSpike, CoMain, 0444B);
      (* Install time and spike info in the end
           slot of EventBuf *)
      WITH EventBuf.buf[EventBuf.end] DO
         activity := EVENT(Drv.DrvInp);
         time := Kwv.KwvBuf;
      END;
      (* Where is the new end of the buffer? *)
      IF EventBuf.end = EbufSize THEN
         newend := 1
      ELSE
         newend := EventBuf.end + 1
      END;
      (* Don't install newend if the buffer
           will overflow *)
      IF newend <> EventBuf.begin THEN
         EventBuf.end := newend
      END;
      (* Re enable the KWV *)
      Kwv.KwvCsr := KwvSet;
   END (* LOOP *)
END SpikeInt;

(* Device driver for overflow interrupts *)
PROCEDURE OvfInt;
VAR
   newend : CARDINAL;
BEGIN
```

```
    LOOP
        IOTRANSFER(CoOvf, CoMain, 0440B);
        (* Install time and spike info in the end
              slot of EventBuf *)
        WITH EventBuf.buf[EventBuf.end] DO
            activity := EVENT { Overflow };
            time := Kwv.KwvBuf;
        END;
        (* Where is the new end of the buffer? *)
        IF EventBuf.end = EbufSize THEN
            newend := 1
        ELSE
            newend := EventBuf.end + 1
        END;
        (* Don't install newend if the buffer
              will overflow *)
        IF newend <> EventBuf.begin THEN
            EventBuf.end := newend
        END;
        (* Re enable the KWV *)
        Kwv.KwvCsr := KwvSet;
    END (* LOOP *)
END OvfInt;

BEGIN
    EventBuf.begin := 1;
    EventBuf.end := 1;
    NEWPROCESS(SpikeInt, ADR(WspSpike),
                    SIZE(WspSpike), CoSpike);
    NEWPROCESS(OvfInt, ADR(WspOvf),
                    SIZE(WspOvf), CoOvf);
    TRANSFER(CoMain, CoSpike);
    TRANSFER(CoMain, CoOvf);
    Kwv.KwvCsr := KwvSet;
END CorInt.
```

Let's look at the advantages and disadvantages of each approach. The major reason that the device driver was originally written in assembly language was performance. Even though the driver is about one hundred lines long, there are only a handful of instructions that get executed each time an interrupt occurs. Notice that only a single general purpose register is used in the assembly language version, hence the "overhead" of this driver is tiny. (You must examine the code closely to appreciate its compactness and efficiency.)

It's impossible for the driver written in Modula–2 to achieve the performance of the assembly language approach. Modula–2's very general coroutine handlers often have significant overhead. Modula–2 must save the entire state of the program before calling the handler, and then the entire state must be restored when the handler is finished. This is much more overhead than the assembly language version, which only saves and restores the single register that it modifies.

Modula–2's advantages are subtle. The built in IOTRANSFER PRO-CEDURE means that programmers don't need to know the details of the interrupt system on the host computer. However in any language the author of a device driver must understand the hardware that is being managed. Another advantage of Modula–2 is the intermodule checking. The checking in this case means the event RECORD will be properly conveyed to the client MODULES. Since this driver only exports one item, the intermodule checking is only marginally significant in this case.

In my opinion, the bottom line is that the Modula–2 version is easier to write. If I were starting from scratch, I would write the handler first in Modula–2. This would allow me to work out the kinks, fix the obvious bugs, and prove the design without strug-gling with assembly language. Then if the performance proved to be inadequate I would translate the driver to assembly language. As an intermediate step, on some systems it is possible to write handlers in Modula–2 without using the general, but computation-ally expensive IOTRANSFER facility.

**Exercise 19.3.** How could you combine the pair of device drivers?

□

**Exercise 19.4.** Write a program MODULE to perform go/nogo testing of this driver.

□

# 19.4. Example — The Interrupt driven Term Program

The previous chapter introduced a polling version of the Term program. In this section we translate the polling version into an interrupt version. The primary advantage of using interrupts rather than polling is *efficiency*. Interrupts are more efficient because each coroutine is only entered when data is actually available. The polling approach spends most of its time moving from coroutine to coroutine, and each polling coroutine usually does nothing more than discover that there is nothing to do except skip to the next coroutine.

The interrupt approach can potentially handle more devices at once because there is less waste. However many people think that interrupts are always a more efficient approach than polling. There is an unavoidable overhead in using interrupts because interrupts force the ongoing activity to be suspended politely. This enables that activity to be resumed when the interrupt service is complete. If there are several data channels each presenting moderate data rates then interrupts are more efficient because the channels are only serviced as needed.

However polling is the preferred method to perform peripheral servicing of a single data channel at the maximum rate possible on a given computer. In a polling situation all other activity is suspended at the outset of polling and there is less overhead each time the interface requires service (because the ongoing task doesn't need to be suspended and then resumed). However a computer engaged in continuous polling of an interface can do nothing else, a usually undesirable situation.

The version of Term given in Example 18.3 only has to be altered slightly to work with interrupts. In the previous version, the RemIO PROCEDURE transferred data to and from the serial port. Here we have separated these two functions. The serial data input is handled by an interrupt coroutine, the data output is performed by polling in the main loop. As before the console data input and output is performed by calls to the host computer's operating system using the DOSCALL PROCEDURE from the SYSTEM MODULE.

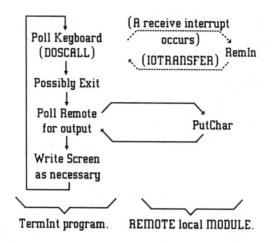

Figure 19.3. In this version of the Term program incoming data causes a hardware interrupt, which automatically activates the RemIN coroutine. The main coroutine manages the local keyboard and the screen, and it activates the PutChar coroutine whenever keyboard data needs to be transmitted to the remote site.

```
                                           (* Example 19.6 *)
MODULE TermInt;

(* Virtual Terminal program for the IBM/PC
 *   running PCDOS. Uses Logitech Modula-2/86
 *   specific imports from SYSTEM
 *)

FROM SYSTEM IMPORT
    PROCESS, TRANSFER, IOTRANSFER, (* standards *)
    NEWPROCESS, SIZE, ADR, WORD, (* standards *)
    ENABLE, DOSCALL, INBYTE, OUTBYTE; (* Dos *)

MODULE REMOTE[4];
IMPORT RemCh, main, remote, IOTRANSFER, INBYTE,
    OUTBYTE, WORD;
EXPORT RemIn, PutChar;

CONST       (* all of the 8250 registers and bits *)
    StatReg = 03FDH;
    DataReg = 03F8H;
    IntEnbReg = 03F9H;
```

```
      ModemCtrlReg = O3FCH;
      RcvIntEnb = {0};
      MasterIntEnb = {3};
      XmtRdy = 5;

   PROCEDURE RemIn;
   (* Interrupting input handler for the 8250 Asnyc
        Serial I/O chip *)
   BEGIN
     OUTBYTE(IntEnbReg,WORD(RcvIntEnb));
     OUTBYTE(ModemCtrlReg,WORD(MasterIntEnb));
     LOOP
         IOTRANSFER(remote, main, OCH);
         INBYTE(DataReg,RemCh);
     END
   END RemIn;

   PROCEDURE PutChar(VAR ch : CHAR);
   (* Polling serial output driver *)
   VAR
      stat : WORD;
   BEGIN
      INBYTE(StatReg,stat);
      IF XmtRdy IN BITSET(stat) THEN (* send it *)
         OUTBYTE(DataReg,ch);
         ch := OC;
      END;
   END PutChar;

   END REMOTE; (* local module *)

   CONST
      Para = 16; (* sixteen bytes in a paragraph *)

   VAR
      main, remote : PROCESS;
      WorkSpace : ARRAY [ 0 .. 255 ] OF CARDINAL;
      KbdCh, RemCh : CHAR;
      ready : BOOLEAN;

   BEGIN
      NEWPROCESS(RemIn, ADR(WorkSpace),
                   lSIZE(WorkSpace) DIV Para, remote);
      TRANSFER(main,remote);
```

```
    ENABLE;
    KbdCh := 0C;
    RemCh := 0C;

    LOOP
        (* Poll kbd *)
        IF KbdCh = 0C THEN
            DOSCALL(6H, 0FFH, KbdCh, ready)
        END;
        (* exit on escape *)
        IF KbdCh = 33C THEN EXIT END;
        (* try to send to remote *)
        IF (KbdCh # 0C) THEN PutChar(KbdCh) END;
        (* write screen *)
        IF RemCh # 0C THEN
            DOSCALL(6H, RemCh); RemCh := 0C
        END;
    END;
END TermInt.
```

In a sense this entire program consists of device driver coroutines. This is often the style of programs where the *entire* program is a systems program. Programs written for real time data collection or process control often consist entirely of systems techniques.

However most programs consist of a systems part and an applications part. On most computers the systems part is supplied and programmers only work on the applications part. On other systems, especially programs for science or industry, it is necessary to include a certain amount of systems code in many programs.

The general approach to writing device driver programs is to have them transfer information between devices and the applications part of a program. Usually each driver is connected to a buffer that is also accessible to the applications part of the program. This general approach makes it easier to analyze the data flowing through the devices. Perhaps more importantly it decouples the systems programming (the drivers) from the applications programming (the data analysis).

**Exercise 19.5.** Modify this program so that it can copy a disk file to the remote system.
□

**Exercise 19.6.** Modify this program so that it can keep a log file of the incoming data.

# Appendices

# Appendix I

# Modula-2's Reserved Words

| + | = | AND | FOR | QUALIFIED |
|---|---|---|---|---|
| − | # | ARRAY | FROM | RECORD |
| * | < | BEGIN | IF | REPEAT |
| / | > | BY | IMPLEMENTATION | RETURN |
| := | < > | CASE | IMPORT | SET |
| & | < = | CONST | IN | THEN |
| , | . | DIV | MOD | TYPE |
| ; | : | DO | MODULE | UNTIL |
| ( | ) | ELSE | NOT | VAR |
| [ | ] | ELSIF | OF | WHILE |
| { | } | END | OR | WITH |
| ^ | \| | EXIT | POINTER | |
| (* | *) | EXPORT | PROCEDURE | |
| , | " | ~ | | |

# Appendix II

# Modula-2's Standard Identifiers

| ABS | CHR | HIGH | LONGREAL | PROC |
|---|---|---|---|---|
| BITSET | DEC | INC | MAX | REAL |
| BOOLEAN | EXCL | INCL | MIN | SIZE |
| CAP | FALSE | INTEGER | NIL | TRUE |
| CARDINAL | FLOAT | LONGCARD | ODD | TRUNC |
| CHAR | HALT | LONGINT | ORD | VAL |

# Appendix III

# Modula-2's Standard Functions

The functions listed below are special because they are built into each Modula-2 compiler. See the DEFINITION MODULES in Chapter 9 for information about standard facilities that are supplied as ordinary global MODULES.

ABS( n ) — Absolute Value

> Function PROCEDURE with value parameter.
> Parameter TYPES: INTEGER (subrange), REAL.
> Result TYPE: Same as the actual parameter.
> Example: x := ABS(x)

CAP( ch ) — Capitalize

> Function PROCEDURE with value parameter.
> Parameter TYPE: CHAR.
> Result TYPE: CHAR
> Example: ch := CAP('a');

CHR( n ) — Convert a CARDINAL to a CHAR

> Function PROCEDURE with value parameter.
> Parameter TYPE: CARDINAL
> Result TYPE: CHAR
> Example: ch := CHR(12B)

DEC( n ) — Decrement n by one.

True PROCEDURE with a variable parameter.
Parameter TYPE: INTEGER (subrange), CARDINAL (subrange),
CHAR, or any enumeration.
Equivalent to n := n - 1
Example: DEC(ch)

DEC(n,i) — Decrement n by i.

Same as DEC except the decrement amount is supplied.
Example: DEC(ch,2)

DISPOSE(p) — Dispose a dynamically allocated datum.

(See NEW)

DISPOSE(p,t1,t2,...) — Dispose a dynamically allocated variant RECORD.

The tag field values are t1, t2, ... (See NEW)

EXCL(s,n) — Exclude n from membership in set s.

True PROCEDURE, variable first parameter, value second
parameter.
First Parameter: Any SET TYPE.
Second Parameter: Base TYPE of the first parameter.
Example:

```
TYPE
   Color = (Red,Green,Blue);
   S = SET OF COLOR;
VAR
   s : S; c : Color;
...
EXCL(s,c);
```

FLOAT(n) — Convert a CARDINAL to a REAL

Function PROCEDURE with value parameter.
Parameter TYPE: CARDINAL
Result TYPE: REAL
Example: r := FLOAT(1)

HALT — Terminate program execution.

True PROCEDURE.

HIGH(a) — Return the upper index of ARRAY a.

> Function PROCEDURE with value parameter.
> Parameter TYPE: Any ARRAY
> Result TYPE: CARDINAL
> Example:

```
PROCEDURE s(a : ARRAY OF REAL);
VAR
   n : CARDINAL;
BEGIN
   n := HIGH(a)
...
```

INC(n) — Increment n by one.

> True PROCEDURE with a variable parameter.
> Parameter TYPE: INTEGER (or subrange), CARDINAL (or subrange), CHAR, or any enumeration.
> Equivalent to n := n + 1
> Example: INC(ch)

INC(n,i) — Increment n by i.

> Same as INC except the increment value is supplied.
> Example: INC(ch,2)

INCL(s,n) — Include n as a member of set s.

> True PROCEDURE, variable first parameter, value second parameter.
> First Parameter: Any SET TYPE.
> Second Parameter: Base TYPE of the first actual parameter.
> Example: see EXCL.

MAX(t) — Return the Maximum of a TYPE

> Function PROCEDURE.
> The parameter is the name of any scalar data TYPE, including INTEGER, CARDINAL, REAL, LONGINT, LONGCARD, LONGREAL, CHAR, BOOLEAN, all enumerations, and all subranges.
> The returned value is the maximum value of the given TYPE.
> Example: CONST MaxCard = MAX(CARDINAL);

MIN(t) — Return the Minimum of a TYPE

> Function PROCEDURE.

The parameter t is the name of any scalar data TYPE, See MAX.

The returned value is the minimum value of the given TYPE.

NEW(p) — Create a new variable.

The TYPE of the new variable is the TYPE pointed at by p. p is assigned the address of the new datum.

True PROCEDURE with a variable parameter.

Parameter TYPE: POINTER.

Equivalent to ALLOCATE(p, TSIZE(T)) where T is the TYPE pointed at by p.

Note: The ALLOCATE and DEALLOCATE PROCEDURES must be imported into any MODULE that uses NEW and DISPOSE.

Example:

```
FROM Storage IMPORT ALLOCATE, DEALLOCATE;
TYPE
    Ptr = POINTER TO REC;
    REC : RECORD x,y,z : REAL; p : Ptr END;
VAR
    r : REC;
 .  .  .
    NEW(r.p); (* ALLOCATE must be visible at this point
```

Warning: NEW and DISPOSE are no longer recommended usage, although they exist in many compilers. Recommended usage is to call ALLOCATE and DEALLOCATE directly. ALLO-CATE and DEALLOCATE must be imported from a global MODULE, usually a MODULE named Storage.

NEW(p,t1,t2,...) — Allocate a new variant RECORD.

This is the same as NEW except the values for the tag fields of a variant RECORD are supplied. This version of NEW dynami-cally allocates a datum large enough to hold a RECORD with the given variants.

ODD(n) — Odd

Function PROCEDURE with value parameter.

Parameter TYPE: INTEGER (or subrange), CARDINAL (or subrange)

Result TYPE: BOOLEAN

Example: IF ODD(n) THEN . . .

ORD(n) — Ordinal number corresponding to n.

Function PROCEDURE with value parameter.
Parameter TYPE: INTEGER (or subrange), CARDINAL (or subrange), CHAR, or any enumeration.
Result TYPE: CARDINAL
Example: n := ORD('a');

SIZE(n) — Return the size of a datum.

Function PROCEDURE with value parameter.
Parameter TYPE: Anything.
Result TYPE: CARDINAL.
The units assumed by SIZE vary; bits, bytes, or machine words are possible.

TRUNC(r) — The value of r converted to a CARDINAL.

Function PROCEDURE with value parameter.
Parameter TYPE: REAL
Result TYPE: CARDINAL (INTEGER in some implementations.)
Example: n := TRUNC(1.0E2)

VAL(T,n) — A value whose TYPE is T and whose ordinal is n.

Function PROCEDURE.
The First Parameter is the name of a TYPE.
The Second Parameter's TYPE: INTEGER (or subrange), CARDINAL (or subrange), CHAR, or any enumeration.
Result TYPE: CARDINAL (INTEGER in some implementations.)
Example:

```
TYPE
   Color = (Red, Green, Blue);
VAR
   c : Color;
   ch : CHAR;
...
   c := VAL(Color,0);
   ch := VAL(CHAR,140B);
```

# Appendix IV

# Standard PROCEDURES from

# SYSTEM

In addition to the PROCEDURES detailed below, the SYSTEM MODULE defines the WORD and ADDRESS data TYPES.

- WORD represents an uninterpreted unit of storage. WORDS are ordinarily incompatible with other data TYPES, except when used as formal PROCEDURE parameters. See Section 16.2.
- ADDRESS is a special POINTER TYPE that is compatible with other POINTER TYPES. In addition the ADDRESS TYPE is compatible with one of the numeric data TYPES so that arithmetic operations can be performed on POINTERS.

ADR(n) — Return the address of a datum.

> Function PROCEDURE with value parameter.
> Parameter TYPE: Anything.
> Result TYPE: ADDRESS.

TSIZE(T) — Return the size of a TYPE.

> Function PROCEDURE.
> Parameter: The name of any TYPE.
> Result TYPE: CARDINAL.
> The units assumed by TSIZE vary; bits, bytes, or machine words are possible.

Note: the SYSTEM MODULE is discussed in Chapter 16.

# Appendix V

# Standard Coroutine PROCEDURES

Most versions of Modula–2 contain the following PROCEDURES to manage coroutines. In some implementations these facilities must be imported from the SYSTEM MODULE, in other implementations these facilities are contained in a standard global MODULE. Some versions of Modula–2 contain a special TYPE called PROCESS for coroutine descriptors.

IOTRANSFER(P,Q,vec) — Wait for an interrupt.

> True PROCEDURE, P is a variable parameter, the others are value parameters.
> P, Q : ADDRESS
> vec : CARDINAL
> IOTRANSFER causes a transfer to the coroutine described by Q. P becomes a descriptor for the calling coroutine. When the hardware interrupt identified by vec occurs, an immediate transfer will be made to P, thereby resuming the coroutine. Only one interrupt is caught each time IOTRANSFER is called. Note: details vary from one system to another — P and Q are PROCESS TYPES in many Modula–2 implementations.

LISTEN — Enable interrupts within a critical region.

> True PROCEDURE.
> In side a prioritized MODULE, interrupts whose priority is less than the MODULE'S priority are disabled. LISTEN is called within a prioritized MODULE to enable interrupts.

Note: LISTEN is not available in all versions of Modula–2.

NEWPROCESS(P,A,N,Q) — Create a coroutine.

True PROCEDURE, Q is a variable parameter, the others are value parameters.
P : PROC (The coroutine PROCEDURE)
A : ADDRESS (Location of coroutine workspace)
N : CARDINAL (Implementation dependent size of coroutine workspace)
Q : ADDRESS (The coroutine descriptor)
NEWPROCESS initializes the coroutine workspace and the coroutine descriptor for the coroutine embodied in the P PROCEDURE. NEWPROCESS must be called before the coroutine can be activated using the TRANSFER PROCEDURE.
Note: Q is a PROCESS TYPE in many Modula–2 implementations.

TRANSFER(P,Q) — Transfer from one coroutine to another.

True PROCEDURE, variable first parameter, value second parameter.
Parameter TYPES: ADDRESS
Transfer to the coroutine described by Q; descriptor P can be used subsequently to transfer back to the calling coroutine. P and Q are PROCESS TYPES in many Modula–2 implementations.

# Appendix VI

# Legal Modula-2 Operations

| Generic TYPES | | | | | | | | | | | | | | |
|---|---|---|---|---|---|---|---|---|---|---|---|---|---|---|
| | := | + | – | * | / | DIV | MOD | < | <= | > | >= | = | # | IN |
| Opaque | ● | | | | | | | | | | | ● | ● | |
| Subrange[1] | ● | ? | ? | | | ? | ? | ● | ● | ● | ● | ● | ● | |
| Enumeration | ● | | | | | | | ● | ● | ● | ● | ● | ● | |
| SETS[2] | ● | ● | ● | ● | ● | | | | ● | | ● | ● | ● | ● |
| ARRAYS | ● | | | | | | | | | | | | | |
| RECORDS | ● | | | | | | | | | | | | | |
| POINTERS[2] | ● | | | | | | | | | | | ● | ● | |
| PROCEDURE[2] | ● | | | | | | | | | | | | | |

Notes:
1.  INTEGER and CARDINAL subranges allow the +, –, DIV, and MOD operators; CHAR and enumeration subranges do not.
2.  Some additional "operations" are available for some data TYPES:
    *   PROCEDURE variables may be activated.
    *   POINTER variables may be dereferenced.
    *   The standard INCL and EXCL PROCEDURES are often used with SETS to form new SETS.

| Built In TYPES | | | | | | | | | | | | | | | | |
|---|---|---|---|---|---|---|---|---|---|---|---|---|---|---|---|---|
| | := | + | − | * | / | DIV | MOD | < | <= | > | >= | = | # | IN | NOT | AND | OR |
| INTEGER | • | • | • | | | • | • | • | • | • | • | • | • | | | | |
| LONGINT | • | • | • | | | • | • | • | • | • | • | • | • | | | | |
| CARDINAL | • | • | • | | | • | • | • | • | • | • | • | • | | | | |
| LONGCARD | • | • | • | | | • | • | • | • | • | • | • | • | | | | |
| REAL | • | • | • | • | • | | | • | • | • | • | • | • | | | | |
| LONGREAL | • | • | • | • | • | | | • | • | • | • | • | • | | | | |
| BOOLEAN | • | | | | | | | • | • | • | • | • | • | | • | • | • |
| CHAR | • | | | | | | | • | • | • | • | • | • | | | | |
| PROC | • | | | | | | | | | | | | | | | | |
| BITSET[2] | • | • | • | • | • | | | | • | | • | • | • | • | | | |
| WORD[1] | • | | | | | | | | | | | | | | | | |
| ADDRESS[1] | • | • | • | • | • | | | • | • | • | • | • | • | | | | |

Notes:
1. WORD and ADDRESS must be imported from the SYSTEM MODULE.
2. The standard INCL and EXCL PROCEDURES are often used with BITSETS.

# Appendix VII

# Strict TYPE Compatibility

Two items are strictly compatible if
- They are the same TYPE.
- One is a subrange of the other.
- Both are subranges of a third TYPE.

In addition, constant character strings of length one are compatible with CHARS.

The special WORD and ADDRESS systems programming TYPES provide the following compatibilities:
- Formal parameters whose TYPE is WORD are compatible an implementation dependent group of TYPES. Usually a WORD formal parameter is compatible with any actual parameter that occupies a single word of storage. Formal parameters whose TYPE is ARRAY OF WORD are usually compatible with any actual parameters.
- The ADDRESS TYPE is compatible with all POINTER TYPES. In some versions of Modula–2 ADDRESSES are compatible with CARDINALS (or LONGCARDS or LONGINTS) and some arithmetic operators.

Strict Compatiblity is required in the following situations:
- All of the elements of an expression must be compatible.
- Actual parameters to a PROCEDURE must be the same TYPE as variable formal parameters.
- The limit expressions in a FOR loop must be compatible with the control variable.

# Appendix VIII

# Assignment TYPE Compatibility

Two variables are assignment compatible if they are strictly compatible. In addition, the following are assignment compatible:

- CARDINALS and INTEGERS.
- Constant character strings and longer or equally long ARRAY OF CHAR variables.

Assignment Compatibility is required in the following situations:

- The variable on the left hand side of an assignment statement must be assignment compatible with the expression on the right.
- The expression following the word RETURN in a function PROCEDURE must be assignment compatible with the declared TYPE of the PROCEDURE.
- Actual parameter expressions to a PROCEDURE must be assignment compatible with value formal parameters.
- Actual ARRAY index expressions must be assignment compatible with the declared TYPE of the index.

# Appendix IX

# The ASCII Character Set

| | | | | | | | |
|---|---|---|---|---|---|---|---|
| 0H nul | 1H soh | 2H stx | 3H etx | 4H eot | 5H enq | 6H ack | 7H bel |
| 8H bs | 9H ht | 0AH nl | 0BH vt | 0CH ff | 0DH cr | 0EH so | 0FH si |
| 10H dle | 11H dc1 | 12H dc2 | 13H dc3 | 14H dc4 | 15H nak | 16H syn | 17H etb |
| 18H can | 19H em | 1AH sub | 1BH esc | 1CH fs | 1DH gs | 1EH rs | 1FH us |
| 20H sp | 21H ! | 22H " | 23H # | 24H $ | 25H % | 26H & | 27H ' |
| 28H ( | 29H ) | 2AH * | 2BH + | 2CH , | 2DH − | 2EH . | 2FH / |
| 30H 0 | 31H 1 | 32H 2 | 33H 3 | 34H 4 | 35H 5 | 36H 6 | 37H 7 |
| 38H 8 | 39H 9 | 3AH : | 3BH ; | 3CH < | 3DH = | 3EH > | 3FH ? |
| 40H @ | 41H A | 42H B | 43H C | 44H D | 45H E | 46H F | 47H G |
| 48H H | 49H I | 4AH J | 4BH K | 4CH L | 4DH M | 4EH N | 4FH O |
| 50H P | 51H Q | 52H R | 53H S | 54H T | 55H U | 56H V | 57H W |
| 58H X | 59H Y | 5AH Z | 5BH [ | 5CH \ | 5DH ] | 5EH ^ | 5FH _ |
| 60H ` | 61H a | 62H b | 63H c | 64H d | 65H e | 66H f | 67H g |
| 68H h | 69H i | 6AH j | 6BH k | 6CH l | 6DH m | 6EH n | 6FH o |
| 70H p | 71H q | 72H r | 73H s | 74H t | 75H u | 76H v | 77H w |
| 78H x | 79H y | 7AH z | 7BH { | 7CH \| | 7DH } | 7EH ˜ | 7FH del |

# Appendix X

# Implementation Notes

Like any language in its infancy, Modula-2 has been growing rapidly. This book conforms to the latest (as of this writing) revisions of the language. Thus Modula-2 as described here is the same as that described in the third edition of Wirth's book "Programming in Modula-2." Note that the first and second editions of Wirth's book described an earlier version of the language. Most of the current compilers were built using the first edition of Wirth's book as their guide, thus as of this writing most working compilers follow that standard rather than the latest standard. I expect that the compilers will be upgraded to reflect the improvements that have been agreed upon in the Modula-2 community.

Here is a list of the recent changes to Modula-2. If you are using an older compiler you may encounter some of these vestiges.

- DEFINITION MODULES used to contain an EXPORT list. This was removed because it was redundant. In the current version of the language everything defined in a DEFINITION MODULE is automatically exported. EXPORT lists are currently only allowed in local MODULES.
- SETS currently can have variables as members. In many older compilers SET membership is restricted to constants and the built in functions INCL and EXCL were used when the vaule of a variable was used to determine SET membership.
- The LONGCARD, LONGINT, and LONGREAL data TYPES are recent additions. The are not found in many implementations.

- The standard PROCEDURES MIN and MAX are recent additions that are not found in older implementations.
- Many older systems use a special PROCESS TYPE for coroutine descriptors. Newer systems use the ADDRESS TYPE for coroutine descriptors.
- Older implementations don't allow an identifer in front of a subrange TYPE declaration. In the current version this feature allows one to dictate the base TYPE of a subrange.
- In many older systems there were dynamic allocation routines called NEW and DISPOSE. These are replaced by calls to ALLOCATE and DEALLOCATE from a standard MODULE (usually Storage).
- The syntax of constants is now the same as the syntax of expressions. In previous versions constants warranted a separate group of rules.
- The syntax of variant FieldLists, cases, and variants has been slightly changed. Both cases and variants may be empty. In a practical sense, this means that you may place superflous bars separating the cases in a CASE statement. Variant FieldLists must always include the colon before the TYPE name.
- The character "~" is now allowed as a synonym for NOT.
- A string of length one is compatible with the CHAR TYPE.
- The ADDRESS TYPE is now required to be compatible with one of the numeric TYPES. This feature was previously optional, although it was implemented in all versions that I've encountered.

# Appendix XI

# Syntax Diagrams

# Modules

**CompilationUnit**

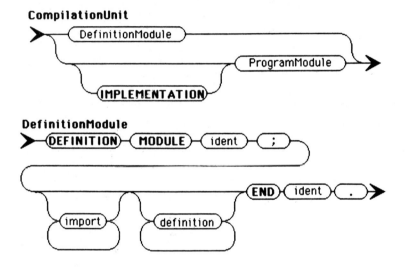

**DefinitionModule**

**definition**

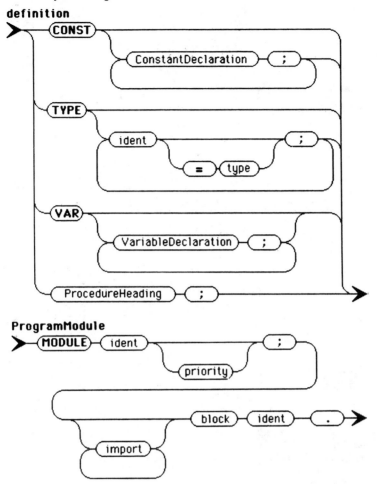

**ProgramModule**

**ModuleDeclaration**

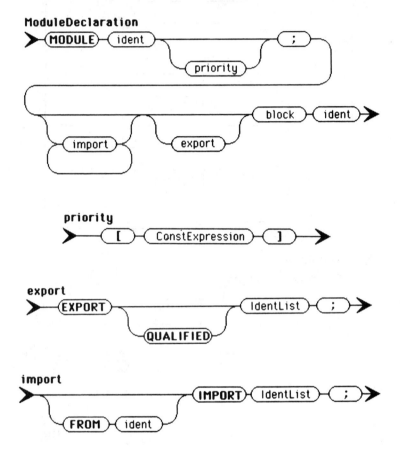

**priority**

**export**

**import**

# Procedures

**ProcedureDeclaration**

**ProcedureHeading**

**FormalParameters**

**FPSection**

**FormalType**

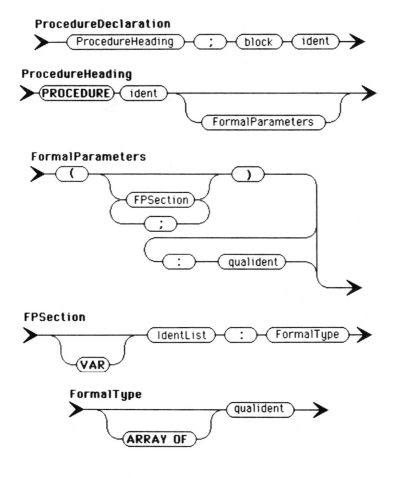

**block**

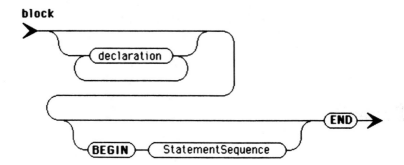

# Types

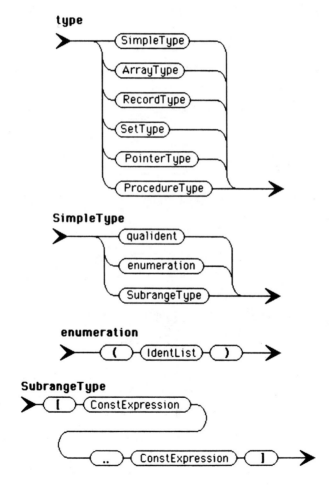

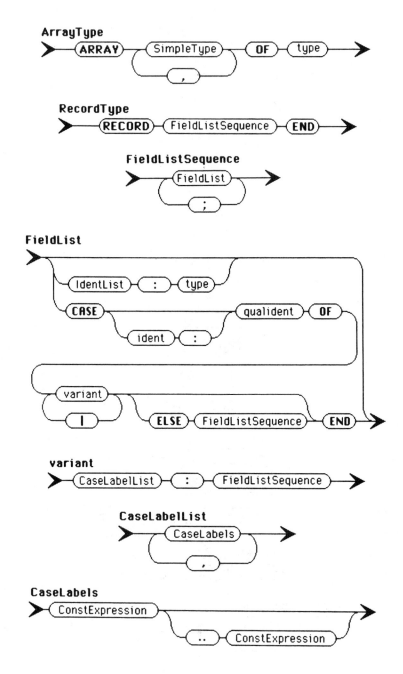

**SetType**

**PointerType**

**ProcedureType**

**FormalTypeList**

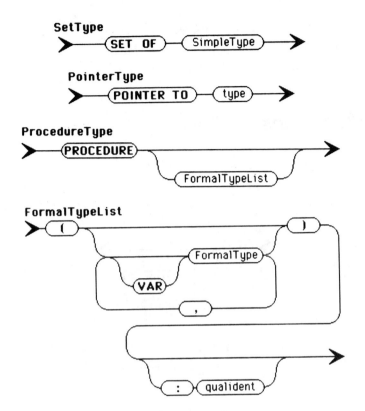

# Declarations

**ident**

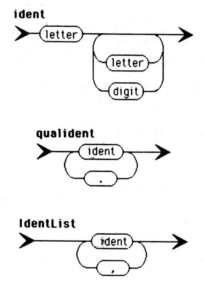

**qualident**

**IdentList**

**declaration**

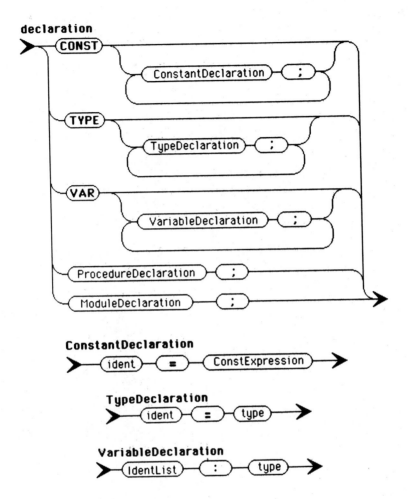

**ConstantDeclaration**

**TypeDeclaration**

**VariableDeclaration**

# Constants

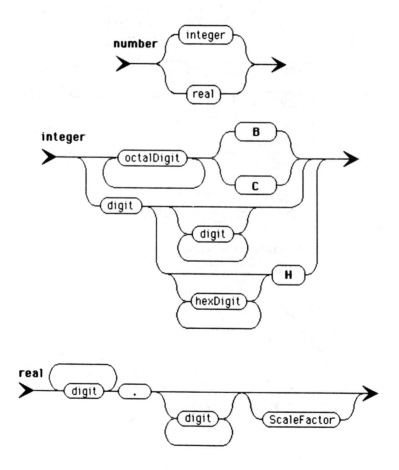

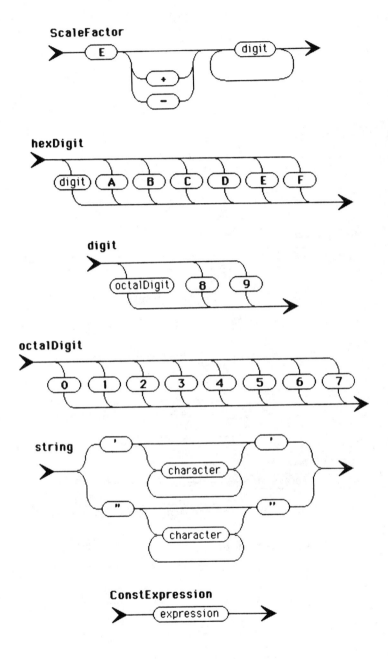

# Variables

**designator**

**ExpList**

**expression**

**SimpleExpression**

**term**

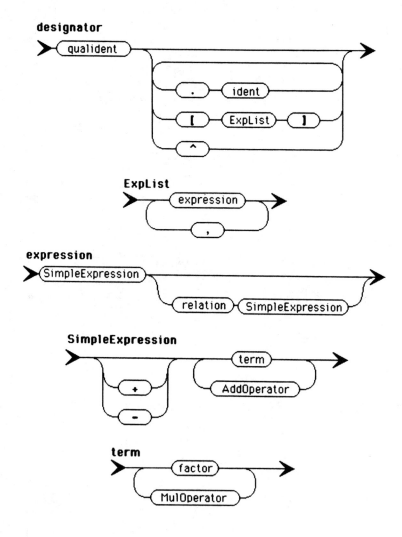

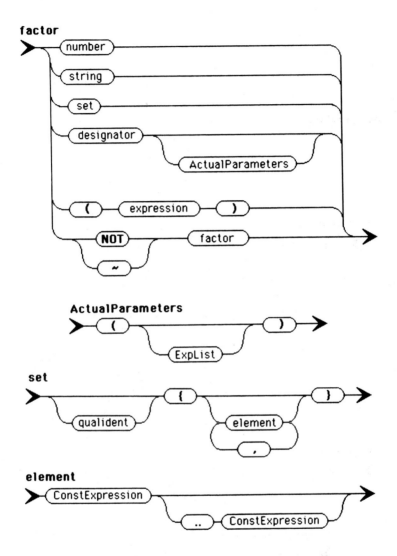

# Operators

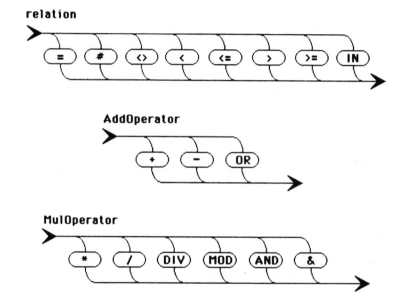

# Statements

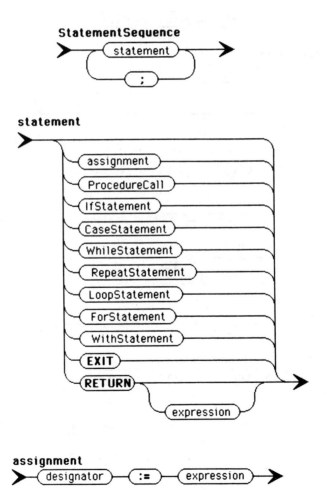

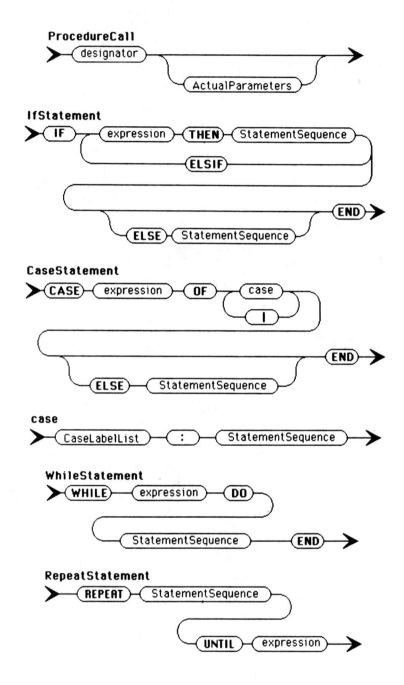

**ForStatement**

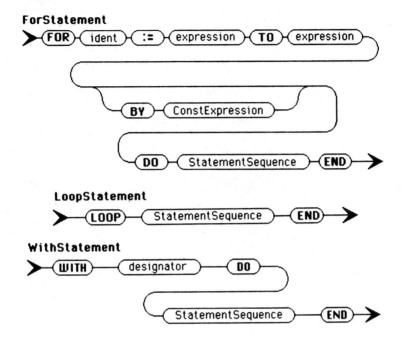

**LoopStatement**

**WithStatement**

# Index